The Invention of the Land of Israel

The Invention of the Land of Israel

From Holy Land to Homeland

Shlomo Sand

Translated by Geremy Forman

VERSO
London • New York

This English-language edition first published by Verso 2012
© Verso 2012
Translation © Geremy Forman 2012
First published as *Matai ve'ekh humtzea eretz israel?* [When
and How the Land of Israel Was Invented?]
© Kinnert, Zmora-Bitan 2012

1 3 5 7 9 10 8 6 4 2

Verso
UK: 6 Meard Street, London W1F 0EG
US: 20 Jay Street, Suite 1010, Brooklyn, NY 11201
www.versobooks.com

Verso is the imprint of New Left Books

ISBN-13: 978-1-84467-946-1

British Library Cataloguing in Publication Data
A catalogue record for this book is available from the British Library

Library of Congress Cataloging-in-Publication Data
Sand, Shlomo.
  [Matai ve-ekh humtse'ah Erets-Yisra'el. English]
  The invention of the land of Israel / Shlomo Sand ; translated by Geremy Forman.
      p. cm.
  Includes bibliographical references and index.
  ISBN 978-1-84467-946-1 (hardback : alk. paper) — ISBN 978-1-84467-947-8 (ebook)
  1. Post-Zionism. 2. Judaism and state—Israel. 3. Palestine in rabbinical literature.
  4. Christian Zionism—History. 5. Jews—Israel—Identity. 6. Territory, National—
Israel. I. Title.
  DS113.4.S2613 2012
  320.54095694—dc23
                              2012031367

Typeset in Minion by Hewer UK Ltd, Edinburgh
Printed in the US by Maple Vail

In memory of the villagers of al-Sheikh Muwannis, who were uprooted long ago from the place where I now live and work

Contents

Introduction: Banal Murder and Toponymy

Zionism and its progeny, the state of Israel, reached the Western Wall through military conquest, in fulfillment of national messianism. They will never again be able to forsake the Wall or abandon the occupied parts of the Land of Israel without denying their historiographic conception of Judaism . . . The secular messiah cannot retreat: he can only die.
—Baruch Kurzweil, 1970

It is entirely illegitimate to identify the Jewish links with the ancestral land of Israel . . . with the desire to gather all Jews into a modern territorial state situated on the ancient Holy Land.
—Eric Hobsbawm, *Nations and Nationalism since 1780*, 1990

The tattered, seemingly anonymous memories underlying this book are vestiges of my younger days and of the first Israeli war in which I took part. For the sake of transparency and integrity, I believe it is important to share them with readers here, at the outset, in order to openly bare the emotional foundation of my intellectual approach to the mythologies of national land, ancient ancestral burial grounds, and large chiseled stones.

MEMORIES FROM AN ANCESTRAL LAND

On June 5, 1967, I crossed the Israeli-Jordanian border at Jabel al-Radar in the Jerusalem Hills. I was a young soldier, and, like many other Israelis, I had been called up to defend my country. It was after nightfall when we silently and carefully traversed the remains of the clipped barbed wire. Those who trod there before us had stepped on land mines, and the blast had torn their flesh from their bodies, flinging it in all directions. I trembled with fear, my teeth chattering wildly and my sweat-drenched shirt clinging to my body. Still, in my terrified imagination, as my limbs continued to move automatically, like parts of a robot, I never once stopped pondering the fact that this would be my first time abroad. I was two years old when I first arrived in Israel, and despite my dreams (I grew up in a poor neighborhood of Jaffa and had to work as a teenager), I never had enough money to go abroad and travel the world.

My first trip out of the country would not be a pleasant adventure, as I quickly learned after being sent directly to Jerusalem to fight in the battle for the city. My frustration grew when I realized that others did not regard the territory we had entered as "abroad." Many of the soldiers around me saw themselves as merely crossing the border of the State of Israel (*Medinat Israel*) and entering into the Land of Israel (*Eretz Israel*). After all, our forefather Abraham had wandered between Hebron and Bethlehem, not Tel Aviv and Netanya, and King David had conquered and elevated the city of Jerusalem located to the east of Israel's "green" armistice line, not the thriving modern city located to the west. "Abroad?" asked the fighters advancing with me during the grueling battle for the Jerusalem neighborhood of Abu Tor. "What are you talking about?! This is the true land of your forefathers."

My brothers-in-arms believed they had entered a place that had always belonged to them. I, in contrast, felt that I had left my true place behind. After all, I had lived in Israel almost my entire life and, frightened by the prospect of being killed, worried I might never return. Although I was lucky and, through great effort, made it home alive, my fear of never again returning to the place I had left behind ultimately proved correct, albeit in a way I could never have imagined at the time.

The day after the battle at Abu Tor, those of us who had not been killed or wounded were taken to visit the Western Wall. Weapons cocked, we walked cautiously through the silent streets. From time to time, we caught glimpses of frightened faces appearing momentarily in windows to steal glances of the outside world.

An hour later, we entered a relatively narrow alleyway overshadowed on one side by a towering wall made of chiseled stones. This was before the homes of the neighborhood (the ancient Mughrabi Quarter) were demolished to make room for a massive plaza to accommodate devotees of the "Discotel" (a play on "discotheque" and *kotel*, the Hebrew word for the Western Wall), or the "Discotheque of the divine presence," as Professor Yeshayahu Leibowitz liked to refer to it. We were worn out and on the edge; our filthy uniforms were still stained with the blood of the dead and wounded. Our chief concern was finding a place to urinate, as we could not stop in any of the open cafés or enter the homes of the stunned locals. Out of respect for the observant Jews among us, we relieved ourselves on the walls of the houses across the way. This enabled us to avoid "desecrating" the outer supporting wall of the Temple Mount, which Herod and his descendants, who had allied themselves with the Romans, had constructed with enormous stones in an effort to exalt their tyrannical regime.

Filled with trepidation by the sheer immensity of the hewn stones, I felt tiny and weak in their presence. Most likely this feeling was also a product of the narrow alleyway as well as my fear of its inhabitants, who still had no idea that they would soon be evicted. At the time, I knew very little about King Herod and the Western Wall. I had seen it pictured on old postcards in school textbooks, but I myself knew no one who aspired to visit it. I was also still completely unaware that the wall had not in fact been part of the Temple and had not even been considered sacred for most of its existence, in contrast to the Temple Mount, which observant Jews are prohibited from visiting in order to avoid contamination by the impurity of death.[1]

But the secular agents of culture who sought to re-create and rein-force tradition through propaganda did not hesitate before initiating their national assault on history. As part of their album of victory images, they selected a posed photograph of three combat soldiers (the middle, "Ashkenazi" soldier bareheaded and helmet in hand, as if in church), eyes mournful from two thousand years of longing for the mighty wall and hearts overjoyed by the "liberation" of the land of their forefathers.

From this point on, we sang "Jerusalem of Gold" nonstop, with unmatched devotion. Naomi Shemer's song of pining for annexation, which she composed shortly before the battles began, played an instant and extremely effective role in making the conquest of the eastern city appear the natural fulfillment of an ancient historical right. All those who took part in the invasion of Arab Jerusalem during those blistering days of June 1967 know that the song's lyrics of psychological preparation for the war—"The wells ran dry of all their

---

1   The Western Wall is not the temple wall referred to in the Midrash Rabbah, Song of Songs (2:4). It was not an internal wall but rather a city wall, and for this reason its name is misleading. It was established as a site of prayer only relatively recently, apparently during the seventeenth century. Its importance cannot be compared to the long-standing sacred status of the Temple Mount (the plaza of the Al-Aqsa Mosque), to which observant Jews are permitted to ascend only after acquiring the ashes of a red heifer.

water, / Forlorn the market square, / The Temple Mount dark and deserted, / In the Old City there"—were unfounded.² However, few if any of us understood the degree to which the lyrics were actually dangerous and even anti-Jewish. But when the vanquished are so weak, the chanting victors waste no time on such minor details. The voiceless, conquered population was now not only kneeling before us but had faded away into the sacred landscape of the eternally Jewish city, as if they had never existed.

After the battles, I, along with ten other soldiers, was assigned to guard the Intercontinental Hotel, which was subsequently Judaized and is known today as the Sheva Hakshatot (Seven Arches). This spectacular hotel was built near the old Jewish cemetery on the summit of the Mount of Olives. When I phoned my father, who was then living in Tel Aviv, and told him I was on the Mount of Olives, he reminded me of an old story that had been passed down in our family but that, due to lack of interest, I had completely forgotten.

Just before his death, my father's grandfather decided to leave his home in Lodz, Poland, and travel to Jerusalem. He was not the least bit Zionist, but rather an ultraorthodox observant Jew. Therefore, in addition to his tickets for the voyage, he also took along a tombstone. Like other good Jews of the day, he intended not to live in Zion but to be buried on the Mount of Olives. According to an eleventh-century midrash, the resurrection of the dead would begin on this elevated hill located across from Mount Moriah, where the Temple once stood. My elderly great-grandfather, whose name was Gutenberg, sold all his possessions and invested all he had in the journey, leaving not a penny to his children. He was a selfish man,

---

2   As with the Western Wall, there were things I did not know about the song so closely associated with the Six-Day War. Like many others at the time, I was unaware that the tune we were humming was actually taken from a Basque lullaby called "Pello Joxepe." This is not unusual. Most people who sing "Hatikvah," the anthem of the Zionist movement that was adopted as the national anthem of the State of Israel, are unaware that its tune was borrowed from a symphonic poem by Smetana known as "Vltava" (My Homeland) or "Die Moldau." The same is true of the Israeli flag; the Star of David is not an ancient Jewish symbol but rather a symbol originating from the Indian subcontinent, where various religious and military cultures made extensive use of it throughout history. National traditions are thus often more the product of imitation and reproduction than of originality and inspiration. On this, see Eric Hobsbawm and Terence Ranger (eds.), *The Invention of Tradition*, Cambridge: Cambridge University Press, 1983.

the type of person who was always pushing to the front of the line. He therefore aspired to be among the first of the resurrected at the coming of the Messiah. He simply wanted his redemption to precede that of everyone else, and this is how he came to be the first person in my family to be buried in Zion.

My father suggested I try to find his grave. However, despite my immediate curiosity, the heavy summer heat and the dispiriting exhaustion that followed the end of the fighting compelled me to abandon the idea. In addition, rumors were circulating that some of the old headstones had been used to build the hotel, or had at least been used as tiles to pave the road ascending to it. That evening in the hotel, after speaking with my father, I leaned against the wall behind my bed and imagined it was made from my egotistical great-grandfather's headstone. Inebriated by the delightful wines that stocked the hotel bar, I marveled at the irony and the deceptive nature of history: my assignment to safeguard the hotel against Jewish Israeli looters, who were certain that all its contents belonged to the "liberators" of Jerusalem, convinced me that the redemption of the dead would not occur anytime soon.

Months after my initial encounter with the Western Wall and the Mount of Olives, I ventured deeper into the "Land of Israel," where I experienced a dramatic encounter that, to a great extent, shaped the rest of my life. During my first tour of reserve duty following the war, I was posted to the old police station at the entrance to Jericho, which, according to ancient legend, was the first city in the Land of Israel to be conquered by the "People of Israel," through the miracle of a long blast of a ram's horn. My experience in Jericho was altogether different from that of the spies who, according to the Bible, found lodging in the home of a local prostitute by the name of Rahab. When I reached the station, soldiers who had arrived before me told me that Palestinian refugees from the Six-Day War had been systematically shot while trying to return to their homes at night. Those who crossed the Jordan River in broad daylight were arrested and, one or two days later, sent back across the river. My assignment was to guard the prisoners, who were being held in a makeshift jail.

One Friday night in September 1967 (as I remember, it was the night before my birthday), we were left alone by our officers, who drove into Jerusalem for their night off. An elderly Palestinian man, who had been arrested on the road while carrying a large sum in

American dollars, was taken into the interrogation room. While standing outside the building on security detail, I was startled by terrifying screams coming from within. I ran inside, climbed onto a crate, and, through the window, observed the prisoner sitting tied to a chair as my good friends beat him all over his body and burned his arms with lit cigarettes. I climbed down from the crate, vomited, and returned to my post, frightened and shaking. About an hour later, a pickup truck carrying the body of the "rich" old man pulled out of the station, and my friends informed me they were driving to the Jordan River to get rid of him.

I do not know whether the battered body was tossed into the river at the very spot where the "children of Israel" crossed the Jordan when they entered the land that God himself had bestowed upon them. And it is safe to assume that my baptism into the realities of occupation did not occur at the site where St. John converted the first "true children of Israel," which Christian tradition locates south of Jericho. In any event, I could never understand why that elderly man had been tortured, as Palestinian terrorism had not yet even emerged and no one had dared put up any resistance. Perhaps it was for the money. Or perhaps the torture and banal murder had simply been the product of boredom on a night offering no alternative forms of entertainment.

Only later did I come to view my "baptism" in Jericho as a watershed in my life. I had not tried to prevent the torture because I had been too frightened. Nor do I know if I could have stopped it. However, not having tried to do so troubled me for years. Indeed, the fact that I am writing about it here means I still carry the murder around inside me. Above all, the inexcusable incident taught me that absolute power not only corrupts absolutely, as attested to by Lord Acton, but brings with it an intolerable sense of possession over other people and, ultimately, over place. I have no doubt that my ancestors, who lived a powerless life in the Pale of Settlement in Eastern Europe, could have never dreamed of the actions their progeny would perpetrate in the Holy Land.

For my next tour of reserve duty, I was again stationed in the Jordan Valley, this time during the celebrated establishment of the first Nahal[3] settlements there. At dawn on my second day in the valley, I

---

3   A program of the Israel Defense Forces that combines military service and the establishment of new agricultural settlements.

took part in an inspection conducted by Rehavam Ze'evi, better known as "Gandhi," who had only recently been appointed head of central command. This was before his friend Defense Minister Moshe Dayan had given him a lioness as a gift, which would become a symbol of the Israeli army's presence in the West Bank. The Israeli-born general stood before us, striking a pose worthy of General Patton himself,[4] and delivered a brief speech. I cannot remember exactly what he said, as I was somewhat drowsy at the time. However, I will never forget the moment he waved his hand toward the mountains of Jordan behind us and enthusiastically instructed us to remember that those mountains, too, were part of the Land of Israel and that our forefathers had lived there, in Gilad and Bashan.

A few of the soldiers nodded their heads in agreement, others laughed, most were focused on getting back to their tents as soon as possible to catch up on sleep. One joked that our general must have been a direct descendant of those ancestors who had lived east of the river three millennia ago, and proposed we immediately set out to liberate the occupied territory from the backward gentiles in his honor. I didn't find the remark funny. Instead, the general's brief address served as an important catalyst for the development of my skepticism toward the collective memory with which I had been infused as a pupil. I knew even then that, according to his biblical (and at least somewhat skewed) logic, Ze'evi was not mistaken. The former Palmach hero and future Israeli government minister was always honest and consistent in his passionate views on the homeland. His moral blindness toward those who had previously been living in "the land of our forefathers"—his indifference to their reality—soon came to be shared by many.

As I have already noted, I felt a powerful sense of connection with the small land where I grew up and first fell in love, and with the urban landscape that had shaped my character. Although never truly a Zionist, I was taught to see the country as a refuge in time of need for displaced and persecuted Jews who had nowhere else to go. Like historian Isaac Deutscher, I understood the historical process that led up to 1948 as the story of a man leaping from a burning building in

---

4   Or at least worthy of actor George C. Scott, who played the well-known American general in the 1970 film *Patton*.

desperation and injuring a passer-by as he landed.[5] At the time, however, I was unable to foresee the monumental changes that would come to reshape Israel as a result of its military victory and territorial expansion—changes that were wholly unrelated to Jewish suffering from persecution and that past suffering could certainly not justify. The long-term outcome of this victory reinforced the pessimistic view of history as an arena for continual role reversal between victim and executioner, as the persecuted and displaced often emerge subsequently as rulers and persecutors.

The transformation of Israel's conception of national space almost certainly played a meaningful role in the formation of Israeli national culture after 1967, although it may not have been truly decisive. After 1948, Israeli consciousness suffered from discontent with limited territory and "narrow hips." This unease openly erupted after Israel's military victory in the 1956 war, when Prime Minister David Ben-Gurion seriously considered annexing the Sinai Peninsula and the Gaza Strip.

Despite this significant but fleeting episode, the mythos of the ancestral homeland declined significantly after the establishment of the state of Israel and did not return forcefully to the public arena until the Six-Day War almost two decades later. For many Judeo-Israelis, it seemed that any criticism of Israel's conquest of the Old City of Jerusalem and the cities of Hebron and Bethlehem would undermine the legitimacy of its previous conquest of Jaffa, Haifa, Acre, and other places of comparatively less importance to the Zionist mosaic of connection with the mythological past. Indeed, if we accept the Jews' "historical right of return to their homeland," it is difficult to deny its applicability to the very heartland of the "ancient homeland" itself. Weren't my comrades-in-arms justified in feeling we had not crossed any borders? Wasn't this why we had studied the Bible as a distinct pedagogical historical subject in our secular high school? Back then, I never imagined that the green armistice line—the so-called Green Line—would disappear so quickly from the maps produced by the Israeli Ministry of Education, and that future generations of Israelis would hold conceptions of the homeland's borders that would differ so greatly from my own. I simply was unaware that, following its establishment, my

5 Isaac Deutscher, *The Non-Jewish Jew and Other Essays*, London: Oxford University Press, 1968, 136–7.

country had no borders except the fluid, modular frontier regions that perpetually promised the option of expansion.

One example of my humanistic political naïveté was the fact that I never dreamed Israel would dare legally annex East Jerusalem, characterize the measure by invoking "a city that is bound firmly together" (Psalms 122:3), and at the same time refrain from granting equal civil rights to one-third of the residents of its "united" capital city, as is still the case today. I never imagined I would bear witness to the assassination of an Israeli prime minister because the lethal patriot who pulled the trigger believed he was about to withdraw from "Judea and Samaria." I also never imagined I would be living in a moonstruck country whose foreign minister, having immigrated there at the age of twenty, would reside outside of Israel's sovereign borders for the entire duration of his term in office.

At the time, I had no way of knowing that Israel would succeed in controlling such a large Palestinian population for decades, bereft of sovereignty. I also could not foresee that, for the most part, the country's intellectual elite would accept the process and that its senior historians—my future colleagues—would continue to refer to this population quite readily as "Arabs of the Land of Israel."[6] It never dawned on me that Israel's control of the local "other" would not be exercised through mechanisms of discriminatory citizenship such as military government and the Zionist-socialist appropriation and Judaization of land, as had been the case within the borders of "good old" pre-1967 Israel, but rather through the sweeping negation of their freedoms and the exploitation of natural resources for the sake of the pioneering settlers of the "Jewish people." Furthermore, I never even considered the possibility that Israel would succeed in settling more than a half million people in the newly occupied territories and keeping them fenced off in complex ways from the local population, who would in turn be denied basic human rights, highlighting the colonizing, ethnocentric, and segregationist character of the entire national enterprise from the outset. In short, I was wholly unaware I would spend most of my life living next door to a sophisticated and unique

---

6   A typical example can be found in the work of Anita Shapira, who refers to the traumatic "encounter with the Arabs in the Land of Israel," as in "From the *Palmach* Generation to the Candle Children: Changing Patterns in Israeli Identity," *Partisan Review* 67:4 (2000), 622–34.

regime of military apartheid with which the "enlightened" world, due in part to its guilty conscience, would be forced to compromise and, in the absence of any other option, to support.

In my younger years, I could never have imagined a desperate Intifada, the heavy-handed suppression of two uprisings, and brutal terrorism and counterterrorism. Most important, it took me a long time to comprehend the power of the Zionist conception of the Land of Israel relative to the fragility of the day-to-day Israeliness that was still in the process of crystallizing, and to process the simple fact that the Zionists' forced separation from parts of their ancestral homeland in 1948 was only temporary. I was not yet a historian of political ideas and cultures; I had not yet begun to consider the role and influence of modern mythologies regarding land, particularly those that thrive on the intoxication caused by the combination of military power and nationalized religion.

RIGHTS TO AN ANCESTRAL LAND

In 2008, I published the Hebrew edition of my book *The Invention of the Jewish People*, a theoretical endeavor to deconstruct the historical supermythos of the Jews as a wandering people in exile. The book was translated into twenty languages and reviewed by numerous hostile Zionist critics. In one review, the British historian Simon Schama maintained that the book "fails to sever the remembered connection between the ancestral land and Jewish experience."[7] Initially, I must admit, I was surprised by the insinuation that this had been my intention. Yet when many more scholars repeated the assertion that my goal had been to undermine the Jews' right to their ancient homeland, I realized that Schama's claim was a significant and symptomatic precursor to the broader attack on my work.

In the course of writing *The Invention of the Jewish People*, I never expected that, at the beginning of the twenty-first century, so many critics would step forward to justify Zionist colonization and the establishment of the State of Israel by invoking claims of ancestral lands, historical rights, and millennia-old national yearnings. I was certain that most serious grounds for the establishment of the State of

---

7   *The Invention of the Jewish People*, London: Verso, 2009. See the review in the *Financial Times*, November 13, 2009.

Israel would be based on the tragic period beginning in the late nine-teenth century, during which Europe ejected its Jews and, at a certain point, the United States closed its doors to immigration.[8] But I soon came to realize that my writing had been unbalanced in a number of ways. To a certain extent, the present book is meant as a modest addition to my previous book and aims both to provide greater accuracy and to fill in some gaps.

I must begin, however, by clarifying that *The Invention of the Jewish People* addressed neither Jewish ties nor Jewish rights to the ancestral Jewish "homeland," even if its content had direct implications for the subject. My aim in writing it had been mainly to use historical and historiographical sources to question the ethnocentric and ahistorical concept of essentialism and the role it has played in past and present definitions of Judaism and Jewish identity. Although it is widely evident that the Jews are not a pure race, many people—Judeophobes and Zionists in particular—still tend to espouse the incorrect and misleading view that most Jews belong to an ancient race-based people, an eternal "*ethnos*" who found places of residence among other peoples and, at a decisive stage in history, when their host societies cast them out, began to return to their ancestral land.

After many centuries of living with the self-image of a "chosen people" (which preserved and reinforced the ability of Jews to endure their ongoing humiliation and persecution), after almost two thousand years of Christian insistence on seeing Jews as the direct descendants of the killers of God's son, and, most important, after the emergence (alongside traditional anti-Jewish hostility) of a new anti-Semitism that cast Jews as members of a foreign and contaminating race, it was no easy task to deconstruct European culture's "ethnic" defamiliarization of the Jews.[9] In attempting to do so, my previous

---

8   As a result of the establishment of the State of Israel and its ensuing conflict with Arab nationalism, the Jewish communities of Arab countries were also uprooted from their homelands; some were either forced to immigrate to Israel or did so by choice.

9   Influential elements within Christianity found it difficult to regard Judaism as a legitimate rival religion and instead preferred to see its followers as a repulsive group of shared ethnic descent and a legacy of punishment by God. The initial crystallization of a modern people, consisting of the large population of Yiddish speakers in Eastern Europe—a nucleus that was just beginning to emerge when it was brutally wiped out during the twentieth century—also played an indirect role in facilitating this mistaken conceptualization of a worldwide "Jewish people."

book employed one basic working premise: that a human unit of pluralistic origin, whose members are united by a common fabric devoid of any secular cultural component—a unit that can be joined, even by an atheist, not by forging a linguistic or cultural connection with its members but solely through religious conversion—cannot under any criteria be considered a people or an ethnic group (the latter is a concept that flourished in academic circles after the bankruptcy of the term "race").

If we are to be consistent and logical in our understanding of the term "people," as used in cases such as the "French people," the "American people," "the Vietnamese people," or even the "Israeli people," then referring to a "Jewish people" is just as strange as referring to a "Buddhist people," an "Evangelical people," or a "Baha'i people." A common fate of holders of a shared belief bound by a degree of solidarity does not make them a people or a nation. Even if human society consists of a linked collection of multifaceted complex experiences that defy all attempts at formulation in mathematical terms, we must nonetheless do our utmost to employ precise mechanisms of conceptualization. Since the beginning of the modern era, "peoples" have been conceptualized as groups possessing a unifying culture (including elements such as cuisine, a spoken language, and music). However, despite their great uniqueness, Jews throughout all of history have been characterized by "only" a diverse culture of religion (including elements such as a common nonspoken sacred language and common rituals and ceremonies).

Nonetheless, many of my critics, who not coincidentally are all sworn secular scholars, remained adamant in defining historical Jewry and its modern-day descendants as a people, albeit not a chosen people, but one unique, exceptional, and immune to comparison. Such a view could be maintained only by providing the masses with a mythological image of the exile of a people that ostensibly took place in the first century BCE, despite the fact that the scholarly elite was well aware that such an exile never really occurred during the entire period in question. For this reason, not even one research-based book has thus been written on the forced uprooting of the "Jewish people."[10]

---

10   The legend of the Jews' mass displacement by the Romans is related to the Babylonian exile referred to in the Bible. However, it also has Christian sources, and appears to have originated with the punitive prophecy articulated by Jesus in the New

In addition to this effective technology for the preservation and dissemination of a formative historical mythos, it was also necessary (1) to erase, in a seemingly unintentional manner, all memory of Judaism having been a dynamic and proselytizing religion at least between the second century BCE and the eighth century CE; (2) to disregard the existence of many Judaized kingdoms that emerged and flourished throughout history in various geographic regions;[11] (3) to delete from collective memory the enormous number of persons who converted to Judaism under the rule of these Judaized kingdoms, providing the historical foundation for most of the world's Jewish communities; and (4) to downplay statements of the early Zionists—most prominently those of David Ben-Gurion, founding father of the State of Israel[12]—who well knew that an exile had never taken place and therefore regarded most of the territory's local peasants as the authentic offspring of the ancient Hebrews.

The most desperate and dangerous proponents of this ethnocentric view sought a genetic identity common to all the world's Jewish offspring, so as to distinguish them from the populations among which they lived. Forswearing negligence, pseudoscientists gathered shreds of data aimed at corroborating presuppositions suggesting the existence of an ancient race. "Scientific" anti-Semitism having failed in its deplorable attempt to locate the uniqueness of the Jews in their blood and other internal attributes, we witnessed the emergence of a perverted Jewish nationalist hope that perhaps DNA could serve as solid proof of a migrating Jewish *ethnos* of common origin that eventually reached the Land of Israel.[13]

Testament: "There will be great distress in the land and wrath against this people. They will fall by the sword and will be taken as prisoners to all the nations" (Luke 21:23–4).

11   Specifically, I am referring to the Adiabene kingdom of Mesopotamia, the Himyarite kingdom of southwestern Arabia, the kingdom of Dahyā al-Kāhina of northern Africa, the kingdom of Semien of eastern Africa, the kingdom of Kodungallur of the southern Indian subcontinent, and the great Khazar empire of southern Russia. It should come as no surprise that we are unable to locate even one comparative study that attempts to explore the fascinating Judaization of these kingdoms and the fate of their many subjects.

12   For an example, see Ben-Gurion's 1917 article "Clarifying the Origins of the *Felahs*," in David Ben-Gurion, *We and Our Neighbors*, Tel Aviv: Davar Press, 1931, 13–25 (in Hebrew).

13   On this, see Sand, *Invention of the Jewish People*, 272–80.

The fundamental, but by no means sole, reason for this uncompromising position, which became only partially clear to me in the course of writing this book, was simple: according to an unwritten consensus of all enlightened worldviews, all peoples possess a right of collective ownership over the defined territory in which they live and from which they generate a livelihood. No religious community with a diverse membership dispersed among different continents was ever granted such a right of possession.

For me, this basic legal-historical logic was not initially self-evident because during my youth and late adolescence, being a typical product of the Israeli education system, I believed without a shadow of a doubt in the existence of a virtually eternal Jewish people. Just as I had been mistakenly certain that the Bible was a history book and that the Exodus from Egypt had occurred in reality, I was convinced, in my ignorance, that the "Jewish people" had been forcibly uprooted from its homeland after the destruction of the Temple, as asserted so officially by Israel's declaration of statehood.

But at the same time, my father had raised me according to a universalist moral code based on sensitivity to historical justice. It therefore never occurred to me that my "exiled people" was entitled to the right of national ownership to a territory in which it had not lived for two millennia, whereas the population that had been living there continuously for many centuries was entitled to no such right. By definition, all rights are based on ethical systems that serve as a foundation which others are required to recognize. In my view, only the local population's agreement to the "Jewish return" could have endowed it with a historical right possessed of moral legitimacy. In my youthful innocence, I believed that a land belonged first and foremost to its permanent inhabitants, whose places of residence were located within its borders and who lived and died on its soil, not to those who ruled it or tried to control it from afar.

For instance, in 1917, when the Protestant colonialist and British foreign secretary Arthur James Balfour promised Lionel Walter Rothschild a national home for the Jews, he did not—despite his great generosity—propose its establishment in Scotland, his birthplace. In fact, this modern-day Cyrus remained consistent in his attitude toward the Jews. In 1905, as prime minister of Britain, he worked tirelessly for the enactment of stringent anti-immigration legislation meant primarily to prevent Jewish immigrants fleeing the pogroms of Eastern Europe from entering Britain.[14] Nonetheless, second only to the Bible, the Balfour Declaration is regarded as the most decisive source of moral and political legitimacy of the Jews' right to the "Land of Israel."

In any case, it always seemed to me that a sincere attempt to organize the world as it was organized hundreds or thousands of years ago would mean the injection of violent, deceptive insanity into the overall system of international relations. Would anyone today consider encouraging an Arab demand to settle in the Iberian Peninsula to establish a Muslim state there simply because their ancestors were expelled from the region during the Reconquista? Why should the descendants of the Puritans, who were forced to leave England centuries ago, not attempt to return en masse to the land of their forefathers in order to establish the heavenly kingdom? Would any sane person support Native American demands to assume territorial possession of Manhattan and to expel its white, black, Asian, and Latino inhabitants? And somewhat more recently, are we obligated to assist the Serbs in returning to Kosovo and reasserting control over the region because of the sacred heroic battle of 1389, or because Orthodox Christians who spoke a Serbian dialect constituted a decisive majority of the local population a mere two hundred years ago? In this spirit, we can easily imagine a march of folly initiated by the assertion and recognition of countless "ancient rights," sending us back into the depths of history and sowing general chaos.

Never did I accept the idea of the Jews' historical rights to the Promised Land as self-evident. When I became a university student and studied the chronology of human history that followed the invention of writing, the "Jewish return"—after more than eighteen centuries—seemed to me to constitute a delusional jump in time. To me, it was not fundamentally different from the mythoi of Puritan Christian settlement in North America or Afrikaner settlement in South Africa, which imagined the conquered land as the Land of Canaan, bestowed by God upon the true children of Israel.[15]

---

14   See chapter titled "The Other Arthur Balfour" in Brian Klug, *Being Jewish and Doing Justice*, London: Vallentine Mitchell, 2011, 199–210.

15   For a discussion of the promised lands of the Puritans and Afrikaners, see Anthony D. Smith, *Chosen Peoples: Sacred Sources of National Identity*, Oxford: Oxford University Press, 2003, 137–44.

On this basis, I concluded that the Zionist "return" was, above all, an invention meant to arouse the sympathy of the West—particularly the Protestant Christian community, which preceded the Zionists in proposing the idea—in order to justify a new settlement enterprise, and that it had proven its effectiveness. By virtue of its underlying national logic, such an initiative would necessarily prove detrimental to a weak indigenous population. After all, the Zionists did not land in Jaffa port with the same intention harbored by persecuted Jews who landed in London or New York, that is, to live together in symbiosis with their new neighbors, the older inhabitants of their new surroundings. From the outset, the Zionists aspired to establish a sovereign Jewish state in the territory of Palestine, where the vast majority of the population was Arab.[16] Under no circumstances could such a program of national settlement be completed without ultimately pushing a substantial portion of the local population out of the appropriated territory.

As I have already indicated, after many years of studying history, I believe neither in the past existence of a Jewish people, exiled from its land, nor in the premise that the Jews are originally descended from the ancient land of Judea. There can be no mistaking the striking resemblance between Yemenite Jews and Yemenite Muslims, between North African Jews and the indigenous Berber population of the region, between Ethiopian Jews and their African neighbors, between the Cochin Jews and the other inhabitants of southwestern India, or between the Jews of Eastern Europe and the members of the Turkish and Slavic tribes that inhabited the Caucasus and southeast Russia. To the dismay of anti-Semites, the Jews were never a foreign "ethnos" of invaders from afar but rather an autochthonous population whose ancestors, for the most part, converted to Judaism before the arrival of Christianity or Islam.[17]

I am equally convinced that Zionism did not succeed in creating a worldwide Jewish nation but rather "only" an Israeli nation, the

---

16   Even the Zionist factions that at times proposed federative schemes did so for pragmatic reasons, primarily in order to facilitate the creation of a Jewish majority, and did not seek integration with the local population.

17   Virtually all the religious groups listed above evolved in the areas ruled by the Judaized kingdoms mentioned in footnote 11 above. For example, see the assertions of Marc Bloch, one of the great historians of the twentieth century, in his book L'Étrange défaite, Paris: Gallimard, 1990, 31, and of Raymond Aron, in Mémoires, Paris: Julliard, 1983, 502-3.

existence of which it unfortunately continues to deny. First and fore-most, nationalism represents people's aspiration, or at least their willingness and agreement, to live together under independent politi-cal sovereignty according to a unique secular culture. However, most people around the world who classify themselves as Jews—even those who, for a variety of reasons, express solidarity with the self-declared "Jewish state"—prefer not to live in Israel and make no effort to immi-grate to the country and live with other Israelis within the terms of the national culture. Indeed, the pro-Zionists among them find it quite comfortable to live as citizens of their own nation-states and continue to take an immanent part in the rich cultural lives of those nations, while at the same time claiming historical rights to the "ancestral land" they believe to be theirs for eternity.

Nonetheless, in order to preclude any misunderstanding among my readers, I again emphasize that (1) I have never questioned, nor do I question today, the right of modern-day Judeo-Israelis to live in a democratic, open, and inclusive state of Israel that belongs to all its citizens; and (2) I have never denied, nor do I today deny, the exist-ence of the strong, age-old religious ties between believers in the Jewish faith and Zion, its holy city. Nor are these two preliminary points of clarification causally or morally linked to each other in any binding manner.

First, to the extent that I myself am capable of judging the matter, I believe my own political approach to the conflict has always been pragmatic and realistic: if it is incumbent upon us to rectify the events of the past, and if we are compelled by moral imperative to recognize the tragedy and destruction we have caused to others (and to pay a high price in the future to those who became refugees), moving back-ward in time will only result in new tragedies. Zionist settlement in the region created not only an exploitative colonial elite but also a society, a culture, and a people whose removal is unthinkable. There-fore, all objections to the right of existence of an Israeli state based on the civil and political equality of all its inhabitants—whether advanced by radical Muslims who maintain that the country must be wiped off the face of the earth or by Zionists who blindly insist on viewing it as the state of world Jewry—are not only anachronistic folly but a recipe for another catastrophe in the region.

Second, whereas politics is an arena of painful compromise, historical scholarship must be as devoid of compromise as possible. I have always held that the spiritual longing for the land of divine promise was a central axis of identity for Jewish communities and an elementary condition for understanding them. However, these strong yearnings for the Heavenly Jerusalem in the souls of oppressed and humiliated religious minorities were primarily metaphysical longings for redemption, not for stones or landscape. In any event, a group's religious connection to a sacred center does not endow it with modern property rights to some, or all, of the places in question.

Despite the many differences, this principle is as true for other cases in history as it is for the case of the Jews. The Crusaders had no historical right to conquer the Holy Land, despite their strong religious ties to it, the extended period of time they spent there, and the large quantity of blood they spilled in its name. Neither did the Templars—who spoke a southern German dialect, identified themselves as the chosen people, and, in the mid-nineteenth century, believed they would inherit the Promised Land—earn such a privilege. Even the masses of Christian pilgrims, who also made their way to Palestine during the nineteenth century, and clung to it with such fervor, typically never dreamed of becoming the lords of the land. Likewise, it is safe to assume that the tens of thousands of Jews who have made pilgrimages to the grave of Rabbi Nachman of Bratslav in the Ukrainian city of Uman in recent years do not claim to be the city's masters. Incidentally, Rabbi Nachman, a founder of Hasidic Judaism who made a pilgrimage to Zion in 1799 during Napoleon Bonaparte's short occupation of the region, considered it not his national property but rather a focal point of the spreading energy of the Creator. It therefore made sense for him to return modestly to his country of birth, where he eventually died and was buried with great ceremony.

But when Simon Schama, like other pro-Zionist historians, refers to "the remembered connection between the ancestral land and Jewish experience," he is denying Jewish consciousness the thoughtful consideration it deserves. In actuality, he is referring to Zionist memory and to his own extremely personal experiences as an Anglo-Saxon Zionist. To illustrate this point, we need look no further than the introduction to his intriguing book *Landscape and Memory*, in which he recounts his experience collecting funds for the planting of trees in Israel as a child attending a Jewish school in London:

The trees were our proxy immigrants, the forests our implantation. And while we assumed that a pinewood was more beautiful than a hill denuded by grazing flocks of goats and sheep, we were never exactly sure what all the trees were for. What we did know was that a rooted forest was the opposite landscape to a place of drifting sand, of exposed rock and red dirt blown by the winds. The Diaspora was sand. So what should Israel be, if not a forest, fixed and tall?[18]

For the moment, let us ignore Schama's symptomatic disregard for the ruins of the many Arab villages (with their orange orchards, *sabr* cactus patches, and surrounding olive groves) upon which the trees of the Jewish National Fund were planted and cast their shadow, hiding them from sight. Schama knows better than most that forests planted deep in the ground have always been an essential motif of the politics of romantic nationalist identity in Eastern Europe. Typical of Zionist writing is his tendency to forget that forestation and tree planting, throughout rich Jewish tradition, were never regarded as a solution to the "drifting sand" of exile.

To reiterate, the Promised Land was undoubtedly an object of Jewish longing and Jewish collective memory, but the traditional Jewish connection to the area never assumed the form of a mass aspiration for collective ownership of a national homeland. The "Land of Israel" of Zionist and Israeli authors bears no resemblance to the Holy Land of my true forefathers (as opposed to the mythological forefathers), whose origins and lives were embedded within the Yiddish culture of Eastern Europe. As with the Jews of Egypt, North Africa, and the Fertile Crescent, their hearts were filled with a deep awe and a sense of mourning for what was, to them, the most important and sacred place of all. So exalted worldwide was this place that, during the many centuries following their conversion, they had made no effort to resettle there. According to most of the rabbinically educated figures whose writings have survived the passage of time, "the Lord gave, and the Lord hath taken away" (Job 1:21), and when God would send the Messiah, the cosmic order of things would change. Only upon the arrival of the redeemer would the living and the dead gather together in eternal Jerusalem. For most, the hastening of collective salvation was considered a transgression to be severely punished; for

---

18   Simon Schama, *Landscape and Memory*, London: Fontana Press, 1995, 5–6.

others, the Holy Land was largely an allegorical, intangible notion—
not a concrete territorial site but an internal spiritual state. This reality
was perhaps best reflected in the reaction of the Jewish rabbinate—
traditional, ultraorthodox, Reform, and liberal alike—to the birth of
the Zionist movement.[19]

History as we define it deals not only with a world of ideas but
also with human action as it plays out in time and space. The human
masses of the distant past did not leave behind written artifacts, and
we know very little about how their beliefs, imagination, and emotions
guided their individual and collective actions. The way they dealt with
crises, however, provides us with a bit more insight into their priori-
ties and their decisions.

When Jewish groups were expelled from their places of residence
during acts of religious persecution, they did not seek refuge in their
sacred land but made every effort to relocate to other, more hospitable
locations (as in the case of the Spanish expulsion). And when the
more malicious and violent protonationalist pogroms began to take
place within the Russian empire, and the increasingly secular persecuted population began to make its way, full of hope, to new shores,
only a tiny, marginal group, imbued with modern nationalist ideology, imagined an "old/new" homeland and set their course for
Palestine.[20]

This was also true both before and after the appalling Nazi genocide. In fact, it was the United States' refusal, between the
anti-immigration legislation of 1924 and the year 1948, to accept the
victims of European Judeophobic persecution that enabled decision
makers to channel somewhat more significant numbers of Jews
toward the Middle East. Absent this stern anti-immigration policy,
it is doubtful whether the State of Israel could have been established.

---

19   Despite the existence of a number of more "Land"-related conceptions,
which (not coincidentally) were among the most ethnocentric, the trickle of pilgrims
and the small minority of immigrants from both Europe and the Middle East confirm
the tendency of the Jewish masses, the Jewish elite, and the Jewish leadership to refrain
from immigrating to Zion.

20   The masses of assimilationists—from Liberal Israelites to international
socialists—were not the only ones to have trouble understanding the essence of
Zionism's new pseudo-religious connection to the Holy Land. The Bund, the most
widespread semi-nationalist movement among Yiddish speakers in Eastern Europe,
was also astounded by the effort to spur Jewish immigration to the Middle East.

Karl Marx once said, paraphrasing Hegel, that history repeats itself: the first time as tragedy, the second as farce. In the early 1980s, US President Ronald Reagan decided to allow refugees of the Soviet regime to immigrate to the United States, an offer greeted with overwhelming demand. In response, the Israeli government exerted pressure to have the gates of immigration to the United States blocked by all possible means. Because the immigrants continued to insist on the United States, and not the Middle East, as their preferred destination, Israel collaborated with Romanian ruler Nicolae Ceauşescu to limit their ability to choose. In return for payoffs to Ceauşescu's Securitate and the corrupt Communist regime in Hungary, more than one million Soviet immigrants were routed to their "national state," a destination they had not chosen and in which they did not want to live.[21]

I do not know whether or not Schama's parents or grandparents had been given the choice to return to the Middle Eastern "land of their forefathers." In any event, like the large majority of immigrants, they, too, chose to migrate westward and continue to endure the torments of "diaspora." I am also certain that Simon Schama himself could have immigrated to his "ancient homeland" anytime he chose to do so, but preferred to use migrating trees as a proxy and to leave immigration to the Land of Israel to Jews who were unable to gain entry into Britain or the United States. This brings to mind an old Yiddish joke that defines a Zionist as a Jew asking another Jew for money to donate to a third Jew in order to make aliyah to the Land of Israel. It is joke more applicable at present than ever before, and a point to which I will return throughout this book.

In sum, the Jews were not forcibly exiled from the land of Judea in the first century CE, and they did not "return" to twentieth-century Palestine, and subsequently to Israel, of their own free will. The role of the historian is to prophesize the past, not the future, and I am fully aware of the risk I am taking by hypothesizing that the mythos of exile and return, so heated an issue during the twentieth century because of the nationalism-driven anti-Semitism of the era, could possibly cool

---

21   On this cynical form of Zionism, see the interview with Yaakov Kedmi, former head of the Nativ espionage agency, which confirms that "in the eyes of the Soviet Jews, the non-Israeli option—the US, Canada, Australia, and even Germany—will always be preferable to the Israeli option." *Yedioth Aharonot*, April 15, 2011 (in Hebrew).

down during the twenty-first. This will be possible, however, only if the State of Israel changes its policies and halts actions and practices that awaken Judeophobia from its slumber and ensure the world new episodes of horror.

NAMES OF AN ANCESTRAL LAND

One goal of this book is to trace the ways in which the "Land of Israel" was invented as a changing territorial space subject to the rule of the "Jewish people," which, as I have argued here in brief and elsewhere at length, was also invented through a process of ideological construction.[22] Before beginning my theoretical journey to the depths of the mysterious land that has proven so fascinating to the West, however, I must first draw the reader's attention to the conceptual system in which the land has been embedded. As is not uncommon with other national languages, the Zionist case contains its own semantic manipulations, replete with anachronisms that frustrate all critical discourse.

In this brief introduction, I address one prominent example of this problematic historical lexicon. The term "Land of Israel," which does not and has never corresponded with the sovereign territory of the State of Israel, has for many years been widely used to refer to the area between the Mediterranean Sea and the Jordan River and, in the recent past, to large areas located to the east of the river as well. For more than a century, this fluid term has served as an instrument of navigation and a source of motivation for the territorial imagination of Zionism. For those who do not live with the Hebrew language, it is difficult to fully understand the weight carried by this term and its influence on Israeli consciousness. From school textbooks to doctoral dissertations, from high literature to scholarly historiography, from songs and poetry to political geography, this term continues to serve as code, unifying political sensitivities and branches of cultural production in Israel.[23]

---

22   For three works related to the subject of this book but that, for the most part, offer different insights and conclusions, see Jean-Christophe Attias and Esther Benbassa, *Israel Imaginaire*, Paris: Flammarion, 1998; Eliezer Schweid, *Homeland and a Land of Promise*, Tel Aviv: Am Oved, 1979 (in Hebrew); and Yoad Eliaz, *Land/Text: The Christian Roots of Zionism*, Tel Aviv: Resling, 2008 (in Hebrew).

23   The term is also used in adjectival form in Modern Hebrew for, e.g., a "Land of Israel experience" (as opposed to an Israeli experience), "Land of Israel poetry," a

Shelves in bookstores and university libraries in Israel hold count-less volumes on subjects such as "the prehistoric Land of Israel," "the Land of Israel under Crusader rule," and "the Land of Israel under Arab occupation." In the Hebrew-language edition of foreign books, the word "Palestine" is systematically replaced with the words *Eretz Israel* (the Land of Israel). Even when the writings of important Zion-ist figures such as Theodor Herzl, Max Nordau, Ber Borochov, and many others—who, like most of their supporters, used the standard term "Palestine" (or *Palestina*, the Latin form used in many European languages at the time)—are translated into Hebrew, this appellation is always converted into the "Land of Israel." Such politics of language sometimes results in amusing absurdities, as, for example, when naïve Hebrew readers do not understand why, during the early-twentieth-century debate within the Zionist movement over the establishment of a Jewish state in Uganda instead of Palestine, the opponents of the plan were referred to as "Palestinocentric."

Some pro-Zionist historians also attempt to incorporate the term into other languages. Here, too, a prominent example is Simon Schama, who titled his book commemorating the colonizing enter-prise of the Rothschild family *Two Rothschilds and the Land of Israel*,[24] despite the fact that during the historical period in question, the name Palestine was customarily used not only by all the European languages but also by all the Jewish protagonists discussed in Schama's book. The British-American historian Bernard Lewis, another loyal supporter of the Zionist enterprise, goes even further in a scholarly article in which he attempts to use the term "Palestine" as little as possible, by making the following statement: "The Jews called the country *Eretz Israel*, the Land of Israel, and used the names Israel and Judea to designate the two kingdoms into which the country was split after the death of king Solomon."[25]

"Land of Israel landscape," etc. Over the years, some Israeli universities have established separate departments, based on the disciplines of history and geography, whose mandate is an exclusive focus on "Land of Israel Studies." For support of the ideological legitimacy of this pedagogy, see Yehoshua Ben-Arieh, "The Land of Israel as a Subject of Historical-Geographic Study," in *A Land Reflected in Its Past*, Jerusalem: Magnes, 2001, 5–26 (in Hebrew).

24   London: Collins, 1978.

25   Bernard Lewis, "Palestine: On the History and Geography of a Name," *The International History Review* 2:1 (1980), 1.

It is no surprise that Judeo-Israelis are certain of the eternal, unequivocal nature of this designation of tenure, which leaves no room for doubt as to ownership in both theory and practice and is believed to have held sway since the divine promise itself. As I have already argued elsewhere in a somewhat different manner, more than Hebrew speakers think by means of the mythos of the "Land of Israel," the mythological Land of Israel considers itself through them and, in so doing, sculpts an image of national space with political and moral implications of which we may not always be aware.[26] The fact that since the establishment of Israel in 1948 there has been no territorial correspondence between the Land of Israel and the sovereign territory of the State of Israel provides good insight into the geopolitical mentality and the consciousness of border (or absence thereof) that are typical of most Judeo-Israelis.

History can be ironic, particularly with regard to the invention of traditions in general and traditions of language in particular. Few people have noticed, or are willing to acknowledge, that the Land of Israel of biblical texts did not include Jerusalem, Hebron, Bethlehem, or their surrounding areas, but rather only Samaria and a number of adjacent areas—in other words, the land of the northern kingdom of Israel.

Because a united kingdom encompassing both ancient Judea and Israel never existed, a unifying Hebrew name for such a territory never emerged. As a result, all biblical texts employed the same pharaonic name for the region: the land of Canaan.[27] In the book of Genesis, God makes the following promise to Abraham, the first convert to Judaism: "And I will give to you and to your offspring after you the land of your sojournings, all the land of Canaan, for an everlasting possession" (17:8). And in the same encouraging, fatherly tone, he later commands Moses: "Go up this mountain of the Abarim,

---

26   Shlomo Sand, *The Words and the Land: Israeli Intellectuals and the Nationalist Myth*, Los Angeles: Semiotext(e), 2011, 119–28.

27   On the nonexistence of a united kingdom, see Israel Finkelstein and Neil A. Silberman, *The Bible Unearthed*, New York: Touchstone, 2002, 123–68. The "land of Canaan" appears in Mesopotamian and, particularly, Egyptian sources. In one instance in the book of Genesis, Canaan is referred to as "the Land of Hebrews" (40:15). Jewish nationalist unease with the region's biblical name resulted in efforts to "correct" somewhat the written texts. See Yohanan Aharoni, *The Land of Israel in Biblical Times: A Historical Geography*, Jerusalem: Bialik, 1962, 1–30 (in Hebrew).

Mount Nebo, which is in the land of Moab, opposite Jericho, and view the land of Canaan" (Deut. 32:49). In this manner, the popular name appears in fifty-seven verses.

Jerusalem, in contrast, was always located within the land of Judea, and this geopolitical designation, which took root as a result of the establishment of the small kingdom of the House of David, appears on twenty-four occasions. None of the authors of the books of the Bible would have ever dreamed of calling the territory around God's city the "Land of Israel." For this reason, 2 Chronicles recounts that "He broke down the altars and beat the Asherim and the images into powder and cut down all the incense altars throughout all the land of Israel. Then he returned to Jerusalem" (34:7). The land of Israel, known to have been home to many more sinners than was the land of Judea, appears in eleven additional verses, most with rather unflattering connotations. Ultimately, the basic spatial conception articulated by the authors of the Bible is consistent with other sources from the ancient period. In no text or archaeological finding do we find the term "Land of Israel" used to refer to a defined geographic region.

This generalization is also applicable to the extended historical period known in Israeli historiography as the Second Temple period. According to all the textual sources at our disposal, neither the successful Hasmonean revolt of 167–160 BCE nor the failed Zealot rebellion of 66–73 CE took place in the "Land of Israel." It is futile to search for the term in 1 or 2 Maccabees or the other noncanonical books,[28] in the philosophical essays of Philo of Alexandria, or in the historical writings of Flavius Josephus. During the many years when some form of Jewish kingdom existed—whether sovereign or under the protection of others—this appellation was never used to refer to the territory between the Mediterranean Sea and the Jordan River.

Names of regions and countries change over time, and it is sometimes common to refer to ancient lands using names assigned to them later in history. However, this linguistic custom has typically been practiced only in the absence of other known and acceptable names for the places in question. For example, we all know that Hammurabi did not rule over the eternal land of Iraq but

---

28   The book of Tobit, which appears to have been written at the beginning of the second century BCE, contains a use of the term "Land of Israel" to refer to the territory of the kingdom of Israel (14:6).

over Babylonia, and that Julius Caesar did not conquer the great land of France but rather Gaul. On the other hand, few Israelis are aware that David, son of Jesse, and King Josiah ruled in a place known as Canaan or Judea, and that the group suicide at Masada did not take place in the Land of Israel.

This problematic semantic past, however, has not troubled Israeli scholars, who regularly reproduce this linguistic anachronism unhindered and unhesitatingly. With rare candor, their nationalist-scientific position was summed up by Yehuda Elitzur, a senior scholar of the Bible and historical geography from Bar-Ilan University:

> According to our conception, our relationship with the Land of Israel should not be simply equated to other peoples' relationship with their homelands. The differences are not difficult to discern. Israel was Israel even before it entered the Land. Israel was Israel many generations after it went into the Diaspora, and the Land remained the Land of Israel even in its barrenness. The same is not true of other nations. People are English by virtue of the fact that they live in England, and England is England because it is inhabited by English people. Within one or two generations, English people who leave England cease to be English. And if England were to be emptied of Englishmen, it would cease to be England. The same is true of all nations.[29]

Just as the "Jewish people" is considered to be an eternal "*ethnos*," the "Land of Israel" is regarded as an essence, as unchanging as its name. In all the interpretations of the above-mentioned books of the Bible and texts from the Second Temple period, the Land of Israel is portrayed as a defined, stable, and recognized territory.

In illustration of this point, I offer the following examples. In a new, high-quality Hebrew translation of the second book of Maccabees, published in 2004, the term "Land of Israel" appears in the volume's introduction and footnotes 156 times, whereas the Hasmoneans themselves had no idea that they were leading a revolt within a territory bearing that name. A historian from the Hebrew University of Jerusalem made a similar leap, publishing an academic study under

---

29 Yehuda Elitzur, "The Land of Israel in Biblical Thought," in Yehuda Shaviv, *Eretz Nakhala*, Jerusalem: World Mizrachi Center, 1977, 22 (in Hebrew).

the title *The Land of Israel as a Political Concept in Hasmonean Literature*, even though this concept did not exist during the period in
question. This geopolitical mythos has proven so prevalent in recent
years that editors of the writings of Flavius Josephus have even dared
to incorporate the term "Land of Israel" into the translation of the
texts themselves.[30]

In actuality, as one of the many names of the region—some of
which were no less accepted in Jewish tradition, such as the Holy
Land, the Land of Canaan, the Land of Zion, or the Land of the
Gazelle—the term "Land of Israel" was a later Christian and rabbinical invention that was theological, and by no means political in nature.
Indeed, we can cautiously posit that the name first appeared in the
New Testament in the Gospel of Matthew. Clearly, if the assumption
that this Christian text was composed toward the end of the first
century CE. is correct, then this usage can truly be considered groundbreaking: "But when Herod died, behold, an angel of the Lord
appeared in a dream to Joseph in Egypt, saying, 'Rise, take the child
and his mother and go to the land of Israel, for those who sought the
child's life are dead. So he got up, took the child and his mother and
went to the land of Israel" (Matt. 2:19–21).

This one-time, isolated use of the phrase "Land of Israel" to refer
to the area surrounding Jerusalem is unusual, as most books of the
New Testament use "Land of Judea."[31] The appearance of the new term
may have stemmed from the first Christians referring to themselves
not as Jews but as the children of Israel, and we cannot rule out the
possibility that "Land of Israel" was inserted into the ancient text at a
much later date.

The term "Land of Israel" took root in Judaism only after the
destruction of the Temple, when Jewish monotheism was showing
signs of decline throughout the Mediterranean region as a result of
the three failed anti-pagan revolts. Only in the second century CE,
when the land of Judea became Palestina by Roman order and an

---

30   *The Second Book of Maccabees*, "Introduction," trans. and commentary by
Uriel Rappaport, Jerusalem: Yad Izhak Ben-Zvi, 2004 (in Hebrew); Doron Mendels,
The Land of Israel as a Political Concept in Hasmonean Literature, Tubingen: Mohr, 1987.
See, for example, *History of the Jewish War against the Romans*, Warsaw: Stybel, 1923,
Book II, 4;1, and 1–15; 6, . For a more recent translation, see Book VII, 3, 3, Ramat Gan:
Masadeh, 1968, 376 (in Hebrew).

31   See, for example, Mark 1:5, John 3:22 and 7:1, Acts 26:20, and Romans 15:31.

important segment of the population began to convert to Christianity, do we find the first hesitant occurrences of the term "Land of Israel" in the Mishnah and Talmud. This linguistic appellation may have also emerged from a deep fear of the growing strength of the Jewish center in Babylonia and its increasing pull on the intellectuals of Judea.

However, as suggested above, the Christian or rabbinical incarnation of the term is not identical in meaning to the term as employed in the context of the Jewish connection to the territory in the age of nationalism. Like the ancient and medieval concepts of "people of Israel," "chosen people," "Christian people," and "God's people"— which meant something completely different from the meanings assigned today to modern peoples—so, too, do the biblical "Promised Land" and "Holy Land" of the Jewish and Christian traditions bear no resemblance to the Zionist homeland. The land promised by God encompassed half the Middle East, from the Nile to the Euphrates, whereas the religious and more limited borders of the Talmudic Land of Israel always demarcated only small, noncontiguous areas assigned different degrees of sacredness. Nowhere in the long and diverse tradition of Jewish thinking were these divisions conceived of as borders of political sovereignty.

Only in the early twentieth century, after years in the Protestant melting pot, was the theological concept of "Land of Israel" finally converted and refined into a clearly geonational concept. Settlement Zionism borrowed the term from the rabbinical tradition in part to displace the term "Palestine," which, as we have seen, was then widely used not only throughout Europe but also by all the first-generation Zionist leaders. In the new language of the settlers, the Land of Israel became the exclusive name of the region.[32]

This linguistic engineering—part of the construction of ethno-centric memory, and later to involve the Hebraization of the names of regions, neighborhoods, streets, mountains, and riverbeds— enabled Jewish nationalist memory to make its astonishing leap back in time over the territory's long non-Jewish history.[33] Much

---

32   Even the song "Hatikvah," written in the late 1880s, still privileged the term "Land of Zion" over "Land of Israel." All other Jewish names for the region lost out and disappeared from the culture of national discourse.

33   David Ben-Gurion explained the rationale behind this effort in 1949: "We are obliged to remove the Arabic names for reasons of state. Just as we do not recognize the Arabs' proprietorship of the land, so also do we not recognize their spiritual

more significant for our discussion, however, is the fact that this territorial designation, which neither included nor related to the vast majority of the population, quickly made it easier to view that majority as an assemblage of subtenants or temporary inhabitants, living on land that did not belong to them. Usage of the term "Land of Israel" played a role in shaping the widely held image of an empty land—"a land without a people," eternally designated for a "people without a land." Critical examination of this prevalent but false image, which was in fact formulated by an Evangelical Christian, better enables us to understand the evolution of the refugee problem during the 1948 war and the revival of the settlement enterprise in the aftermath of the 1967 war.

My main goal in this book is to deconstruct the concept of the Jewish "historical right" to the Land of Israel and its associated nationalist narratives, whose only purpose was to establish moral legitimacy for the appropriation of territory. From this perspective, the book is an effort to critique the official historiography of the Zionist Israeli estab-lishment and, in the process, to trace the ramifications of Zionism's influential paradigmatic revolution within a gradually atrophying Judaism. From the outset, the rebellion of Jewish nationalism against Jewish religion involved a steadily increasing instrumentalization of the latter's words, values, symbols, holidays, and rituals. From the onset of its settlement enterprise, secular Zionism was in need of formal religious attire, both to preserve and fortify the borders of the "*ethnos*" and to locate and identify the borders of its "ancestral land." Israel's territorial expansion, together with the disappearance of the Zionist socialist vision, made this formal attire even more essential, bolstering the status of Israel's ethnoreligious ideological constituen-cies toward the end of the twentieth century within the government and the military.

But we must not be deceived by this relatively recent process. It was the nationalization of God, not his death, that lifted the sacred veil from the land, transforming it into the soil on which the new nation began to tread and build as it saw fit. If for Judaism the

proprietorship and their names." Quoted in Meron Benvenisti, *Sacred Landscape: The Buried History of the Holy Land since 1948*, Berkeley: University of California Press, 2000, 14.

opposite of metaphysical exile was primarily messianic salvation, embracing a spiritual connection to the place though lacking any concrete claim to it, for Zionism the opposite of the imagined exile was manifested in the aggressive redemption of the land through the creation of a modern geographic, physical homeland. Absent permanent borders, however, this homeland remains dangerous for both its inhabitants and its neighbors.

CHAPTER ONE

Making Homelands:
Biological Imperative or National Property?

What is a country? A country is a piece of land surrounded on all sides by boundaries, usually unnatural. Englishmen are dying for England, Americans are dying for America, Germans are dying for Germany, Russians are dying for Russia. There are now fifty or sixty countries fighting in this war. Surely so many countries can't all be worth dying for.

—Joseph Heller, *Catch-22*, 1961

The "external frontiers" of the state have to become "internal frontiers" or— which amounts to the same thing—external frontiers have to be imagined constantly as a projection and protection of an internal collective personality, which each of us carries within ourselves and enables us to inhabit the space of the state as a place where we have always been—and always will be—at home.

—Étienne Balibar, "The Nation Form: History and Ideology," in *Race, Nation, Class: Ambiguous Identities*, 1988

The theoretical discussions of nations and nationalism conducted during the late twentieth and early twenty-first century dedicated only marginal attention to the construction of modern homelands. The territorial space, the "hardware," in which a nation actualizes its own sovereignty was not paid the same academic consideration as the "software"—the relations between culture and political sovereignty, or the role of historical myths in sculpting the national entity. Nonetheless, just as nation-making projects cannot be carried out without a political mechanism or an invented historical past, they also require a geo-physical imagination of territory, in order both to provide support and to serve as a constant focus of nostalgic memory.

What is a homeland? Is it the place for which Horace once said "it is sweet and fitting" to die? This well-known adage has been quoted by many devotees of nationalism over the past two centuries,[1] although with a different meaning than the one intended by the eminent Roman poet of the first century BCE.

Because many of the terms we use today are derived from ancient languages, it is difficult to distinguish the mental substance of the past from the modern sensitivities of the present. All historical conceptualization undertaken without meticulous historiographical effort presents a potential for anachronism. The concept of "homeland" is one case in point: though the concept exists in many other languages, it does not always carry the same moral baggage, as we have noted.

In the more ancient Greek dialects, we find the term *patria* (πατρίδα) and, somewhat later, *patris* (πατρίς), which found its way into ancient Latin as *patria*. Derived from the noun "father" (*pater*), the term left its imprint on a number of modern European languages, as in the Italian, Spanish, and Portuguese *patria*, the French *patrie*, and incarnations in other languages, all of which were derived from the ancient language of the Romans. The meaning of the Latin term gave rise to the English "fatherland," the German *vaterland*, and the Dutch *vaderland*. However, some synonyms base their conception of homeland on the concept of mother, such as the English "motherland," or the concept of home, such as the English "homeland," the German *heimat*, and the Yiddish *heimland* (הײמלאַנד). In Arabic, by contrast, the term *watan* (وطن) is etymologically related to the concept of property or inheritance.

The Zionist scholars who devised the modern Hebrew language, whose mother tongue was typically Russian (and/or Yiddish), adopted the term *moledet* (מולדת) from the Bible, apparently following the example of the Russian *rodina* (Родина), which means something closer to place of birth or family origin. *Rodina* is somewhat similar to the German *heimat*, and its echoes of romantic (and perhaps sexual) longing appear to have been consistent with the Zionist connection to the mythological Jewish homeland.[2]

---

1   "Dulce et decorum est pro patria mori." Horace, *Odes* 3.2 in *Odes and Epodes*, Cambridge: Harvard University Press (Loeb Classical Library), 2004, 144–5. These lines were written between 23 and 13 BCE. In its Zionist incarnation, the same sentiment was articulated using the words "It is good to die for our country," which were attributed to Josef Trumpeldor, a pioneering Jewish settler who was killed in 1920 in a clash with local Arabs. As Trumpeldor had studied Latin in his younger years, he may have in fact quoted Horace just before his death.

2   On the relationship between the Russian term *rodina* and the German term

In any event, the concept of homeland, which made its way to the threshold of the modern era from the ancient Mediterranean via medieval Europe, is associated with various meanings that typically do not correspond with the way it has been understood since the rise of nationalism. But before I delve into the thick of the matter, we must first acknowledge and rid ourselves of a few widely held preconceptions regarding the relationship between humans and the territorial spaces they inhabit.

THE HOMELAND—A NATURAL LIVING SPACE?

In 1966, the anthropologist Robert Ardrey dropped a small sociobiological bombshell that, at the time, had surprisingly potent reverberations throughout a relatively wide readership. His book *The Territorial Imperative: A Personal Inquiry into the Animal Origins of Property and Nations*[3] aimed at challenging how we think about territory, borders, and living space. For everyone who until then had believed that defending a home, a village, or a homeland was the product of conscious interests and historical cultural development, Ardrey sought to prove that defined space and the consciousness of borders are deeply ingrained in biology and evolution. He maintained that humans have an instinctual drive to appropriate territory and to defend it by all means necessary, and that this hereditary drive dictates the manner in which all living creatures behave under different conditions.

After extended observations of a variety of animals, Ardrey reached the conclusion that even if not all species are territorial, many are. Among animals of different species, territorialism is a congenital instinct that developed through mutation and natural selection. Meticulous empirical research showed that territorial animals launch ferocious attacks against trespassers on their living space, particularly those of the same species. Conflicts between males in a given space, which scholars formerly viewed as reflecting competition over females, are actually brutal contests over property. Much more surprising was Ardrey's finding that control of territory imbues those

---

heimat, see Peter Bickle, *Heimat: A Critical Theory of the German Idea of Homeland*, New York: Camden House, 2002, 2–3.

3   New York: Atheneum, 1970.

who control it with energies not possessed by outsiders attempting to penetrate it. Among most species, there is "some universal recognition of territorial rights" that conditions and guides all systems of power relations among them.

Why do animals need territory? asks Ardrey. The two most important of the many reasons are (1) animals select specific areas where they can sustain their material existence through access to food and water; and (2) territory serves as a defensive cushion and as protection against enemy predators. These primal spatial needs are rooted in the long process of evolutionary development and became part of the genetic inheritance of "territorialists." This natural inheritance produces an awareness of borders and provides the basis for flocks and schools. The need of animals to defend their living space impels their collective socialization, and the resulting unified group enters into conflict with other groups of the same species.

Had Ardrey limited himself to an account of animal behavior, his study would have attracted much less attention and remained a subject for debate between experts in ethology, despite his considerable rhetorical skills and colorful language.[4] His theoretical goals and conclusions, however, were much more ambitious. Going beyond empirical premises within the field of zoology, he also sought to understand the "rules of the game" of human behavior as passed down through the generations. Exposing the territorial dimension of the living world, he believed, would enable us to better understand the nations of the world and the conflicts between them throughout history. On this basis, he reached the following decisive conclusion:

> If we defend the title to our land or the sovereignty of our country, we do it for reasons no different, no less innate, no less ineradicable, than do lower animals. The dog barking at you from behind his master's fence acts for a motive indistinguishable from that of his master when the fence was built.[5]

---

4   For more on this, see Geoffrey Gorer, "Ardrey on Human Nature: Animals, Nations, Imperatives," in Ashley Montagu (ed.), *Man and Aggression*, London: Oxford University Press, 1973, 165–7.

5   Ardrey, *Territorial Imperative*, 5.

The territorial aspirations of human beings, then, are manifestations of an ancient biological imperative that shapes the most basic aspects of human behavior. Yet Ardrey goes even further by maintaining "that the bond between a man and the soil he walks on should be more powerful than his bond with the woman he sleeps with," an assertion he backs up with the rhetorical question, "How many men have you known of, in your lifetime, who died for their country? And how many for a woman?"[6]

This final statement leaves us with no doubt as to its author's generational identity. As an American born in 1908 and thus a child during the First World War and its aftermath, Ardrey was well aware of the casualties of war. As an adult, he knew many members of the Second World War generation and witnessed the wars in Korea and Vietnam. Written at the beginning of the Vietnam War, his book embodies significant aspects of the international situation of the 1960s. The process of decolonization that commenced in the wake of the Second World War more than doubled the number of hitherto existing "national territories." Although the First World War was followed by the establishment of a wave of new nations, the process reached its height with the rise of the states of the so-called Third World. Moreover, the wars of national liberation waged in places such as India, China, Algeria, and Kenya paint a picture of an all-encompassing struggle aimed at the acquisition of defined independent national territories. At the end of the fighting, the spread of nationalist sentiment outside the borders of the West endowed the globe with broad diversity and decorated it with close to two hundred colorful national flags.

The scientific imagination of sociobiology typically turns history on its head. Like the rest of the social sciences, sociobiology ultimately tailors its terminology to suit conceptual by-products of social and political processes witnessed by its practitioners in the course of their lives. Sociobiologists, however, are typically unaware that later events in history usually provide a better explanation for earlier events than vice versa. Borrowing most of their terms from social experience, these researchers of nature then adapt them to the task of better understanding the living environment they are studying. Next, they retrain their focus on human society and attempt to better

---

6   Ibid., 6–7.

understand it by using terminology and images from the natural world, which were originally borrowed from the conceptualization that accompanies and is produced by historical processes. Consider, for example, how the nationalist wars for territory fought in the 1940s, and the arduous struggles for national homelands waged between the late 1940s and the 1960s, were regarded as catalysts for evolutionary processes genetically ingrained in most living creatures.

Despite the significant differences between the two, the biological determinism of sociobiology bears some resemblance to the equally well-known approach of geographic determinism developed by the German geographer and ethnographer Friedrich Ratzel and, later, by Karl Haushofer and others. Although Ratzel himself did not coin the term "geopolitics," he is nonetheless considered one of its founders. He was also one of the first to firmly incorporate a sophisticated consideration of biological conditions into political geography. Though averse to simple racialist theories, he nonetheless believed that inferior peoples were obligated to support advanced civilized nations and that through such contact they, too, could reach cultural and spiritual maturity.

As a former student of zoology who became a staunch supporter of Darwinist theories, Ratzel was convinced that a nation was an organic body whose development required the constant change of its territorial borders. Just as the skin of all living creatures stretches as they grow, homelands also expand and must necessarily enlarge their borders (although they may also contract and even cease to exist). "A nation does not remain immobile for generations on the same piece of land," Ratzel declared. "It must expand, for it is growing."[7] Although he believed that expansion was contingent on cultural, and not necessarily on aggressive, activity, Ratzel was the first to coin the phrase "living space" (*lebensraum*).

Karl Haushofer went one step further by developing a theory of national living space; it was no coincidence that his field of research, geopolitics, became popular in territorially frustrated Germany between the two world wars. This academic profession, which had many proponents in Britain, the United States, and, even earlier, in Scandinavia, sought to explain international power relations on the

_____

7   Quoted in David Thomas Murphy, *The Heroic Earth: Geopolitical Thought in Weimar Germany, 1918–1933*, Ohio: Kent State University Press, 1997, 9.

basis of patterns of natural processes. The thirst for space came to play a central role in the theoretical apparatus aimed at providing a general explanation for aggravated tensions between nation-states in the twentieth century.

Geopolitical logic maintained that every nation in the midst of demographic consolidation and growth was in need of living space— that is, the expansion of the original homeland. And because Germany had a smaller per-capita territorial area than the surrounding countries, it had the national and historical right to expand outside its borders. Expansion should supposedly take place in economically weaker regions that had, either in the present or the past, been home to an "ethnic" German population.[8]

Germany's late entry into the colonial race that began in the late nineteenth century also provided an appropriate environment for popular theories of "living space" to thrive. Germans felt deprived by the division of the territorial spoils of the imperialist superpowers and even more frustrated by the terms of the peace settlement the nation had been forced to accept at the end of the First World War. In this context, according to the above-mentioned theses, it had to strengthen itself territorially, in accordance with the natural law that controlled relations between nations throughout history. Non-German geographers were initially enthusiastic at the prospect.

But when natural law is based entirely on ethnic origin and land, there arises an extremely volatile linkage between geopolitics and ethnocentrism. As a result, the situation in Germany soon exploded. Haushofer and his colleagues did not influence Hitler and his regime so much as they effectively served it, albeit indirectly, by providing the Führer with ideological legitimacy for his insatiable desire for conquest. After the Nazis' military defeat, their theories were "scientifically" eradicated.[9] Ardrey's popular theories were also rather quickly forgotten, and although sociobiological explanations would periodically gain increased attention, their application to the evolution of homelands continued to fade. Despite the appeal of Ardrey's

---

8   For more on Haushofer, see ibid., 106–10.

9   It took geopolitics quite some time to recover from its experience under Nazi rule, but by the 1970s it had already been reintroduced as a legitimate field of study. See David Newman, "Geopolitics Renaissant: Territory, Sovereignty and the World Political Map," in David Newman (ed.), *Boundaries, Territory and Postmodernity*, London: F. Cass, 1999, 1–5.

analysis, ethology ultimately moved away from the strict determinism that characterized his and some of his colleagues' approaches to territorial behavior.[10]

First, it became evident that the developed primates most closely related to human beings—chimpanzees, gorillas, some baboons—are not "territorialists" at all, and that the behavior of animals vis-à-vis their environment is much more diverse than Ardrey's account might suggest. Even birds, which are arguably the most territorial type of animal, exhibit behaviors that are much more dependent on changes in their surroundings than on hereditary impulses. Experiments involving alterations in animals' living conditions have proven that aggressive behavior can take on new manifestations in the wake of geo-biological change.[11]

Anthropologists with broader historical knowledge must never disregard the fact that the human species, which to the best of our knowledge originated on the African continent, flourished and prospered demographically due precisely to the fact that it did *not* cling to familiar territory but migrated onward and continued to conquer the world with its light legs and swift feet. As time passed, the planet came to be increasingly populated by migrating tribes of human hunters and gatherers who incessantly moved forward in their search for new fields of sustenance and more abundant shores for fishing. Only when nature provided for their basic needs did humans stop in a given area and turn it, to some degree, into their home.

What later bound humans to the land in a stable and permanent manner was not a biological predisposition to acquire permanent territory but the beginning of agricultural cultivation. The transition from nomadism to sedentary settlement first took place around the alluvial soil left by rivers, which improved the land for agriculture without the complex human knowledge typically required to do so. Gradually and increasingly, the sedentary way of life became familiar. It was the cultivation of land that alone provided the basis for the development of territorial civilizations, led by a number of societies that, over time, emerged as great empires.

---

10   See especially Konrad Lorenz's famous book *On Aggression*, London: Methuen, 1967.

11   On this subject, see John Hurrell Crook, "The Nature and function of territorial aggression," in Montagu (ed.), *Man and Aggression*, 183–217.

Yet early kingdoms of this kind—such as Mesopotamia, Egypt, and China—developed no collective territorial consciousness shared by all those who worked the land. The borders of these immense empires could not be ingrained in popular consciousness as boundaries delineating the living space of farmers or slaves. In all agrarian civilizations, we can assume that land was important to the producers of food. We can also assume that such subjects had a psychological attachment to the land they themselves worked. It is doubtful, however, whether they possessed any sense of connection to the broader territories of the kingdom.

In ancient traditional civilizations, nomadic and agricultural alike, land was sometimes conceived of as a female deity responsible for birthing and creation of everything that lived upon it.[12] Tribes or villages on different continents deemed sacred parts of the land they inhabited, but this attribution of sacred status bore no resemblance to modern patriotism. Land was almost always thought of as the property of the gods, not of human beings. In many cases, ancient humans regarded themselves as paid workers or tenants who were using the land temporarily and were by no means its owners. By means of its religious agents, the gods (or God, with the emergence of monotheism) granted the land to their followers and, when there were lapses in ritual obedience, reclaimed it from them at will.

PLACE OF BIRTH OR CIVIL COMMUNITY?

Unlike Ardrey, who traced the origin of national territorialism to the living world of nature, historians linked the birth of the "homeland" we know today to the emergence of the term in ancient texts. It has been widespread practice for scholars of the past to write about nations as if they had existed since the beginning of civilization. Indeed, not only many popular but also many academic history books have depicted eternal, universal homelands.

Because the historian's primary raw material, unlike that of the anthropologist, is the written text, historical constructions of the past always begin with and are based on what are usually called

---

12   Examples include Gaia, the primordial earth goddess of Greek mythology, and the Canaanite goddess Asherah.

primary sources. Historians are of course interested in knowing who produced the source in question, as well as the circumstances of its production, and it is commonly accepted that a "good" historian must first be a cautious philologist. However, we rarely encounter scholars who never lose sight of the fact that almost all the sources that have been passed down from generation to generation (except material remains) were produced by a small class of educated elites who consistently accounted for only a miniscule percentage of all premodern societies.

Such accounts are of extreme importance, as without them we would know very little about history. Nevertheless, any assumption, determination, or conclusion regarding the worlds of the past that does not take into consideration the subjectivity and narrow intellectual perspective of all written testimony—whether literary, legal, or from some other realm of social activity—is ultimately worth very little. Historians, who presumably are aware of the technology of their own narrative reconstructions, must recognize that they will never know the true thoughts and feelings of those who worked the land, the silent majority of all past societies who left behind no written remnants. As we know, every tribe, village, and valley had its own dialect. Members of nomadic tribes and land-bound farmers, who possessed extremely limited means of communication and lacked basic knowledge of reading and writing, did not need to develop sophisticated vocabulary to work, to give birth, or even to pray. In the world of agriculture, communication was frequently based on direct contact, gestures, and vocal tone, rather than on the all-encompassing abstract concepts formulated by the few educated members of the community and recorded in written texts, some of which we have at our disposal today.

The royal court scribes, philosophers, clergymen, and priests, in cultural and social symbiosis with the landed nobility, the wealthy urban classes, and the warrior class, provided future generations with a great deal of information. The problem is that historians all too often treat this material as an easily accessible, criterionless bank of comprehensive data regarding the basic systems of conceptualization and practices of the society as a whole. This has resulted in the widespread misleading and indiscriminate application to premodern societies of terms such as "race," *ethnos*, "nation," "migration of peoples," "exile of peoples," and "national kingdoms."

Primary sources are like the beam of a searchlight, illuminating small, isolated regions within an otherwise overwhelming sea of darkness. Every historical narrative is ultimately held captive by written remains. Careful researchers know that they must navigate such artifacts with caution and hesitation. They must work with no illusions, knowing that their writing relies on historical products indicative of the spirit of a small elite, representing the very tip of an iceberg that has melted away and can never be fully recreated.

This section offers a brief survey of a number of ancient Mediterranean texts and well-known European texts. Although the following discussion will unfortunately be extremely Eurocentric, its narrow perspective stems much less from any ideological position on my part than from the limitations of my own knowledge.

We begin in ancient Mediterranean society, where we encounter the concept of homeland in relatively early literary works. When the classical poet Homer refers to someone's land of birth in his epic poem *The Iliad*, he makes repeated use of the term *patrida* (πατρίδα). The beloved homeland is also the place for which warriors yearn while away on expeditions or in faraway battles, and where their wives, children, parents, and other family members remain. It is the idealized home to which mythological heroes return—for despite their heroism and great endurance, they too grow weary. It is also the sacred place where fathers are buried.[13]

Some three hundred years later, in his play *The Persians*, the oldest surviving tragedy, Aeschylus passionately describes the famous battle of Salamis fought between the Hellenic coalition and the Persian armies in 480 BCE. In it, he attributes this cry to his heroes: "Sons of Greece, go!/Free fatherland,/free children, wives,/shrines of our fathers' gods,/tombs where our forefathers lie./Fight for all we have!" The remains of the invading Persian army also return vanquished to the *patrida* and their family members in order to bemoan their bitter defeat.[14] But we must also pay heed to the fact that neither Greece nor Persia constituted the homeland of the warriors. Their homeland was

---

13   For example, see Homer, *The Iliad*, Ann Arbor: University of Michigan Press, 2007, 5.212; 9.41, 46.

14   Aeschylus, *The Persians*, New York: Oxford University Press, 1981, 59. Herodotus' *The History* also makes sparing use of the term, primarily to indicate place of origin. See, for example, Herodotus, *The History*, Chicago: University of Chicago Press, 1987, 3.140, 4.76.

their home, their city, their place of origin. It was the small territory where they were born, of which all of its children, its descendants, and its close neighbors possessed firsthand physical knowledge.

Later plays, such as Sophocles' *Antigone*, Euripides' *Medea*, and other works from the fifth century BCE, also feature the homeland as a place of incomparable importance that must not be abandoned, regardless of the cost. Being displaced from a homeland is always perceived of as eviction from a warm and protective home, as a major disaster, and, albeit rarely, as an exile worse than death. The homeland is the known, the safe, and the familiar, outside of which everything is foreign, threatening, and alienating.[15]

A short time later, when the warriors of Syracuse did battle with the Athenians, Thucydides wrote that the former fought to defend their homeland, while their enemies, the Athenians, waged war to annex a foreign land.[16] The concept of homeland appears many times in *The History of the Peloponnesian War*, but it is not a single place universal to all Hellenes. Although modern proponents of Greek nationalism would have liked it to be otherwise, the *patrida* of ancient literature is not identical to the land of Greece and cannot be conceived of as such. Historians use the term "homeland" only to refer to a single city-state, a specific polis. For this reason, in Thucydides' recreation of Pericles' famous funeral oration, it is Athens that is described as an object of admiration and worship.[17]

Greek references to the idea of the homeland suggest a unique and fascinating form of politicization of a territorial site. The homeland and its emotional baggage not only relate to geographic location but are also frequently applied within specific political frameworks. Just as territory was politicized, Hellenic politics were always territorial. To better understand this point, we momentarily direct our attention to the logic of Plato.

---

15   See, for example, Sophocles, *Antigone*, ll. 183, 200. and Euripides, *Medea*, ll. 34, 797ff.

16   Thucydides, *The History of the Peloponnesian War*, 6.69.

17   Ibid., 2.34–46. The Stoic school sometimes employed the term "homeland" to refer to the entire cosmos. In addition, although Greece was never recognized as a homeland, some educated Hellenes possessed a consciousness of shared cultural identity that stemmed from "shared blood" or linguistic and ritual similarity. For example, see Herodotus, *The Histories*, 8.144, and the famous words of Isocrates in *Panegyricus* 50.

Like Thucydides, the Athenian philosopher employs the term "homeland" to refer not to greater Greece but to an individual polis. Here, it is the sovereign city-state, together with its institutions and system of laws, that constitutes the true *patrida*. Plato repeatedly uses the term not merely in the simple sense of a place of birth or a physical area with its own longed-for landscapes, but primarily for the political entity, including its entire apparatus of civil administration. For example, in his well-known dialogue *Critias*, Plato attributes the following words to Socrates, in admonishment of his interlocutor:

> Has a philosopher like you failed to discover that our country is more to be valued and higher and holier far than mother or father or any ancestor, and more to be regarded in the eyes of the gods and of men of understanding? . . . and if she leads us to wounds or death in battle, thither we follow as is right; neither may anyone yield or retreat or leave his rank, but whether in battle or in a court of law, or in any other place, he must do what his city and his country order him; or he must change their view of what is just: and if he may do no violence to his father or mother, much less may he do violence to his country.[18]

As in other cases, here, too, the Platonic homeland is a city that constitutes a supreme value to which all other values are subordinate. Its uniqueness and moral power lies in its existence as an area of self-government exercised by sovereign citizens. Because of their great personal interest in this political entity, its members are obligated to defend their homeland—their community. This is also the origin of the need to sanctify it, to incorporate it into religious rituals, to worship it on holidays. Plato's unconditional patriotic demands revolved around a city-homeland that subordinated individual interests to the needs and values of the collective.

In many ways, the Athenian discourse concerning homeland resembles the modern-day understanding of the term. Loyalty, dedication to place, and willingness to make sacrifices in its name are considered sacred values, not to be questioned and certainly not to be discussed in tones of sarcasm. Superficially, this discourse appears to

---

18   Plato, *The Trial and Death of Socrates: Four Dialogues*, trans. Benjamin Jowett, New York: Dover Publications, 1992, 51.

represent the beginnings of nationalist consciousness, which in the past two centuries has come to enjoy a dominant status in human society. But was the homeland of Thucydides, Plato, and the other Athenians the same national homeland imagined by Benito Mussolini, Charles de Gaulle, Winston Churchill, and millions of other twentieth-century nationalists? At the end of the day, is there indeed nothing new under the sun?

In actuality, these two incarnations of homeland are as different as they are similar. Just as ancient Athenian society employed not representative democracy but direct participatory democracy, so too was it completely unfamiliar with the modern abstract, nationalist concept of homeland. The notion of homeland in the democratic states of ancient Greece was limited to patriotic loyalty to the polis, the small and supremely tangible city-state whose human and physical landscape was well known to all its citizens, owing to their firsthand knowledge of its size and borders. Daily they met its other inhabitants in the agora and joined them in general meetings, celebrations, and theatrical performances. From unmediated experience sprang the essence and intensity of patriotic sentiment, which was, for them, one of the most important areas of social consciousness.

In truth, the level of communication and the limited means of cultural dissemination were insufficient for facilitating the emergence of a large democratic homeland. Despite Aristotle's dictum (as usually and loosely translated) about man being, by nature, a political animal, that classical human animal was the citizen of a city-state devoid of form, precise maps, newspapers, radio, compulsory education, and other such provisions. Therefore, when the Hellenic world was later united under the leadership of Alexander of Macedonia, the old patriotism of the polis dissolved, just as the democratic dimension disappeared from the everyday life of much of Greece.

In addition, the ethical lines demarcating democracy in the ancient city-state were far from identical to the political boundaries of the modern democracy. The sovereign citizens of the Athenian polis constituted a minority of the city's overall population and the farmers who cultivated the surrounding lands. Only free males born to parents who already held citizenship were considered to be autochthonous and were incorporated into the electorate and its elected institutions. Women, immigrants, people of mixed descent, and the many slaves possessed no rights and were excluded from self-sovereignty. The universal conception of humanity that would emerge and splinter in the modern era was still unknown in the Mediterranean world, which was rich, refined, and thoroughly elitist.[19]

Loyalty to the homeland in the form of devotion to a league of citizens possessing representative self-government would appear in some of the literary works written in Rome during the Republican era. On the eve of its disappearance and its transformation into an immense empire, numerous scholars decorated it with verbal praises that would be preserved in European culture up to the modern era. We have already noted Horace's famous declaration in *Odes* about the sweetness of dying for the homeland. More than intending to sanctify national soil, however, the great poet meant to express his devotion to the Republican homeland, or the *res publica*, just after Julius Caesar buried it forever.

In *The Catiline Conspiracy*, Roman historian Gaius Sallustius Crispus, a loyal follower of Caesar's, identified the homeland with liberty, as distinct from to the rule of the few.[20] The same was true of Marcus Tullius Cicero, the statesman whose contribution to thwarting this anti-Republican conspiracy earned him the distinguished status of "father of the homeland." In his famous oration against the conspirator, he berates his opponent:

> Should your parents dread and hate you, and be obstinate to all your endeavors to appease them, you would doubtless withdraw somewhere from their sight. But now the country, the common parents of us all, hates and dreads you and has long regarded you as a parricide, intent upon the design of destroying her. And will you neither respect her authority, submit to her advice, nor stand in awe of her power?[21]

---

19   On the complex relationship between autochthonism and politics in Athens, see the articles in Nicole Loraux's fascinating book *Né de la terre. Mythe et politique à Athènes*, Paris: Seuil, 1996, and also Marcel Detienne, *Comment être autochtone*, Paris: Seuil, 2003, 19–59. On the Spartans' startling concept of space and their unique attitude toward ancestral land, see Irad Malkin, *Myth and Territory in the Spartan Mediterranean*, Cambridge: Cambridge University Press, 1994.

20   Gaius Sallustius Crispus, *The Catiline Conspiracy*, 58.

21   Cicero, *The Catiline Conspiracy*, Oration 4.7, in William Duncan, *Cicero's Select Orations Translated into English*, London: Printed for G. G. J. and J. Robinson and J. Evans, 1792, 127.

In the end, this highly acclaimed orator, known for his rhetorical acuity, lost his life in the events that led to the decline and demise of the republican structure that was so dear to his heart. Shortly before his death, however, he put down in writing his unswerving views on the homeland in a Socratic-style dialogue echoed in many writings that appeared in Western Europe on the eve of the modern era. Cicero's well-known *Treatise on the Laws* considers the common association between homeland and republic in a dualistic formulation:

> I should say, that Cato [a well-known Roman statesman], and municipal citizens like him, have two countries, one, that of their birth, and the other, that of their choice . . . In the same way, we may justly entitle as our country, both the place from where we originated, and that to which we have been associated. It is necessary, however, that we should attach ourselves by a preference of affection to the latter, which, under the name of the Commonwealth, is the common country of us all. For this country it is, that we ought to sacrifice our lives; it is to her that we ought to devote ourselves without reserve; and it is for her that we ought to risk and hazard all our riches and our hopes. Yet this universal patriotism does not prohibit us from preserving a very tender affection for the native soil that was the cradle of our infancy and our youth.[22]

Like devotion to the Hellenic polis, loyalty to the Roman Republic was a supreme value, an extolled attribute transcending even nostalgia for one's birthplace and the landscapes of childhood, inasmuch as it was the republic where one was his own sovereign, an equal partner in the ruling collective. Here an army of civilian volunteers, as distinct from a paid army, could be mobilized; here an individual could be required to die for the place. It was considered justified to be asked to sacrifice oneself for the sake of the public, as the public was the manifestation of one's own sovereignty. As has already been stated, this conception of political homeland, which would remain unique in the premodern world, resembles the homeland of the modern nationalist era.

---

22   Marcus Tullius Cicero, *The Political Works of Marcus Tullius Cicero*, London: Edmund Spettigue, 1841, 78–9.

Indeed, many enlightened intellectuals of the eighteenth century were enchanted by the patriotic declarations they retrieved from the ancient Mediterranean world, and regarded them as evidence of an ideal regime of liberty, a realm without tyrants or kings. Nevertheless, one of these thinkers, the Neapolitan philosopher and historian Giambattista Vico, reminded his readers that Roman nobles "did not hesitate for the safety of their various fatherlands, to consecrate themselves and their families the will of the laws, which by maintaining the common security of the fatherland kept secure for each of them a certain private monarchical reign over his family."[23] Vico also did not refrain from criticizing his own Latin forefathers, noting that "the true fatherland was the interest of a few fathers . . ."[24]

Cicero's Republican homeland was indeed an oligarchy, consisting of a limited body of civilians, with the electorate and the elected always belonging to the same small elite. Most important for our discussion of the concept of homeland is the fact that only those who were physically present in the Roman capital were eligible to take part in elections. Citizens residing outside the limits of the city itself were stripped both of the right to vote and the right to be elected. And because in Cicero's time most citizens were already living outside the city, they were ineligible to play an active role in their beloved homeland.

The expansion and growing power of imperial Rome divested it of its connection to the civil homeland. In a number of ways, the empire was a great league of many city-states that each lacked any real practical independence. The third century CE transformation of the empire's nonslave inhabitants into citizens who lacked the right to participate in the shaping of sovereignty obscured even further the emotional and political connections to the republic homeland. By this means, it facilitated the consolidation and dissemination of a universal monotheism—with ties to specific holy places—that would come to be based on different psychological mechanisms and different intellectual associations.

The founders of the Christian Church would attempt to shift this loyalty from the republican homeland to the heavenly kingdom. As all

---

23   Thomas G. Bergin and Max H. Fisch (eds.), *The New Science of Giambattista Vico*, Ithaca: Cornell University Press, 1984, 23–4.
24   Ibid., 255.

people are equal before God, the old devotion to the Greek polis and the Roman Republic of slave owners would ostensibly be replaced by devotion to the eternal life that would follow life in this world. As early as Augustine, we see expression of the idea that citizenship, in the true and pure sense of the word, could be found only in the city of God. If it was appropriate to die for the homeland, its appropriateness derived from being a sacrifice by a faithful believer in God's heavenly kingdom.[25] This approach to love for the *patria aeterna* would reverberate throughout large circles within the Church and serve as a central foundation of Christian faith.

The civilian armies of the Roman Republic disappeared with the expansion of the empire; mercenaries carried the flag of Rome not only throughout the Mediterranean basin but deep into conquered Europe. This historic encounter triggered change on the dormant wooded continent, although the weakness and disintegration of the empire is what ultimately freed the European tribes and localities from the Roman yoke. Only then do we see the beginning of the long, gradual process that concluded in the creation of a new civilization with a completely different structure of social relations. Emergent European feudalism had no citizens, invited no heroic patriotic death, and produced no loyalty to a political-territorial homeland. Nonetheless, elements of the Mediterranean conceptual world trickled into the culture and languages of Europe via a variety of channels, primarily through the works and the increasing power of the Christian Church.

As effectively described by Ernst Kantorowicz in *The King's Two Bodies*, the Athenian and Roman Republican concept of homeland faded away completely in societies in which loyalty and personal dependence were hegemonic.[26] Although *patria* became a commonly used word, it was typically employed to refer to a person's place of birth or residence. "Homeland" became synonymous with the concept of "little country"—*pays* in the French dialects and *heimat* in the German dialects—the region in which one's home was located, in which children were born and raised, and in which the extended family continued to live.

---

25   See Augustine's discussion in *The City of God*, 5.16, 17.

26   Ernst H. Kantorowicz, *The King's Two Bodies*, Princeton: Princeton University Press, 1981, 233–4. See also Kantorowicz's brilliant article "*Pro Patria Mori* in Medieval Political Thought," *American Historical Review* 56:3 (1951), 472–92.

Kings and princes employed the term differently. Elite segments of society applied the concept to a variety of political entities, turning kingdoms, dukedoms, earldoms, and jurisdictions of taxation and judicial activity into "homelands." The papacy also did not refrain from making use of it, periodically calling for the rescue of the homeland in order to defend Christian harmony and the security of all the faithful.

Typically, the willingness of knights to die was a sacrifice on behalf of either the feudal lord, the Church, or, later, the king and kingdom. The formula *pro rege et patria* (for king and country) grew increasingly popular in the thirteenth and fourteenth centuries and would survive until the modern revolutions. But even in the more organized kingdoms, there was a persistent tension between loyalty to the heavenly homeland and loyalty to the national identities that were always subordinated to hierarchical structures. In addition, the military ethos of premodern European societies encompassed devotion to the homeland in the form of substantive values such as honor, glory, and appropriate financial remuneration for one's willingness to sacrifice.

The slow decline of feudal society and upheavals within the Church also resulted in reinvigoration of the beleaguered concept of *patria*. The gradual rise of the medieval city, not only as a commercial and financial center but as an active force in the regional division of labor, caused many in Western Europe to regard it as their primary homeland. According to Fernand Braudel, these cities were the site of crystallization of a primal form of nascent patriotism that informed later national consciousness.[27]

At the same time, Renaissance society's fondness for the classical tradition of the Mediterranean resulted in another widespread, albeit unoriginal, invocation of the ancient "homeland," as various humanists attempted to apply the concept to the new city-states that emerged as oligarchic republics.[28] At an extraordinarily prophetic moment in history, Machiavelli was even enticed to apply it to the entire Italian

---

27   Fernand Braudel, *Capitalism and Material Life 1400–1800*, Glasgow: Collins, 1973, 399.

28   On the people of the Renaissance period, see Maurizio Viroli, *For Love of Country: An Essay on Patriotism and Nationalism*, Oxford: Clarendon Press, 1995, 24–40.

peninsula.²⁹ Nowhere at this point, however, did the idea of homeland reverberate the way it had in ancient Athens or the Roman Republic, not to mention in the territorial contexts of the later nation-states.

Nor were the evolving absolutist monarchies capable of producing the expressions of loyalty and the willingness to sacrifice for the sake of the homeland that would become familiar after these monarchies' demise in the late modern period. For example, let us consider Montesquieu and Voltaire. These eighteenth-century thinkers clearly understood why kingdoms were not perceived as homelands, and explained it to their readers. In his 1748 work *The Spirit of the Laws*, Montesquieu, who possessed broad historical knowledge, asserted:

> The state continues to exist independently of love of the homeland, desire for true glory, self-renunciation, sacrifice of one's dearest interests, and all those heroic virtues we find in the ancients and know only by hearsay.³⁰

Voltaire, whose historical knowledge was as broad as that of Montesquieu, addressed the value of "homeland" in his witty *Philosophical Dictionary* of 1764:

> A fatherland is a composite of several families; and as we usually stand by our family out of self-love when we have no conflicting interest, so because of the same self-love we support our town or village which we call our fatherland. The bigger the fatherland the less we love it, because divided love is weaker. It is impossible to love tenderly too numerous a family which we hardly know.³¹

In fact, though incisive in their analyses, both thinkers were firmly rooted in an era on the verge of vanishing. They were quite familiar with

---

29   Niccolò Machiavelli, "An Appeal to Take Back Italy and Liberate Her from the Barbarians," *The Prince*, Wellesley: Dante University Press, 2003, 131–4. Despite this chapter and a few other comments in his other writings, it would be an exaggeration to portray Machiavelli as a patriotic idealizer of Italy, as does William J. Langdon in *Politics, Patriotism and Language*, New York: Peter Lang, 2005.

30   Charles de Secondat Montesquieu, *The Spirit of the Laws*, Cambridge: Cambridge University Press, 1989, 25.

31   François Voltaire, *Philosophical Dictionary*, New York: Penguin Classics, 2004, 327.

the term's application to the relationship between people and their places of birth and the areas in which they grew up, but had no way of knowing that this array of personal mental connections would be transformed and transferred to broad political structures. The monarchies established on the eve of the modern era lay the foundation for the rise of nationalism by setting into centrifugal motion the administrative languages that would soon emerge as national languages. Most important for our discussion here is the fact that, though lacking the territorial sensitivities that would accompany the rise of national democracies, they began to draw what, in some cases, would become the future borders of the homeland.

Both Montesquieu and Voltaire were liberal pioneers and consistent and courageous advocates of human freedoms. However, both men also exhibited a clearly antidemocratic temperament; they had no interest in the illiterate masses as political subjects and thus were incapable of imagining mass collective identification with a kingdom or political homeland.

It is no coincidence that the first theoretical patriot to emerge from the European Enlightenment was in many ways also its first anti–liberal democrat. Jean-Jacques Rousseau did not address the concept of homeland in a systematic manner and found it virtually unnecessary to clarify his intended meaning when he made use of the term, as he did abundantly. However, some of his writings contain explicit exhortations to preserve patriotic values, employing rhetoric more characteristic of modern statesmen than of eighteenth-century philosophers.

In his moving "Dedication to the Republic of Geneva," which he wrote in 1754 and used as an introduction to the *Discourse on the Origin of Inequality between Men*, he already explains the kind of homeland he would prefer if afforded the ability to choose one for himself:

> I would have chosen ... a state where, with all private individuals being known to one another, neither the obscure maneuvers of vice nor the modesty of virtue could be hidden from the notice and the judgment of the public ... I would therefore have sought for my homeland a happy and tranquil republic, whose antiquity was somehow lost in the dark recesses of time ... I would have wanted to choose for myself a homeland diverted by a fortunate impotence

from the fierce love of conquest . . . I would have searched for a country where the right of legislation was common to all citizens, for who can know better than they the conditions under which it suits them to live together in a single society? . . . And if in addition providence had joined to it a charming location, a temperate climate, a fertile country and the most delightful appearance there is under the heavens, to complete my happiness I would have desired only to enjoy all these goods in the bosom of that happy homeland, living peacefully in sweet society with my fellow citizens.[32]

His entire life, Rousseau yearned to see the establishment of sovereign egalitarian societies within defined territories that could serve as natural homelands. At the same time, in his *Social Contract*, this republican son of Geneva, with his many internal contradictions, did not hesitate to ponder: "How could a man or a people seize a vast territory and keep out the rest of the human race except by a criminal usurpation since the action would rob the rest of mankind of the shelter and food that nature has given them all in common?"[33]

Despite these ethical and "anarchistic" declarations, Rousseau remained a completely political thinker. His egalitarian conception of man and the universalist perspective on which it was based led him to search for freedom, which was always dear to his heart, only in the realm of politics: that is, in the construction of political community. Yet the father of the idea of modern democracy also maintained that the freedom he sought could be realized only in small units, or, more precisely, in the form of direct democracies. For this reason, the ideal homeland, according to Rousseau's basic theory, must remain small and tangible.[34] A prophet waiting for the gates of the nationalist era to open, Rousseau watched keenly from his great height and distance but remained unable to enter.

---

32   Jean-Jacques Rousseau, *Discourse on the Origin of Inequality*, Indianapolis: Hackett Publishing Co., 1992, 2–5.

33   Jean-Jacques Rousseau, *The Social Contract* 1.9, New York: Penguin Classics, 1968, 67.

34   True to form, in his advice to the sizable Polish confederation, Rousseau also articulated a contradictory view: to implement aggressive patriotic policies, including indoctrination of the masses. See, for example, *Considérations sur le gouvernement de Pologne* (1771), Paris: Flammarion, 1990, 172–4.

TERRITORIALIZATION OF THE NATIONAL ENTITY

Patriotic battle cries could be heard during the Low Countries' revolt against the Spanish kingdom in the late sixteenth century and even more so in the early seventeenth century. During the English revolution of the mid-sixteenth century, the radical wing of the Levellers identified the homeland with the free community, which was fully mobilized against monarchic tyranny. And if at the outset of the American Revolution the rebels regarded Britain as their motherland, their attitude had changed by its conclusion, when a new conception of patriotism began to percolate among them. "The land of the free and the home of the brave"[35] was on its way, soon to make its mark on history.

One of the most important milestones in the new and promising career of the homeland in the modern era was undoubtedly the French Revolution, particularly its Republican phase. If until then the concept of homeland had served as a point of reference for the political and intellectual elite—state officials, ambassadors, scholars, poets, philosophers, and the like—it now strode confidently into the alleyways of the people. For example, "La Marseillaise," composed by a junior officer from Alsace, became a popular refrain sung by the large revolutionary battalion that arrived in Marseille and was quickly learned by many more. "Franche-Comté, children of the fatherland, the day of glory has arrived! Against us stands tyranny," sang the volunteer fighters as they marched, trembling, to the battle of Valmy in September 1792 to fight the hired armies of the old world. And those who were not wounded by the salvo of cannon fire were even able to finish the words to the song: "Sacred love of the fatherland, support our avenging arms. Liberty, cherished liberty, fight with thy defenders!" For good reason, the song was later adopted as France's national anthem.[36]

In the meantime, however, Napoleon's conquests were arousing a new wave of patriotic demands outside France, in areas such as the future territories of Germany and Italy. One by one, the seeds of

---

35   Excerpt from the lyrics of the patriotic US song "The Star-Spangled Banner," which was written in 1814 and became the national anthem of the United States in 1931.

36   On the patriotic awakening during the Revolution, see Philippe Contamine, "Mourir pour la Patrie: Xe–XXe siècle," in Pierre Nora (ed.), *Les Lieux de mémoire II, La Nation*, Paris: Gallimard, 1986, 35–7.

patriotism were planted, soon to transform old Europe into a spectacular garden of nations and, thus, of homelands.

From the stormy 1790s in France to the popular uprisings that rocked the Arab world at the beginning of the second decade of the twenty-first century, almost all revolutionaries and rebels have pledged their love to liberty and, at the same time, declared their loyalty to homeland. The homeland would reemerge on a large scale in the European Spring of Nations of 1848 and would also unite the rebels of the Paris Commune of 1871. And although the Russian Revolution took pride in its internationalism, when put to the test during its war of survival against the Nazi invasion, the Soviet Union revived patriotism as an effective ideological mechanism for mass mobilization. The two world wars of the twentieth century were brutal conflicts fought in the name of a guiding superideology that regarded the state as the entity responsible for protecting the homeland, or at least attempting to work for its benefit by expanding its borders. As we have seen, the acquisition of territory was regarded as a major aim of the nationalist struggles in the great campaigns for decolonization that swept the world from the 1940s to the 1970s. Both the socialists and the communists of the Third World were first and foremost patriots, and only later focused on distinctions of sociopolitical affiliation.

The major question that still needs to be answered is how deep emotion toward a small and familiar physical place was translated into a conceptual composite, applied to vast territories that humans could never know firsthand in their entirety. Perhaps the answer lies in the slow yet decisive territorialization of politics in the age of nationalism.

Despite their great historical importance, the patriots of the English revolution, the volunteers who sang the "Marseillaise" while marching into battle during the French Revolution, the rebels against Napoleonic occupation, and even the revolutionaries of 1848 in the capital cities of Europe still constituted minorities of the populations in which they conducted their activities—large minorities, but minorities nonetheless. And even if homeland had become a key concept in the restless capital cities, most people remained tillers of the soil, relatively untroubled by the qualities of the political leadership, which was already swaying to the cultural and linguistic tones of modernity.

What beckoned them into the new homeland or, perhaps more accurately, what began to construct the concept of national territory in their consciousness was the legislation emanating from the political centers and applied throughout the territories. These laws exempted significant numbers of farmers from feudal obligations, taxes, and other burdens, and in some cases also provided decisive recognition of their ownership to the land they cultivated. The new land laws and agrarian reforms served as the primary means for the transformation of dynastic monarchies and large principalities into increasingly stable nation-states and, as a result, for the evolution of multidimensional homeland areas.

The great urbanization that was responsible for much social change in the nineteenth and twentieth centuries, and for the detachment of the masses from their "small homelands," constituted another important precondition for enabling many to come to terms, at least conceptually, with a large, unfamiliar national territory. Mobility gave rise to hitherto unknown variations of the need for social belonging, and this need was met by national identity, which offered the enticing promise of facilitating individual and collective adherence and rootedness within a larger geographic area.

These and many other political, legal, and social processes were only the starting gun or, rather, the invitation. The invitees still had a long and exhausting road to travel before finding safe haven in their expansive imagined homelands.

It is important to remember that homelands did not produce nationalism, but rather the opposite: homelands emerged from nationalism. The homeland would prove to be one of the more surprising, and perhaps the most destructive, creations of the modern era. The establishment of nation-states imbued with new meaning the areas under their rule and the borders that delineated them. Through the construction of a deep sense of belonging to a national group, a cultural-political process created Britons, Frenchmen, Germans, Italians, and, later, Algerians, Thais, and Vietnamese, from diverse mixtures of local cultures and languages. This process invariably produced an array of emotions related to a defined physical spaces. Landscape became a fundamental component of collective identity, forming the walls, so to speak, of the home in which the evolving nation was being invited to reside. Thai historian Thongchai Winichakul offers a persuasive analysis of this dynamic in his delineation of the evolution of the Siamese nation-state. The "geo-body" of the new nation, he contends, was one condition for its own formation, and it was first and foremost modern mapping that facilitated the creation of this territorial entity.[37] It is customary to refer to historians as the first authorized agents of a nation, but this appellation must also be bestowed on the geographers who undertook its mapping. While historiography helped the national state to discipline its primeval past, it was cartography that helped it actualize its imagination and its power over its territory.

The material, technological precondition for the expansion of territorial imagination was the slow development and spread of mass communications. Political and cultural factors completed the process by creating effective state vehicles for the formulation and dissemination of ideology. From the printing revolution of the fifteenth century—which grew increasingly sophisticated as it evolved into comprehensive and invasive multi-channel media—to the opening of schools and the advent of compulsory education during the late nineteenth and twentieth centuries, the relationship between elite culture and popular culture changed completely, as did the relationship between the cultures of the urban centers and the rural periphery. If not for printing, the kingdoms' maps and the geographers' increasingly sophisticated diagrams of the physical world would have been seen by very few. If not for the provision of public education for all, only a small number of people would have known and been able to identify the borders of their own countries. Mapmaking and education became a natural, integrated complex that served to carve out a defined, familiar space. For this reason, maps that propagate and inculcate the borders of the homeland deep within the consciousness of every student still adorn the walls of today's classrooms. Often beside these maps hang large pictures of the landscapes of the homeland's different regions. Such reproductions and photographs feature valleys, mountains, and villages, but never urban settings.[38] Nearly always, the visual representation of the homeland is accompanied by a touch of romantic longing for an ancient rootedness in the land.

As part of the intensive nationalization of the masses, imbuing the population with a love for the homeland naturally depended on knowledge of its geography. And just as physical cartography enabled

37   Thongchai Winichakul, *Siam Mapped: A History of the Geo-Body of a Nation*, Honolulu: University of Hawaii Press, 1997.

38   Paul Gilbert, *The Philosophy of Nationalism*, Boulder: Westview Press, 1998, 97.

humans to conquer the earth and acquire its many treasures, political mapping helped states to capture the hearts of its citizens. As we have already seen, alongside the history lessons concerning the national entity's past, geography lessons established and sculpted its territorial embodiment. By these means, the national entity was simultaneously being imagined and shaped in both time and space.

Among the results of this was the complicated relationship between the laws of compulsory education and the laws of compulsory military conscription. Previously, in order to defend the territory under their control or to appropriate the territory of others, kingdoms had been forced to hire armies who had no knowledge of the territory and borders of the kingdoms that hired them—a problem gradually resolved for the modern nation-states by compulsory military conscription, based on the willing agreement of most citizens to serve in the armies of their respective states as long as a defined territory stood at their disposal. Thus, modern wars grew longer and increasingly "total" in nature, and, as a result, the number of lives thereby taken increased exponentially. In the new global world, willingness to die for the homeland, which in the ancient Mediterranean world had been the privilege of the few, now became the entitlement—and obligation—of all.

However, we would be mistaken to conclude that so many people were transformed into sworn patriots solely as a result of indoctrination or the manipulations of modern ruling elites. Had it not been for the systematic mechanical reproduction achieved by newspapers, books, and, later, radio broadcasts and cinema newsreels, and for the intensive pedagogic formation of a general system of compulsory state education, citizens would have remained much less aware of the role of national space in their lives. In order to identify their homeland, people had to know how to read and write and had to consume healthy servings of the extensive buffet known as "national culture." We can therefore conclude that as ideological mechanisms of the state, the new schools and the new communications media were directly responsible for the systematic creation of homelands and patriots.

Still, the primary reason for the broad consensus regarding the obligation of mass sacrifice for the sake of the people and the land on which it lived was the remarkable process of democratization that began in the late eighteenth century and spread across the globe. Throughout history, empires, kingdoms, and principalities had belonged to individuals; the Greek polis and the Roman Republic were controlled by the few. The modern state, whether liberal democratic or authoritarian democratic, was now supposed to be subject to the formal authority of all its citizens. Beginning at a defined age, all inhabitants were to hold citizenship and therefore be, in principle, the state's sovereign and legal rulers. The civil body's collective ownership of the state also meant collective ownership of its territorial space.[39]

As we know, the emergence of the modern state, with its criminal code and its civil-legal system, was one of the first conditions for the establishment of bourgeois property. The legitimization of private property within the modern state was stabilized and reinforced by the democratization and sovereignty gaining ground within it. In other words, society's abstract sense of collective ownership of the land within its state borders also served indirectly to reinforce recognition of the capital amassed by wealthy members of society, and the thriving of capital was not facilitated solely by the state's monopoly over violence but also by its absolute control over all its territory.

In this sense, territory is the common property of all shareholders in the nationalist enterprise. Even the completely destitute have something that belongs to them, and small property owners are still masters of the great national assets. This conception of collective ownership engenders a sense of satisfaction and security with which no political utopia or promise for the future can compete. This dynamic, which escaped most socialists and anarchists of the nineteenth century, proved itself during the twentieth century. Workers, clerks, artisans, and farmers marched together during the bloody nationalist conflicts, motivated by the political imagination that they were fighting for the homeland beneath their feet, which strengthened their steadfastness, as well as for a state whose leaders were their official representatives. These democratic representatives were charged with administering the property of the masses—that is, with defending the territory without which the state could not survive.

---

39   For one of the first discussions of the relationship between sovereignty and territory, see Jean Gottman's fascinating but ahistorical work *The Significance of Territory*, Charlottesville: University Press of Virginia, 1973.

This leads us to one source of the strong collective sentiments that would roil and inflame national modernity. When Samuel Johnson declared in the late eighteenth century that "patriotism is the last refuge of the scoundrel," he accurately foresaw the sort of political rhetoric that would dominate for the next two centuries: whoever could present himself as the most loyal watchdog of national property would become the uncrowned king of modern democracy.

Just as all property has its legal limits, every national space is bounded by borders now subject to international law. However, whereas it is possible to quantify the exact value of private property, including land, this is not true of collective national property; because the assets in question have no market, it is difficult to calculate their exact worth.

At the beginning of the nineteenth century, Napoleon could still sell the great Louisiana Territory of North America without eliciting any protest on the part of those who had just started to become French. And in 1867, when Russia sold Alaska (for the paltry sum of $7.2 million), the Russians hardly complained, and some Americans even protested the acquisition as a pointless waste of their money. Such acts of financial quantification and transfer of state property subsequently lost all validity and would not be repeated in the twentieth century.

In contrast, from the beginning of the twentieth century onward, new patriotic wars took the lives of massive numbers of victims. One example was the 1916 Battle of Verdun, one of the bloodiest and fiercest battles of the First World War. On a small patch of no-man's-land just a few square kilometers in area, more than 300,000 French and German soldiers were killed over a period of months, and far more than half a million were left wounded and disabled. Certainly, not all the soldiers remained in the wet, putrid trenches of their own free will. Although by that stage in the so-called Great War they thirsted for it much less than they had at its outset, most were still devoted to the supreme imperative of defending the homeland and suffused with a patriotic desire to avoid giving up even one kilometer of its territory. During the twentieth century, the prospect of dying for the homeland imbued male fighters with the sense that no other death could achieve such timeless nobility.

BORDERS AS BOUNDARIES OF SPATIAL PROPERTY

"Territory is no doubt a geographical notion, but it's first of all a jurid-ico-political one: the area controlled by a certain kind of power."[40] Despite the accuracy of this assessment by Michel Foucault, it fails to capture the true status of national space. The final sculpting of national territory is undertaken with the enthusiastic support of the subjects-turned-citizens: that is to say, its legal proprietors. It also requires the agreement of neighboring states and, at some stage, the authorization of international law. As in the case of all socio-legal manifestations, the border is primarily a historical product of power relations that at a certain point in time were recognized and frozen.

Fluid borders between large and small territories have existed throughout history, but they differed from the borders of the modern era. They were not geometrical lines but, rather, wide strips that lacked definition and permanence; in the case of natural objects—mountains, rivers, valleys, forests, deserts—that separated kingdoms from one another, the entire object served as the border. In the past, it was uncer-tain to which political authority many villages belonged, and, truth be told, many were uninterested in finding out. It was rulers who had a vested interest in recording their not-always-so-loyal taxpayers.

Many of today's international borders were delineated in an arbi-trary and incidental manner, and the delineation took place before the emergence of the nations in question. Empires, kingdoms, and principalities demarcated the areas under their control through diplo-matic agreements at the conclusion of wars. But the numerous territorial conflicts of the past did not result in prolonged world wars, and, in many cases, the primary impetus for armed struggle was not a craving for land itself. Prior to the growth of nationalism, territorial boundaries were never an issue about which no concessions could be made under any circumstances.

In this context, Peter Sahlins's rich empirical work offers particu-larly cogent insight.[41] Sahlins closely traced the evolution of the border

---

40   Michel Foucault, *Power/Knowledge: Selected Interviews and Other Writings 1972–1977* (edited by Colin Gordon), New York: Pantheon Books, 1980, 68.

41   Peter Sahlins, *Boundaries: The Making of France and Spain in the Pyrenees*, Berkeley: University of California Press, 1989.

between France and Spain in the Pyrenees from the seventeenth century onward, and observed that sovereignty under the old regime was applied much more to inhabitants than to territory. The slow, prolonged formation of the border, which began as an imaginary line marked in an extremely inaccurate manner by means of noncontiguous stones, reached a turning point during the French Revolution. By 1868, however, when the final border was agreed upon, territory had become the official property of the nation. The transition from a breached frontier zone to clearly demarcated territorial areas represented the domestication of space and its transformation into a homeland.[42]

Benedict Anderson advanced the same idea in his pioneering book *Imagined Communities*:

> In the modern conception, state sovereignty is fully, flatly, and evenly operative over each square centimeter of a legally demarcated territory. But in the older imagining, where states were defined by centers, borders were porous and indistinct, and sovereignties faded imperceptibly into one another.[43]

Like all first-time capitalists vis-à-vis their initial accumulation of assets, all nation-states at their first stage of evolution are hungry for space and thus driven to expand their borders and increase their landed property. For example, the United States came into being with an inherent inclination to annex additional territory. It refused, in fact, to recognize its own borders and acknowledged only flexible "frontier" areas that would presumably get incorporated into it at some point in the future. This was typical behavior for all settler states, whether in Africa, Australia, or the Middle East.[44]

The French Revolution, on the other hand, pursued the idea of "natural borders," on whose basis the revolutionaries strove to expand their state in the direction of major rivers and tall mountains that were often located far outside its "artificial" borders. In this manner, the French revolutionary imagination, followed by the Napoleonic

---

42   Ibid., 6–7, 191–2.

43   Benedict Anderson, *Imagined Communities: Reflections on the Origin and Spread of Nationalism*, London: Verso, 1996, 19.

44   On the difference between borders and frontier areas, see J. R. V. Prescott, *Political Frontiers and Boundaries*, London: Unwin Hyman, 1987, 12–51.

imagination, claimed the Rhine region and the Low Countries as organic parts of greater France. From its outset, the National Socialist revolution in Germany invoked the logic of "living space," which for the Nazis included Poland, the Ukraine, and western Russia, and which had a decisive impact on the outbreak of the Second World War.

It is no coincidence that the first nation-states also became the leading colonial powers. The causes and conditions for their territorial expansion were undoubtedly economic impulses and the increasing power and technological superiority of Western Europe. However, the patriotic masses' enthusiastic support for colonial expansion also played an important role in the insatiable drive to enlarge the territory under imperial control. At the same time, the frustration felt by large masses in states that missed out on the division of territorial spoils pushed many into the arms of a more aggressive radical nationalism.

Even nation-states that emerged in the Third World in opposition to colonial rule began to establish their territories in fierce border conflicts. The disputes between Vietnam and Cambodia, Iran and Iraq, and Ethiopia and Eritrea, for instance, did not differ substantially from the conflicts of a century earlier between Britain and France, France and Prussia, and Italy and Austria. The wave of democratic nationalism in Eastern Europe resulted in the final battles fought in the former Yugoslavia for the formation of the "correct" borders of the old continent.

The process of transforming land into national property typically began in the ruling centers but subsequently entered the broader social consciousness, fueling and complementing the process of appropriation from the bottom up. Unlike the situation in premodern societies, the masses themselves served as the high priests and guardians of the new sacred land. And as in the religious rituals of the past, the sacred area was unequivocally separated from the secular area surrounding it. Thus, in the new world, every centimeter of common property became part of the hallowed national territory that could never be relinquished. That is not to say that the external secular space would never become internal and sacred, as the annexation of additional land to national territory was always regarded as a classic act of patriotism. From the homeland, however, it was forbidden to take even one clump of earth.

Once borders become the indicator of the extent of national property, not merely as a line on the surface of the land but rather as a line of separation that also runs deep beneath the ground and demarcates airspace as well, it immediately assumes an essential aura of honor and a sense of sublimity. Some of these markings have been based on distant history, others on pure mythology. In such contexts, every shred of primordial knowledge that indicates the presence or control of the ostensible core or majority "ethnic" group of a modern nation over any parcel of land is used as a pretext for annexation, occupation, and colonization. Every marginal mythos or trivial legend from which it is possible to exploit an ounce of legitimacy for territorial rights and demarcation becomes an ideological weapon and an important building block in the construction of national memory.[45]

Ancient battlefields become sites of pilgrimage. The graves of the dictatorial founders of kingdoms as well as those of brutal rebels become official state historical sites. Consistently secular proponents of nationalism imbue inanimate landscapes with primordial and even transcendental elements. Democratic revolutionaries, including socialists who preach the brotherhood of nations, invoke wistful memories of monarchical, imperial, and even religious pasts in order to affirm and establish their control of as large a territory as possible.

In addition to aggressively gaining immediate ownership, it was generally necessary to invoke an extended dimension of time that enveloped the national space and endowed it with an air of timeless eternity. Being relatively abstract, the large political homeland was always in need of both stable points of reference in time and tangible spatial features. For this reason, as has already been asserted above, geographers, like historians, became part of the new pedagogic theology. According to this theology, national land ate into the long-term hegemony of the divine and, to a great extent, converted the heavens: in the modern era, god could be spoken of with much more irony than could ancestral lands.

During the nineteenth and twentieth centuries, the large, abstract homeland was by far the most dominant force in national and international politics. Millions died in its name, others died for its sake,

---

45   For a discussion of this subject based on a completely different theoretical approach, see Anthony D. Smith, "Nation and Ethnoscape," in *Myths and Memories of the Nation*, Oxford: Oxford University Press, 1999, 149–59.

and multitudes sought to continue living only within its borders. Like all other historical phenomena, however, its power was neither absolute nor (perhaps it is needless to say) eternal.

Not only did the homeland have external borders that delineated its territory, it also had an internal border that limited its psychological presence. People who struggled under the burdens of life or were unable to support their family with dignity tended to migrate to other countries. In doing so, they also exchanged national territories the way most people replace a garment that was once attractive but is now frayed—nostalgically, but with determination.

Mass immigration is no less characteristic of modernization than are the nationalization of populations and the construction of homelands. Despite the pain of pulling up roots and journeying to unknown destinations, many millions of people facing poverty, economic crises, persecution, and other such threats in the modern era have attempted to relocate to a living space that appeared to promise a more secure livelihood than did their country of origin. The difficult process of laying down new roots in an acquired homeland also turned immigrants into patriots, and even if the process was not always successful in the first generation, the new homeland inevitably struck deep roots within the hearts and minds of subsequent generations.

Throughout history, political phenomena emerge and ultimately vanish. The national homeland that started to take form in the late eighteenth century and turned into the "normal" and normative space of all those who became its citizens began to show the first signs of exhaustion at the end of the twentieth century. The phenomenon is, of course, still far from disappearing, and in "remote" corners of the globe people are still dying for tracts of national land. In other regions, however, traditional borders are already starting to dissolve.

The market economy that long ago demolished the small homeland and played an important role in constructing national homelands and delineating them within impenetrable borders has begun to partially erode its own previous creations, aided in this effort by the political elite and, to a greater extent, audiovisual and online media. The decline in value of agricultural cultivation as a means for creating economic wealth has also helped weaken the psychological power of the patriotism of the past. Today when Frenchmen, Germans, or Italians leave their homeland, neither the state nor its watchdogs are present at the border. Europeans now move within territorial spaces that have adopted completely new boundaries.

Verdun, which may be a symbol of the folly of twentieth-century patriotism, has become a popular tourist site. Ironically, today at Verdun no notice is taken of the passports or national identities of the Europeans who visit it. Although Europe's newly ordained land borders are undoubtedly steeper and at times no less brutal than the previous ones, the territories that lie within them no longer possess all the attributes of the old political homelands.

Frenchmen will apparently never again die for France, and Germans will most likely never again kill for Germany (or vice-versa). The Italians, on their part, will most likely continue the tradition embodied in the rant by the cynical elderly Italian man from Joseph Heller's *Catch-22* that appears as an epigraph at the beginning of the present chapter.

Although conventional mass killing has become increasingly problematic and complicated in the nuclear age, we cannot rule out the possibility that humans will find new ways of killing and being killed in the future. If they do, however, most likely it will be for the sake of a new, and as yet unknown, version of politics.

CHAPTER TWO

Mytherritory: In the Beginning, God Promised the Land

When you father children and children's children, and have grown old in the land, if you act corruptly by making a carved image in the form of anything, and by doing what is evil in the sight of the Lord your God, so as to provoke him to anger, I call heaven and earth to witness against you today, that you will soon utterly perish from the land that you are going over the Jordan to possess. You will not live long in it, but will be utterly destroyed.

—Deut. 4:25–6

What was the purpose of those three adjurations? One, that Israel shall not go up by a wall; one by which the Holy One, blessed be He, adjured Israel not to rebel against the nations of the world; and one by which the Holy One, blessed be He, adjured the idolaters [the nations of the world] that they not oppress Israel too much.

—Babylonian Talmud, Ketubot 13:111

The word "homeland" (*moledet*) appears in the books of the Bible a total of nineteen times, almost half in the book of Genesis. All the meanings assigned to the word have to do with a person's land of birth or familial place of origin, and never contain the civil or public dimensions encountered in the cultures of the Greek polis or the ancient Roman Republic. Biblical heroes never set out to defend their homeland in order to attain freedom, nor do they articulate expressions of civil love for it. They were also unfamiliar with the meaning of the "ultimate sacrifice" and the "sweetness" of dying for the homeland. In short, the idea of patriotism that developed in the northern Mediterranean basin was barely known on its southern shores and known even less in the Fertile Crescent.

Devotees of the Zionist idea that began to take shape toward the end of the nineteenth century appear to have been faced with a thorny issue. Because they employed the Bible as a title deed to Palestine, which would quickly become the "Land of Israel," they needed to use all means necessary to effect its transformation from an imagined foreign land from which all Jews were supposedly exiled into an ancient homeland once owned by their mythological ancestors. To fulfill this purpose, the Bible now began to take on the character of a nationalist book. From a collection of theological texts incorporating historical plots and divine miracles aimed at inculcating faith in its readers, it became a compilation of historiographic texts that bore only a smattering of optional religious meaning. In this context, it was necessary to obscure the metaphysical entity of God to the greatest extent possible and to distill from it a completely patriotic personality. The Zionist intellectuals all tended to be at least somewhat secular and were therefore uninterested in deep theological discussion. From their perspective, God, whose existence had been undermined, promised a land to his "chosen people" as a reward for devotedly maintaining their faith in him. In this way, he was converted into a sort of voice-over in a historical movie guiding a nation to strive for a homeland and to immigrate there.

It was no simple endeavor to persist in using the term "Promised Land" when the force that had done the promising was dying or, according to many, was already deceased.[1] It could not have been easy to plant an imagined sense of patriotism in theological works that were completely foreign to the nationalist spirit. Despite being complicated and problematic, the undertaking was ultimately successful. But its goal was not achieved by the talent of Zionist thinkers and writers alone. The true secret of its success was the historical circumstances in which it was carried out, which I will discuss later in this book.

GIFTED THEOLOGIANS BESTOW A LAND UPON THEMSELVES

The books of the Bible make no mention of the political dimension of a national homeland.[2] Unlike later Christianity, they do not teach

---

1   Amnon Raz-Krakotzkin articulated this point nicely in the title of his short article "There Is No God, but He Promised Us the Land," *Mita'am* 3 (2005), 71–6 (in Hebrew).

2   Three informative articles questioning whether the "Land of Israel" can be regarded as a homeland for the Jews have been published in Hebrew, although their theoretical underpinnings and conclusions are somewhat different from those proposed here. See Zali Gurevitz and Gideon Aran, "On the Spot (Israeli Anthropology),"

that the true homeland lies in the eternal heavens. Territory, however, does play a leading role in the stories. The word "land" appears in the Bible more than a thousand times and, in the vast majority of the texts, carries great significance.

In contrast to Jerusalem, which is not mentioned in the Pentateuch,[3] the land of Canaan is introduced in the beginning, in Genesis, and subsequently serves as a destination, an arena of action and of compensation, an inheritance, a place that is chosen, and plays other roles as well. It is described as "an exceedingly good land" (Num. 14:7), "a land of wheat and barley, of vines and fig trees and pomegranates" (Deut. 8:8), and of course "a land flowing with milk and honey" (Lev. 20:24; Exod. 3:8; Deut. 27:3). The fundamental assumption of the Jewish and non-Jewish general public alike is that the land was granted to the "seed of Israel" until the end of days, and numerous Biblical verses appear to confirm this assumption.

Like other masterpieces in the history of human literature, Biblical verses can be interpreted in different ways, and this versatility is one source of the power they hold. But this does not mean that every verse can be interpreted in completely contradictory ways. Paradoxically, despite the Christian scripts that trace the belief in Jesus to the land of Judea, the texts of the Bible repeatedly indicate that the Yahwistic religion neither appeared nor developed in the territory that God designated for his chosen ones. Surprisingly, the two first instances of theophany that played a decisive role in establishing God's following and lay the foundation for monotheism in the Western Hemisphere (Judeo-Christian-Islamic civilization) both in theory and in practice did not take place in the land of Canaan.

In the first instance, God appeared in Harran, in what is today Turkey, and issued the following instructions to Abram the Aramaean: "Go from your country and your kindred and your father's house to the land that I will show you" (Gen. 12:1). Indeed, the first follower of Yahweh abandoned his homeland and embarked on a journey to the

---

Alpayim 4 (1991), 9–44 (in Hebrew); Daniel Boyarin and Jonathan Boyarin, "The People of Israel Have No Motherland: On the Place of the Jews," *Teorya Uvikoret* 5 (1994), 79–103 (in Hebrew); Hagai Dagan, "The Concept of 'Homeland' and the Jewish Ethos: Chronicles of a Dissonance," *Alpayim* 18 (1999), 9–23 (in Hebrew).

3   Jerusalem is first introduced relatively late in the Bible, initially referred to as a hostile city in the book of Joshua (10:1) and only conquered and set ablaze by the tribe of Judah in the book of Judges (1:8).

unknown Promised Land. Because of the famine, he did not stay there long, and quickly relocated to Egypt.

According to the founding mythos, the second major dramatic encounter took place in the desert, during the Exodus from Egypt.[4] Yahweh engaged Moses directly during the giving of the Torah on Mount Sinai. After the Ten Commandments, in addition to his instructions, commandments, and advice, God also spoke of the Promised Land: "Behold, I send an angel before you to guard you on the way and to bring you to the place that I have prepared . . . When my angel goes before you and brings you to the Amorites and the Hittites and the Perizzites and the Canaanites, the Hivites and the Jebusites, and I blot them out" (Exod. 23:20, 23). Although the listeners should have already known that the land was not empty, the divine commitment now, for the first time, contains an explicit promise to remove its original inhabitants, who may disrupt the colonization.

That is to say, neither Abraham, the father of the nation, nor Moses, its first great prophet—both of whom enjoyed a close and exclusive relationship with the Creator—were born in the land; instead, they migrated there from elsewhere. Rather than an autochthonous mythos praising the antiquity of the local inhabitants as an expression of their ownership of the land, the Yahwistic faith repeatedly highlighted the foreign origin of its founders and those who established the subsequent political entity in the land.

When Abraham, the "convert," who migrated to Canaan from Mesopotamia with his Aramaean wife, sought to marry off his favored son, he told his servant, "You will not take a wife for my son from the daughters of the Canaanites, among whom I dwell, but will go to my country and to my kindred, and take a wife for my son Isaac" (Gen. 24:3–4). Not at all surprised, the servant returned to his master's homeland and imported the attractive Rebecca from abroad. This antipatriotic custom was practiced by the following generation as well, as reflected in the words spoken by Rebecca—who, like her father-in-law, came from abroad—to her aging husband: "I loathe my life because of the Hittite women. If Jacob marries one of the Hittite women like these, one of the women of the

---

4   In actuality, God reveals himself to Moses in private somewhat earlier in the desert of Midian (the Arabian Peninsula) in the well-known story of the burning bush. Here, God informs Moses, quite remarkably, that "the place where you are standing is holy ground" (Exod. 3:5). He makes a minor, earlier appearance in the land of Canaan, not on the ground but in Jacob's dream (Gen. 28:12–15).

land, what good will my life be to me?" (Gen. 27:46). Isaac gave in to his domineering wife and instructed his eldest son accordingly: "You must not take a wife from the Canaanite women" (Gen. 28:1).

As an obedient son, Jacob had no choice but to leave Canaan and journey to Mesopotamia, the homeland of his grandfather, his grandmother, and his mother. There, amid the not-so-distant Diaspora, he married Leah and Rachel, two local sisters who were also Jacob's first cousins, ultimately fathering with them twelve sons and one daughter. The sons, eleven of whom (together with the two sons of Joseph) constituted the eponymous fathers of the tribes of Israel, were all born in a different land, except for one who was born later in Canaan. In addition, as we have seen, the four "mothers of the nation" also came from a distant homeland. Abraham, his wife, his son's bride, the wives and concubines of his grandchild, and almost all of his great-grandchildren were, according to legend, natives of the northern Fertile Crescent who migrated to Canaan as commanded by the Creator.

The antipatriotic saga continues as the story progresses. As we know, all of Jacob's sons "went down" to Egypt, where all his descendants, the entire "seed of Israel," would be born for the next four hundred years, which was longer than the period between the Puritan Revolution in England and the invention of the atomic bomb. Like their forefathers, they, too, would not hesitate to marry local women (a permissible arrangement as long as the women were not Canaanites). A notable instance is Joseph, who married Osnat, whom he was given by Pharaoh. (Abraham's concubine Hagar was also not Canaanite but rather Egyptian.) Moses, first great leader of the "seed of Israel," took Zipporah the Midianite as a wife. As a result of such marriages, which fully contradicted the later custom, it is no surprise that "the people of Israel were fruitful and increased greatly; they multiplied and grew exceedingly strong, so that the land was filled with them" (Exod. 1:7).[5] The land in question here, we must remember, was Egypt,

---

5   Sergio Della Pergola of the Hebrew University of Jerusalem, an authority on the demography of world Jewry, recently stated that "the Bible speaks of 70 men who went down to Egypt with Jacob and 600,000 men who left it 430 years later. That estimate is certainly possible demographically . . ." Quoted in Amiram Barkat, "Study traces worldwide Jewish population from Exodus to modern age," *Haaretz* (English edition), April 29, 2005. It is interesting to note that over the same period, the initial overall population of ancient Egypt, multiplied by the same factor of almost 8,600, would have yielded a population of at least four or five billion.

not Canaan. Thus, according to the biblical story itself, the "people" was emerging demographically in a place that was not promised to it, but that, according to the ancient cultural map, was considered a prestigious and praiseworthy cultural center. Moses, Aaron, and Joshua—who led the people to Canaan—were also born, educated, and transformed into devoted followers of Yahweh in the great pharaonic kingdom.

As we have seen, this mythological, anti-autochthonous formation of the "holy nation" outside the land must be understood in conjunction with another integral dynamic. Not only did the authors of the Bible oppose the inhabitants of the land but also repeatedly expressed a deep hostility toward them. Most authors of the biblical texts loathed the local ("popular") tribes, who were tillers of the soil and idol worshippers; step by step, they lay the ideological foundation for the tribes' eradication.

As we have noted, Yahweh made an early promise—at Mount Sinai, immediately following the giving of the Ten Commandments—to expel the autochthonous inhabitants of the land in order to make room for his chosen ones.[6] Moses, the former Egyptian prince, reiterated God's promise on a number of occasions. In the book of Deuteronomy, the prophet repeatedly emphasized to the "children of Israel" that their god would "cut off the nations whose land the Lord your God is giving you" and that they would "dispossess them and dwell in their cities and in their houses" (19:1). Moreover, after issuing instructions containing a relatively moderate approach toward the conquered non-Canaanite inhabitants, Moses again emphasized: "But in the cities of these peoples that the Lord your God is giving you for an inheritance, you shall save alive nothing that breathes" (Deut. 20:16).

"Blot out," "cut off," and take the life of "anything that breathes" are clear imperatives, but the term used most widely throughout the

---

6   On this historic occasion, God also revealed a sophisticated strategy: "And I will send hornets before you, which shall drive out the Hivites, the Canaanites, and the Hittites from before you. I will not drive them out from before you in one year, lest the land become desolate and the wild beasts multiply against you. Little by little I will drive them out from before you, until you have increased and possess the land" (Exodus 23:28–30). The fact that this promise appears just two chapters after the giving of the Ten Commandments is indicative that the dominant Biblical ethos was one of in-group morality, devoid of any universal dimension.

Bible to indicate the overall eradication of the land's inhabitants is "completely destroy." Indeed, according to biblical legend, the physical extermination of the local population begins immediately after the tribes of Israel crossed the Jordan River and entered the Promised Land following the conquest of Jericho. It was then that "they completely destroyed everything in the city with the sword—every man and woman, both young and old, and every ox, sheep, and donkey" (Josh. 6:21), a practice they repeated after the fall of every other city. As it is written: "So Joshua conquered the whole region— the hill country, the Negev, the Judean foothills, and the slopes—with all their kings, leaving no survivors. He completely destroyed every living being, as the Lord, the God of Israel, had commanded" (Josh. 10:40). The conquest ended with a looting spree and general bloodshed: "And all the spoil of these cities and the livestock, the people of Israel took for their plunder. But every person they struck with the edge of the sword until they had destroyed them, and they did not leave any who breathed" (Josh. 11:14).

After the mass murder, the army of conquerors was somewhat pacified, and the "people" born in Egypt again split up into tribes, dividing among themselves the various regions of the land. Now, the "Land" was larger than what God had promised Moses, suddenly incorporating the other side of the Jordan River as well. Two and a half tribes settled east of the river, marking the onset of their local history in the Promised Land, which, as noted, was larger than the land of Canaan. The Bible recounts this history in detail and with great imagination, and is replete with denunciations of the repeated sins that led to the final punishment of double exile: the exile of the inhabitants of the kingdom of Israel to Assyria (in the eighth century BCE), and the exile of the inhabitants of the kingdom of Israel to Babylonia (in the sixth century BCE). Much of the narrative recreating the stories of the Hebrews in the land of Canaan seeks to clarify the factors that resulted in these traumatic exiles.

This raises a number of questions for historians and biblical scholars who neither believe in the divine sacredness of the books nor accept the anachronistic and untenable chronology of events: (1) Why did the authors of the ancient texts repeatedly emphasize the revelation of the deity in places outside the Promised Land? (2) Why are most of the heroes of this fascinating epos not of autochthonous descent? (3) What purpose was served by the cultivation of burning hatred toward the indigenous population, and why was this troubling and, by all assessments, strange story of mass extermination told in the first place?

Although many scholars have taken exception to the book of Joshua due to the campaign of extermination it describes,[7] the book was until relatively recently the favored text in many Zionist circles, of which David Ben-Gurion was a prominent representative. The accounts of the colonization and the return of the people of Israel to their promised land lent power and fervor to the founders of the State of Israel, and they pounced upon the inspiring similarity between the Biblical past and the nationalist present.[8]

Yeshiva students have always been aware that the Bible should not be read literally—that it requires guidance and a tempering interpretation of God's stern and ambiguous words. Nevertheless, Jewish students nine and ten years old learn in Israeli schools about Joshua's campaigns, without the benefit of the rationalist and protective filters of Talmudic Judaism. The Israeli Ministry of Education has never found it necessary to distance itself from such shocking parts of the Bible, and instead facilitates its instruction without any censorship. Because the Pentateuch and the books of the early prophets are regarded as historic texts recounting the history of the "Jewish people" since ancient times, there has been a consensus that even if it is not mandatory to study the more abstract books of the later prophets, under no circumstances is it permissible to skip over the book of Joshua. Moreover, even though the teaching of this "past" has been proven ethically and pedagogically destructive, the Israeli education system refuses to exclude from the curriculum these shameful accounts of extermination.[9]

---

7 The initial decline of the Christian faith in the eighteenth century facilitated the voicing of disapproval regarding the disturbing themes of the book of Joshua. A variety of figures expressed harsh criticism of the biblical imperative of extermination, from British deists such as Thomas Chubb to French Enlightenment figures such as Jean Meslier. For example, see Voltaire's assessment in the entry on "Jews" in his *Philosophical Dictionary* (*Dictionnaire philosophique*).

8 See, for example, David Ben-Gurion, *Biblical Reflections*, Tel Aviv: Am Oved, 1969 (in Hebrew), and Moshe Dayan, *Living with the Bible*, Jerusalem: Idanim, 1978 (in Hebrew). This subject is also explored by Gabriel Piterberg in *The Returns of Zionism: Myths, Politics, and Scholarship in Israel*, London: Verso, 2008, 267–82.

9 On the teaching of the book of Joshua in Israel, see Galia Zalmanson Levi, "Teaching the Book of Joshua and the Conquest," in Haggith Gor Ziv (ed.), *The*

Perhaps it is fortunate that Zionist biblical scholars and Israeli archaeologists alike have recently begun to express doubts about the veracity of the narrative. Fieldwork has provided increasingly decisive evidence that the Exodus from Egypt never happened and that the land of Canaan was not suddenly conquered during the period identified in the Bible. These scholars are finding it reasonable to assume that the horror stories of mass murder were fabrications. It now appears likely that the local inhabitants, who underwent a long and gradual process of transition from nomadic life to agricultural work, evolved into an autochthonous mixed population of Canaanites and Hebrews that later gave rise to two kingdoms: the large kingdom of Israel and the small kingdom of Judea.[10]

The theory that has become commonplace among new scholarly circles is that the stories of conquest arose in the late eighth century BCE or, at the very latest, a century later, during the reign of Josiah, at the time of the consolidation of ritual in Jerusalem and the ostensible discovery of the Torah. According to scholars who have espoused this theory, the main goal of the theological-historical writing in question was to imbue the inhabitants of Judea, as well as the refugees of Israel who arrived after the destruction of their northern kingdom, with the belief in a single god. In the struggle for monotheism, all means of persuasion were regarded as legitimate. One result was the hostile and indiscriminate incitement against widespread idol worship and the concomitant moral corruption.[11]

Although such hypotheses can be refreshing, they remain extremely unconvincing. While partly relieving us of the literary nightmare of ancient genocide, they fail to answer the cardinal question: Why does the Biblical story portray the first monotheists as

---

Militarization of Education, Tel Aviv: Babel, 2005 (in Hebrew). In 1963 Georges R. Tamarin, a lecturer in Tel Aviv University's Department of Psychology, conducted a pioneering survey on how the book was understood by Israeli schoolchildren. The study's findings sent shock waves through the Ministry of Education. At the time, it was even argued that the study constituted grounds for Tamarin's dismissal. On the survey, see Tamarin, *The Israeli Dilemma: Essays on a Warfare State*, Rotterdam: Rotterdam University Press, 1973, 183–90. See also John Hartung, "Love Thy Neighbor: The Evolution of In-Group Morality," *Skeptic* 3:4 (1995), and Richard Dawkins, *The God Delusion*, New York: Mariner Books, 2008, 288–92.

10   Israel Finkelstein and Neil A. Silberman, *The Bible Unearthed*, New York: Touchstone, 2002, 98, 118.

11   Ibid., 72–96.

migrants and conquerors who are completely foreign to the land they have reached? Nor do these hypotheses assist us in understanding how the horrifying idea of a massacre of the local population evolved. The brutality of the ancient period is well known and is reflected in many sources; stories of mass killings can be found in the legends of the ancient Assyrians and in the *Iliad*, and every undergraduate history student is familiar with Roman brutality toward the inhabitants of defeated Carthage. However, although acts of extermination have occasionally been mentioned in documents, I know of no group from among those who have carried out such acts that has boasted of its deeds or offered theological or moral justifications for the annihilation of an entire population merely in order to inherit their land.

First, it is highly unlikely that the historiographical core of the Bible was written prior to the destruction of the kingdom of Judea in the sixth century BCE. Before the destruction, it was not possible to write about a large, spectacular kingdom with a capital city consisting of great palaces and glorious halls, as the archaeological findings show that historical Jerusalem was no more than a large village that gradually evolved into a small campus. Second, writings about the systematic subordination of the ruling dynasty of kings to the sovereignty of God—and, even more so, to the angry, preaching prophets who were God's representatives on earth—could not have been done by scribes of the court or temple priests, who were devoid of all intellectual autonomy. And not even the smallest sovereign kingdom would be willing to accept that the ruling dynasty was established by the initiative of the people and that almost all its kings were repeat sinners. Third, it is difficult to explain how a monotheistic revolution that was so significant and so rich in daring insight might have begun to take form in a small kingdom in a sleepy rural region that bore no resemblance to the teeming centers of culture of the Near East.

It seems much more likely, as asserted by many non-Israeli scholars and as concluded by the sharp logic of Spinoza, that the main books of the Bible were written and theologically engineered only after those who left Babylon arrived in Jerusalem, and even later, during the Hellenistic period.[12] There is almost no doubt that the

---

12 Bendedict de Spinoza, *Theological-Political Treatise*, Cambridge: Cambridge University Press, 2007, 118–43. For example, see the groundbreaking recent classic by British Bible scholar Philip R. Davies, *In Search of Ancient Israel*, London: Clark Publishers, 1992.

skilled authors had firsthand knowledge of the significance and the punishment of exile. They incessantly expressed their shock at the event and persistently tried to provide an ideological explanation for its occurrence. Throughout the Pentateuch and the books of the prophets, the exile reverberates as a concrete experience and serves repeatedly as a threat. This is the case in Leviticus: "And I will scatter you among the nations, and I will unsheathe the sword after you, and your land shall be a desolation . . . And you shall perish among the nations, and the land of your enemies shall eat you up. And those of you who are left shall rot away in your enemies' lands because of their iniquity" (26:33, 38–9). It is also the case in Deuteronomy: "And the Lord will scatter you among the peoples, and you will be left few in number among the nations where the Lord will drive you" (4:27). These sentences are virtually identical to references made in openly "post-exile" books such as Nehemiah: "If you are unfaithful, I will scatter you among the peoples" (1:8).

As a working premise, we may posit that when the Persian conquerors reached Babylon and there encountered priests and former court scribes who were descendants of estranged exiles from Judea, the latter acquired some experience with Zoroastrianism, which at the time was struggling against polytheism but was still loyal to divine dualism. A characteristic expression of the decisive epistemological detachment between Zoroastrian dualism and monotheistic Yahwism is found in the words of the prophet Isaiah, who decisively declares: "Thus says the Lord to his anointed, to Cyrus . . . I am the Lord, and there is no other. I form light and create darkness, I make well-being and create calamity, I am the Lord, who does all these things" (45:1, 6–7).

In my opinion, the degree of abstraction present in the young monotheism could have emerged only within an official state material culture with considerable technological control over nature. At the time, such control had been achieved only in the great civilizations located on rivers, such as Egypt and Mesopotamia. The remarkable encounter between exiles and their descendants on the one hand and this center of high culture on the other appears to be what provided the foundation for the pioneering theses.[13]

---

13   The idea of the resurrection of the dead and the very term "dat" (religion) were also taken from Persian culture. Yet it is still unclear why the exiles of Judea were the ones to light the flame of monotheism.

As is typical of decisive intellectual revolutions, these daring and educated thinkers were forced to develop their radical ideas outside established cultural circles. By writing in an unfamiliar language and, in the case of some individuals, migrating to Canaan under the protection of the Persian sovereign, they found it possible to evade head-on confrontations with a hostile, hegemonic priesthood and court writers who were still semi-polytheistic. In this way, moving between Babylonia and Canaan, they took the first step in the slow historical movement toward a completely new kind of theological tradition.

The small Jerusalem of the fifth century BCE became a place of refuge and an intellectual seedbed for these exceptional intellectuals. Some appear to have remained in Babylon and provided the migrants with material and spiritual logistics that helped create the revolutionary corpus. Canaan, therefore, would serve as a spiritual bridge between the faith born in the northern Fertile Crescent and the cultures of the Mediterranean region. Jerusalem would become the first stop in the mighty theological (Jewish-Christian-Muslim) campaign that would eventually conquer a large portion of the earth.

If we adopt this hypothesis, the accounts of the birth of monotheism outside the Promised Land become much more plausible and more easily understood, and literary figures such as Abraham and Moses, who imported their faith in one god to Canaan, can be understood as a legendary mimesis of the actual migration of the Babylonian importers of a single god, who began arriving in Zion in the early fifth century BCE. During the fifth and fourth centuries BCE—a magnificent period that bore witness to the birth of Greek philosophy, Greek plays, the spread of Buddhism and Confucianism—the pioneers of Western monotheism assembled in small Jerusalem and began to cultivate their new faith.

This work was carried out under the watchful eyes of the agents of the Persian kingdom through respectable figures such as Ezra and Nehemiah. The narrative strategies selected were meant to create a community of loyal believers while at the same time preventing this community from becoming strong enough to pose a threat to the supreme imperial authority. It was therefore permitted in *Yehud Medinata* (Aramaic for the "province of Judea") to imagine the conquest of a large land in the name of God, to recount tales of great kingdoms of the past, and to dream of unrealistic borders of a Promised Land that reached all the way to the new migrants' land of origin, while in practice refraining from demands for actual sovereignty, making do with a modest temple, repeatedly thanking the "benevolent" Persian rulers, and preventing the empowerment of the new community of believers from becoming excessive.

Unlike the monarchies that ruled them and the educated stratum that had formerly served the local rulers, the native-born Hebrews—the "people of the land" whose fathers had lived under the kingdoms of Judea and Israel—and the Canaanite tribes that lived alongside them were never exiled to Assyria or Babylonia. They had been, and remained, faithful pagans lacking in education. These tillers of the soil, who spoke a mixture of dialects, did not acknowledge the exclusivity or uniqueness of Yahweh, although they did worship him as the preeminent deity among the other gods. The aim of the monotheistic migrants was to assemble the elite of the local idol worshippers, to dissuade them of their faith thereby isolating them from the masses of the land's inhabitants, and to mold them into dedicated corps of believers. The result was what appears to be the first emergence of the idea of the "chosen people."

As was customary among the kings of Babylonia, detailed official chronicles of events were set down, formulated in a manner similar to that of the Mesha Stele. In all likelihood, these remained in Jerusalem or were taken into exile after the destruction,[14] melting into a rich reservoir of migrating cosmic mythoi and traditions imported from the northern Fertile Crescent. Together, these sources served as the nucleus for the story of the Creation of the world and the revelation of its only god. God himself, originally known as *elo*, was lifted from the Canaanite tradition and became *elohim* (the Hebrew name for God used most commonly in the Bible). Rhythms, rhymes, and linguistic structures from Ugaritic poetry were plundered, and legal codices of the Mesopotamian kingdoms were incorporated into the biblical commandments. Even the long, complicated account of the division

---

14   The Bible itself contains references to the preservation of chronicles from the kingdom of Israel and the kingdom of Judah that provided the initial raw material for later theological writings. See 1 Kings 14:29: "Now the rest of the acts of Rehoboam and all that he did, are they not written in the Book of the Chronicles of the Kings of Judah?" and 22:39: " Now the rest of the acts of Ahab and all that he did, and the ivory house that he built and all the cities that he built, are they not written in the Book of the Chronicles of the Kings of Israel?"

into the twelve tribes of Israel appears to be based on a Greek political tradition articulated by Plato in his description of the ideal colonization and its division into twelve parts and tribes, giving it a well-known and familiar literary expression.[15]

Glorification of a materially and politically modest and forlorn present required a well-established, glorious past, and because the education and propaganda were meant to foster monotheism, they required and thus gave rise to a new genre. At the same time that Herodotus was crossing Canaan (or Palestine, as he referred to it), educated circles in Jerusalem and Babylon began formulating their doctrine. Their writing, however, cannot be thought of as historical, and is much better classified as original "mythistory."[16] In this new, unfamiliar genre we no longer find the stories of various gods, but we also do not yet find the investigation of human events and actions as a goal in itself, as we do in the Greek world. The primary motivation for writing was the powerful need to recreate the past as proof of the plan and wonders of the single God and as evidence of the inferiority of humans, who were destined to move eternally and cyclically between sin and punishment.

For this purpose, it was necessary to persistently separate the wheat from the chaff—to determine which past king had been chosen by God and would have his transgressions forgiven, and who would remain an evildoer in God's eyes, spurned until the end of his days. It was necessary to determine which past kings had remained loyal to Yahweh and which were to be eternally cursed. The major figures in this undertaking were historical, their names taken from the detailed chronicles. Other priests, operating in Samaria, claimed their own relationship with the great kingdom of Israel, reinforcing the remarkably long-lived mythos of the united kingdom of David and Solomon, which split in two as a result of sinful factionalists. Even though the leaders of the northern kingdom turned into detestable idol worshippers, this did not prevent the theft of their prestigious name, Israel, and its assignment to the "chosen people."

---

15   See Plato, *The Laws* 5.744–6.

16   When Herodotus traveled through the region in the fifth century BCE, he knew nothing of the modest community in Jerusalem and made no mention of it in his writings, which describe the inhabitants of the country as Syrians that are referred to as "Palestinians." See Herodotus, *The History* 3–4, New York: Penguin Books, 2003, 172, 445.

Despite Spinoza's pioneering conclusions, it is illogical to presume that these extraordinary texts could have been written by one or two authors alone. The community of authors was most certainly large and diverse and maintained constant contact with the centers in Babylon. The nature of the texts reflect that they were repeatedly written and rewritten over a period of many generations, resulting in repeated accounts, individual stories linked through patchwork, the absence of narrative consistency, lapses in memory, changes in style, the use of different names for God, and a significant number of ideological contradictions. Of course, the authors were unaware that all the texts would one day be assembled into a single canonical book.

Despite a broad consensus regarding the existence of one god, there remained numerous disagreements regarding the moral values that should be inculcated. Variations in the politics of the treatment of others also cropped up.[17] The later authors appear to have been less inclined to exclusion than their pioneering counterparts, as the Deuteronomists differed from the priestly authors both in style and in their conception of the divine presence. In any event, even if the profuse writing was meant to create an immediate community core, it was also, and perhaps much more intentionally, directed toward the distant future.

The increasing prominence of the arrivals from Aram-Naharaim and their profound disdain for the native-born inhabitants is reflected in most books of the Bible and the books of the first prophets. The homeland is located elsewhere—in Babylonia or Egypt, the two most highly regarded cultural centers of the ancient period. The spiritual leaders of the "children of Israel" had originated from a well-respected place with a good reputation, whence they brought their exclusive faith and their god's most important commandments. By comparison to them, the inhabitants of Canaan were ignorant, corrupt, and inclined to engage recurrently in idol worship.

Contempt for and alienation from the autochthonous population

---

17   See Moshe Weinfeld, "Universalist and Isolationist Trends during the Period of the Return to Zion," *Tarbitz* 33 (1964), 228–42 (in Hebrew). We must not forget that the Bible also contains exceptional verses contradicting this overall trend, such as, "When a stranger sojourns with you in your land, you shall not do him wrong. You shall treat the stranger who sojourns with you as the native among you, and you shall love him as yourself, for you were strangers in the land of Egypt: I am the Lord your God" (Lev. 19:33–4). See also Deut. 10:19.

were ultimately translated into disturbing literary descriptions of their expulsion and extermination. The pioneering authors who arrived in Canaan had no state administration and no army. They bore no resemblance to the Crusaders and had no institutionalized Inquisition. Imagination, words, and intimidation were all they had at their disposal.

They did not address the general public. Instead, their literary activity took place among a small, literate elite and a limited number of curious listeners, congregating on the outskirts of small Jerusalem. Step by step, however, the circle expanded and the "seed of Israel" continued to flourish until, in the second century BCE, they were able to establish the first monotheistic regime in history: the small, though short-lived, Hasmonean kingdom.

After negating the proprietorship and the right to life of the chosen land's indigenous inhabitants, the authors of the biblical texts bestowed the land upon themselves and those who agreed to adhere to their doctrine. Monotheism was still an uncertain faith, deeply concerned with the threat posed by polytheism. Only after monotheism had grown strong, following the Maccabean revolt of the second century BCE, would it begin proselytizing and indiscriminately converting those in its midst. But for now, the community of monotheists engaged in fierce struggles with the masses of idol worshippers who surrounded them and against whom they forged uncompromising positions of isolationism.

The prohibition of marrying local women became a supreme directive among the "returnees to Zion" (*shavei zion*), those who did so were ordered to divorce them,[18] and those who had migrated to Canaan were forced to import wives from Babylonia. This denunciation of the local population appears to have been consistent with the overall strategy of the Persian Empire, which was engaged in the familiar principle of divide and rule. The new "holy nation" operating in Jerusalem and its surrounding area was forbidden to integrate with the simple, rural people of the land. Therefore, in acts of literary retroactivity, Isaac and Jacob were also obligated to marry Aramaean virgins, and Joseph and Moses were permitted to take Egyptian and Midianite, but not Canaanite, wives. And when "later," among his seven hundred wives and three hundred concubines, the insatiable

18   See Ezra 10:10–11 and Neh. 13:23–6.

lecher King Solomon also took beautiful local women, his actions were regarded unfavorably by Yahweh, and the imaginary kingdom was split in two. This, among other things, would provide the theological legitimacy for the future existence of the kingdoms of Israel and Judea (1 Kings 11:1–13).

The prohibition against marrying male or female Canaanites from local pagan families that were related to large clans or tribes was strict and sweeping. Such unions were permitted only to the excommunicated or the cursed, such as Isaac's eldest son, Esau, and resulted in a considerable decline in social status. In this context, it is fascinating to trace the interweaving of the biblical story and God's commandments from inception to implementation. Moses, for instance, issued the following instructions:

> When the Lord your God brings you into the land that you are entering to take possession of it, and clears away many nations before you, the Hittites, the Girgashites, the Amorites, the Canaanites, the Perizzites, the Hivites, and the Jebusites, seven nations more numerous and mightier than you, and when the Lord your God gives them over to you, and you defeat them, then you must devote them to complete destruction. You shall make no covenant with them and show no mercy to them. You shall not intermarry with them, giving your daughters to their sons or taking their daughters for your sons. (Deut. 7:1–3)

Strange though it seems, God first ordered the complete extermination of the local population and then issued instructions not to marry those who had been annihilated. The extermination and the prohibition on marriage blended together in the isolationist imagination of the zealous authors into one solid compound of destruction.

After providing an account of Joshua's acts of extermination, the authors went on to inform their amazed readers that the genocide, like every other genocide in history, had not been complete. Indeed, many pagans continued to live in Canaan even after the return to Zion, including after the legendary conquests of Joshua. We know about the mercy shown to Rahab the prostitute and to the Gibeonites, who become cutters of wood and drawers of water. Moreover, before his death, Joshua, a stern military leader, assembled his followers and issued the following warning to them: "For if you turn back and cling to the remnant of these nations remaining among you and make marriages with them, so that you associate with them and they with you, know for certain that the Lord your God will no longer drive out these nations before you. But they shall be snares and traps to you . . ." (Josh. 23:12–13).

In the book of Judges, which appears in the Bible as a direct continuation of the story of Joshua, we are surprised to learn that the local population was in no way exterminated and that the obsession with the threat of assimilation into the local population still ran high:

> So the people of Israel lived among the Canaanites, the Hittites, the Amorites, the Perizzites, the Hivites, and the Jebusites. And their daughters they took to themselves for wives, and their own daughters they gave to their sons, and they served their gods. And the people of Israel did what was evil in the sight of the Lord. They forgot the Lord their God and served the Baals and the Asherahs. (Judg. 3:5–7)

However, it is even more surprising that, supposedly later, in the book of Ezra, great anxiety still surrounds the subject of integration with the ancient, exterminated peoples:

> After these things had been done, the officials approached me and said, "The people of Israel and the priests and the Levites have not separated themselves from the peoples of the lands with their abominations, from the Canaanites, the Hittites, the Perizzites, the Jebusites, the Ammonites, the Moabites, the Egyptians, and the Amorites. For they have taken some of their daughters to be wives for themselves and for their sons, so that the holy race has mixed itself with the peoples of the lands." (Ezra 9:1–2)

The separation and compartmentalization between the solitary deity (*elohim*) and his colorful family—his wife, Asherah, herself a land goddess, and his talented children, the tempestuous Baal, the desirable Astarte, the fierce Anat, and Yam, god of the sea—appears to have been an ongoing Sisyphean enterprise in which the first monotheists were incessantly engaged. In order to inculcate a single, supreme god, it was necessary to uproot the deities of the past, and if this was not done and the children of Israel were to revert to worshipping many deities, they would be punished and dispossessed of the land they had been granted. Although he had a positive opinion of himself and was "merciful and compassionate," Yahweh was a stern and vengeful god. Like a zealously possessive husband, he would not forgive someone who betrayed him, and when his believers sinned, sanctions were activated immediately. At the end of the story, the recurrent themes of destruction and exile are actualized.

The entire book of Kings was meant to establish that the expulsion of the Israelites was the result of the abominations of the House of Omri, just as the inhabitants of Judea were sent into exile due to the sins of King Manasseh. Almost all the prophets, from Jeremiah and Isaiah through Amos and Micah, voice unremitting warnings regarding the calamity that will beset the country and turn it into wilderness, uprooting sinners and causing their brutal dispossession of the land. This is the ultimate weapon of the authors of the Bible, who tirelessly guide and caution the slowly expanding community of believers to adhere to one god.

In the theological discourse of the Bible, the promise of the land to the treasured people is almost always conditional. Nothing is meant for eternity; everything depends on the degree to which they adhere to God. The Promised Land is neither a one-time grant nor an irrevocable gift. It remains a loan, never to be regarded as territorial property. The children of Israel are not granted collective ownership of the Promised Land, which will eternally remain the property of God, who merely gave it to them temporarily and conditionally, albeit in great generosity.

"For all the earth is mine" (Exod. 19:5) repeatedly emphasizes the omnipotent divine landlord. To dispel all doubts regarding the nature of the people's possession and proprietorship, he states it clearly and decisively: "The land shall not be sold in perpetuity, for the land is mine. For you are strangers and sojourners with me" (Lev. 25:23).[19] Since John Locke, modern political thought has always envisaged land as belonging to its cultivators. This, however, was not the philosophy of the Bible. The land was neither the property of the peoples of

---

19   Biblical scholar William David Davies was the first to argue that Yahwism derived the concept of divine ownership of territory from the Canaanite tradition of the deity Baal. See *The Gospel and the Land: Early Christianity and Jewish Territorial Doctrine*, Berkeley: University of California Press, 1974, 12–13.

ancient Canaan nor the property of the Hebrew tribes. To a considerable extent, all who lived on it could be regarded as its orphans.

Notwithstanding their powerful connection to the holy city of Jerusalem, the Land of Israel was never the ancestral land of the descendants of the children of Israel, for, as we have seen, the majority of their imagined forefathers were born elsewhere. Moreover, the heroes of the Bible had no homeland, not only in the Greco-Roman political sense of the word but also in its more limited sense as a familiar, protected, and safe area. The territory, according to the doctrine of early monotheism, would be neither a refuge nor a shelter for ordinary or weary human beings; it would forever be a challenge—a piece of land that one had to prove worthy to hold, even temporarily.

In other words, in all the books of the Bible, the land of Canaan never served as a homeland for the "children of Israel," and for this reason, among others, they never refer to it as "the Land of Israel."

FROM THE LAND OF CANAAN TO THE LAND OF JUDEA

Unlike the vast majority of modern-day Israelis, who are unaware that the conventional term "Land of Israel" (*Eretz Israel*) is not found in the books of the Bible in its inclusive meaning, the authors of the Mishnah and Talmud had a keen understanding of this fact, because they were fortunate enough to read the Bible without the mediating prism of nationalism. One Midrash Halakha (a form of rabbinic literature aimed at the clarification of Jewish law and practice), most likely from the third century CE, contained the following text:

> Canaan merited that the land should be called by his name. But what did Canaan do? Simply this: As soon as he heard that the Israelites were about to enter the land, he got up and moved away from before him. God then said to him: You have moved away from before my children; I, in turn, will call the land by your name. (Mekhilta, Pisha, 18, 69)[20]

As indicated in the introduction to this book, both in the Bible and during the long period preceding the destruction of the Temple in the

---

20   Jacob Z. Lauterbach, *Mekhilta De-Rabbi Ishmael*, Philadelphia: Jewish Publication Society, 2004, 107.

year 70 CE, the region was conceived of as the Land of Israel neither because of the language of its inhabitants nor by its immediate neighbors.

Place names and nicknames, however, do not last for eternity, and social and demographic changes often result in the emergence of new ones. As would be expected over a four-century period in any region of the globe, the political morphology of the land of Canaan changed between the second century BCE and the second century CE. During this time, the region came increasingly to be known as the land of Judea, although its former name did not completely disappear. For example, Flavius Josephus, writing at the end of the first century CE, refers to it as the "land of Canaan" when speaking about the past but draws readers' attention to the fact that the land "then called Canaan" was "now called Judea."[21]

Unfortunately, we know very little about the events that took place in Canaan between the fifth and second centuries BCE, when the books of the Bible were written, edited, and reworked. Such knowledge would tell us a great deal about the circumstances in which these books were written and would better enable us to interpret their meaning. The history of the inhabitants of the small province of Judea that existed in the land until its conquest by Alexander of Macedonia is virtually unknown, owing to the lack of sources, and the same is true of the beginning of the Hellenistic period. What is clear is that the holy books were repeatedly copied and passed down from genera-tion to generation, and that the dissemination of the Yahwistic religion in the small localities around Jerusalem began to bear fruit. As we have already noted, by the second century, the single God already had a large community of believers that was capable of adhering to its own views and even of rebelling against a pagan ruler in order to defend its religious principles and ritual practices.

The Hasmonean revolt of 167–160 BCE was a pivotal event in the historical rise of monotheism in the Western world. Despite the rebels' decisive defeat on the battlefield, the weakening of the Seleucid Empire created a rare situation that facilitated the establishment of an autonomous religious regime, which in 140 BCE emerged as a sover-eign theocratic kingdom. Even if the independence of the kingdom of

---

21   Flavius Josephus, *The Complete Works of Flavius Josephus*, London: T. Nelson and Sons, 1860, 38.

Judea would be short-lived, lasting only seventy-seven years, until the arrival of Pompey of Rome, it would serve as a springboard for the dissemination of Judaism around the world.

Our knowledge of the revolt itself is based on only a few sources, the first and foremost of which is the first book of Maccabees. We also have the later, second book of Maccabees, a number of general comments by Hellenistic and Roman historians, and the subsequent common adages of the Talmud. The revolt is addressed by Flavius Josephus' *Antiquities of the Jews* and *Jewish Wars*, but the Jewish historian bases most of his narrative on the first book of Maccabees, to which he adds no additional significant information. The biblical book of Daniel and a few other texts classified as "outside" or apocryphal were also composed during the Hasmonean period, although their ahistorical character does little to facilitate reconstruction of the events in question.

Even though the identity of the author (or possibly authors) of the first book of Maccabees is unknown, scholars believe that he lived in Judea some thirty years after the revolt and was closely affiliated with the Hasmoneans during the rule of John Hyrcanus. The text was written in Hebrew but was rejected by Jewish heritage and excluded from the Jewish canon.[22] As the original text was lost, all that remains is a Greek version in the Septuagint ("translation by seventy"), which, like the writings of Philo of Alexandria and Flavius Josephus, survived thanks only to Hellenistic Christians. It is an irony of history that had it not been for ancient Christianity's approach to the preservation of ancient texts, we most likely would possess little or no knowledge about the history of the Jews between the Hasmonean revolt and the destruction of the Temple.

A close reading of the first book of Maccabees reveals a remarkable gap between the insights that can be gained from a reading of the text itself and the interpretation of the revolt that is promoted by the Israeli education system. Just as the Zionist enterprise nationalized the traditional holiday of Hanukkah, it also tried to obfuscate the religious aspects of both the biblical book and the revolt itself.[23] The

---

22   To a certain extent, Boas Evron is correct in his assertion that the books of Maccabees and the works of Flavius Josephus are not actually "Jewish." Evron, *Athens and the Land of Uz*, Binyamina: Nahar, 2010, 133 (in Hebrew).

23   For example, the first line of the well-known Hanukkah song "Who Can Retell" ("Mi Yimalel," lyrics by Menashe Rabina, traditional melody, 1936) is a

ancient narrative says nothing about a "national" uprising erupting during a struggle against foreign, Latin culture or a "patriotic" revolt aimed at defending the country from foreign invaders. And just as the name Land of Israel appears nowhere in the narrative, despite the insistence of Zionist historians, the narrative also makes no reference to the concept of "homeland," even though the book's author was well versed in the Bible and extremely familiar with Greek literature, from which he was certainly capable of borrowing.

For many years, Jewish believers were accustomed to living under rulers who did not share their faith. As long as the kings of Persia, and subsequently the first Hellenistic rulers, left them to their own devices and allowed them to worship their singular God, they mounted no protests that left a mark on history. It was the extraordinary religious persecutions of Antiochus IV Epiphanes and the desecration of the Temple that incited their daring revolt. Mattathias and his sons rebelled against the Empire because "at that time, the king's officers were enforcing the decrees to give up Jewish practice. They came to the town of Modein to make its people offer pagan sacrifice" (1 Macc. 2:15). The old Hasmonean priest killed not a Jew attempting to adopt a foreign "national culture" but rather an inhabitant of Judea who was trying to sacrifice an animal to other gods. He mobilized his supporters by exhorting: "Everyone who is zealous for the Law and supports the covenant should come with me!" (1 Macc. 2:27).

In order to convey the significance of terms such as "Hellenists" as distinct from authentic "Hebrews"—words that play a major role in the popular Zionist historiographical interpretations—the author of Maccabees would have had to be buried in a time capsule and emerged in the modern era. As this was an option he obviously did not enjoy, such adjectives do not appear in the text. Like other biblical authors before him, he simply distinguished between believers

---

secularized version of the biblical verse "Who can retell the mighty deeds of the Lord?" (Pss. 106:2). The lyrics of the popular holiday song "We Are Carrying Torches" ("Anu Nosim Lapidim") also reflect such a nationalization of tradition: "A miracle never happened to us. No vessel of oil did we find. We quarried in the stone until we bled. 'Let there be light'" (lyrics by Aharon Zeev, music by Mordechai Zeira; English trans. Noam Zion and Barbara Spectre, *A Different Light: The Hanukkah Book of Celebration*, New York: Devora Publishing, 2000, 14). This transition from heavenly power to human blood typically occurs unbeknownst to the singer. In my youth, this was true of me as well.

and sinners—between dedicated worshippers of the heavens, and detested idol worshippers and the uncircumcised. The inhabitants of Judea at the time still included a significant number of people who engaged in idol worship or were being encouraged to resume such rituals, and leaders of the Jewish community felt it imperative to separate themselves from this population and to overpower it. Key to the entire story of the revolt is the dreadful tension between piety and desecration of the commandments of the Pentateuch, not a self-conscious Hebrew culture on the one hand and Hellenic culture and the Greek language on the other hand.

Judah Maccabee incited his followers to rise up and fight for their lives and religious laws, not for their land (1 Macc. 3:21). Later his brother Simon would attempt to mobilize a new army by explaining, "You know how much my father's family, my brothers, and I have done for the sake of the Law of Moses and the Temple. You also know about the wars we have fought and the troubles we have had" (1 Macc. 13:3). He does not, however, say anything about "national" sacrifice or suffering for the sake of the homeland, a concept which did not even exist in Judea.

Unlike the hired soldiers of the future Hasmonean kingdom, the army of the Maccabees consisted of volunteer believers who were fed up with the moral corruption of the priests in the capital city and the heavy taxes levied by their Seleucid rulers. The combination of intense monotheistic zealousness and ethical protest endowed the rebels with extraordinary mental fortitude and swelled their ranks to startling dimensions. Nevertheless, it is safe to assume that they always constituted a minority of the peasant population.[24] After a number of difficult clashes, they manage to enter Jerusalem and liberate the Temple. Their victory is crowned by purification of the center and construction of a new altar for the single God. Throughout the years, the dedication of this altar would be marked by a Jewish religious holiday.

It is interesting to note that the struggle between the monotheistic Jews and the pagan non-Jews continues after the conquest of Jerusalem. In this context, the rebel army crosses the border of the land of Judea, invades remote regions such as the Galilee, Samaria, the Negev,

---

24 For more on this subject, see William David Davies, *The Territorial Dimension of Judaism*, Berkeley: University of California Press, 1982, 67.

and Gilad across the Jordan River, and returns faithful Jews to "their land," enabling them to worship God peacefully and without idolatrous distraction from their neighbors. At the end of the battles, the land of Judea is expanded through the annexation of adjacent regions, which come under the sovereignty of the new dynasty of priests (1 Macc. 10:30, 41). The Seleucid king Alexander Balas authorizes the annexation and appoints John, one of Mattathias's sons, to serve as the high priest under his royal protection.

When the drama and the battles come to an end and the emissary of the new king, Antiochus VII, demands the return of a number of areas annexed by the Maccabees, the author attributes the following words to Simon the priest, ruler of the Hasmonean kingdom: "We have never taken land away from other nations or confiscated anything that belonged to other people. On the contrary, we have simply taken back property that we inherited from our ancestors, land that had been unjustly taken away from us by our enemies at one time or another" (1 Macc. 15:33). This unusual assertion, which stands out as exceptional in the text, is indicative of the advancement of a new claim for an autochthonous right that begins to transcend the traditional biblical conceptualizations and bring us closer to the territorialist heritage of the Hellenists.

Significant elements of the text (attire, gold, acknowledgments within Simon's court, cordiality toward Hellenic leaders who were supportive of the Hasmoneans) indicates that the wholly religious court writer harbored no ill feeling toward the Hellenization that had started to spread within the new priestly regime. For good reason, John, the high priest and perhaps a patron of the author, chose the typical Greek name Hyrcanus, a precedent followed by all his heirs to the Hasmonean dynasty, who would adopt non-Hebrew names and the practices of other rulers in the region. Ultimately, the Hasmonean kingdom would accelerate the pace of cultural Hellenization among the inhabitants of Jerusalem no less than it would preserve, with effective and sometimes brutal direction, the belief in one God.

At the same time, we must not forget that the term "the land of our forefathers" (*nahalat avoteinu*) means something very different from the concept of *patris* in its original political sense. The ancient concept that arose in the independent polis long before the conquests of Alexander of Macedonia, and that expressed sovereign citizens' connection to their city, was now stripped of its original patriotic meaning and became, during the Hellenistic period, an increasingly distant echo of a faded historical reality. As with the hereditary priestly regime, the dynastic monarchy that ruled the kingdom of Judea until its final conquest by Rome bore no resemblance to the elected leadership of the democratic Greek cities.

The second book of Maccabees is more Hellenistic and theologically Jewish than the first. Unfortunately, however, it is also less historical.[25] It is more Jewish and less historical because God plays an active role in the events and openly directs the revolt, and it is more Hellenistic because, unlike the first book, it makes unexpected use of the term *patris* (πατρίς) as one of the reasons for the uprising. In contrast to the earlier book, which was written in Jerusalem, 2 Maccabees, which was composed during a later period in a Greek dialect, most likely in Hellenistic Egypt, informs us that following Judah's mobilizing speech, his followers were "willing to die for their religion and their country" (2 Macc. 8:21).[26] Yet this rhetoric, which is completely foreign to the Hebrew language, does not turn the text into an especially patriotic declaration because here, too, the main aim of the rebellion remains purification of the Temple, not the establishment of an independent polis or Jewish "nation-state." The book begins with the dedication of the altar and concludes with the beheading of Nicanor, the enemy Seleucid military leader, and with the commemoration of victory as a holiday of Jewish thanksgiving for the acts of god.

Although the transformation from a purely religious rebellion to a sovereign Jewish kingdom is fascinating, evidence of this change is not only meager and reticent but also difficult to use for purposes of

---

25   2 Maccabees was originally written in the Greek Koiné dialect much later, after 100 BCE, in either Egypt or in a more remote region of North Africa. It includes a short summation of five volumes written by their author, Jason of Cyrene, which did not survive the passage of time.

26   See also how this text incorporates the term *patris* among the laws and the sections on the Temple (2 Macc. 13:11, 15). I originally consulted the edition edited by Daniel Schwartz, *The Second Book of Maccabees*, Jerusalem: Yad Ben-Zvi, 2004 (in Hebrew). Here too, the term "Land of Israel" is used in the introduction and in the footnotes on thirty-eight occasions, but never actually appears in the ancient text itself. On the Greek conceptual influence on the author of the Second Book of Maccabees, see Yitzhak Heinemann, "The Relationship between a People and Its Country in Judeo-Hellenistic Literature," *Zion* 13-14 (1948), 5.

recreating an accurate history. In any event, the Hasmonean kings' conceptualization of geographic space was completely different from that of the rebels, as attested to not necessarily by their deliberations, which took place in private, but by their military and religious actions. As we saw in 1 Maccabees, Simon the priest's territorial hunger grew increasingly insatiable with every new victory on the battlefield. Like all other political entities in the region, the kingdom of Judea would try to expand its borders as much as possible and would be successful in its efforts. At the end of the Hasmonean kings' continuing campaign of conquest—which is to say, at the height of their rule—the Land would contain Samaria, the Galilee, and the region of Edom. Thus would the kingdom of Judea come relatively close to the dimensions of the pharaonic land of Canaan.

In order to establish themselves within their new territories, the new Jews employed a different strategy than the one employed by their forefathers, the isolationist "returnees to Zion," who were most likely responsible for shaping the image of Joshua as the destroyer. As we have seen, the earlier generations were fearful of and estranged from their pagan neighbors. The Hellenistic rulers of Judea, however, were more sure of themselves and ignored the biblical directive of extermination; instead, they passionately and forcefully sought to convert the inhabitants of the neighboring conquered territories. The Edomites in the Negev and the Itureans of the Galilee were compelled by the Hasmoneans to part with their foreskins and become Jews in the full sense of the word. Thus, the community of Jewish believers grew both in size and in strength, and the land of Judea expanded.

Such mass conversion was not unique to the kingdom of Judea. Beginning in this period, and particularly as a result of the fertile encounter between monotheism and Greek culture, Judaism became an actively proselytizing religion and began to spread around the Mediterranean, acquiring many new adherents.[27] And whereas a monotheistic community had existed continuously in Babylonia since the fifth century BCE, migrants began to leave Judea three centuries later for all the centers of the Hellenistic world, where they now began disseminating their faith en masse.

---

27   On this, see Uriel Rappaport, "Jewish Religious Propaganda and Proselytism in the Period of the Second Commonwealth," Ph.D. diss., Jerusalem: Hebrew University, 1965 (in Hebrew). Despite its importance, this study was never published in book form.

What was the connection between the Judean migrants and the new Jewish converts, on the one hand, and the land of Canaan, which had gradually become the land of Judea, on the other hand? It is at this point that this issue germinates—an issue that henceforth maintains a presence in the research on Judaism in the communities and kingdoms that adopted the religion up to the modern era. An appreciation of the various connections between Jewish believers and the land of the Bible enables us to better understand the religion itself. Owing to the dearth of sources, however, this section will focus only on the presence of the land of Judea in the hearts of the pioneering Jewish intelligentsia, or, to be more specific, in the hearts of two figures who may perhaps not be strongly representative of larger circles. Most important for our discussion is the fact that it is impossible to determine the degree to which their writings articulated the mood among the masses of Jewish converts with whom they lived and with whom they prayed in the new synagogues.

Philo of Alexandria can be thought of as the first Jewish philosopher, if we omit from this category the authors of the biblical books of the prophets and Ecclesiastes. Although this original Jewish intellectual did not know Hebrew, the Greek translation of the Bible, which played an integral role in attracting educated polytheists to Jewish monotheism, enabled him to construct an organized theological doctrine. In any event, this important thinker not only hoped for the conversion of the entire world but also did not conceal his deep bond to Jerusalem.[28]

As I have already highlighted, the term "Land of Israel" was unknown in Hellenistic Jewish literature, and yet the term "Holy Land," which appeared to a limited extent in the biblical texts, had come to be commonplace and was used frequently by Philo.[29] His writings also contain the Hellenistic term "homeland," although in principle, and quite logically, he did not link his precious Holy Land to the idea of a national homeland:

---

28   See Philo, *On the Life of Moses* 1.41–2.

29   See, for example, *On the Embassy to Gaius*, 202, 205, 230. This concept already appears in 2 Macc. 1:7 and in Wisd. of Sol. 12:3. The term "holy ground" appears in the Hebrew version of the *Sibylline Oracles* 3.267, in *The External Books* II, Tel Aviv: Masada, 1957, 392 (in Hebrew), as well as in other texts.

[I]t is the holy city where the sacred temple of the Most High God stands, that they regard as their mother city, but the regions they obtained from their fathers, grandfathers, great-grandfathers, and even more remote ancestors, to live in [they regard] as their fatherland where they were born and brought up.[30]

In some ways, Philo's words are reminiscent of the distinction Cicero had tried to make a few years earlier. Here, too, we find the nonpolitical homeland, in which people are born and grow up and which shapes their character, alongside another longed-for place, the connection with which does not contradict the sense of connection with the first region of affiliation. However, for Cicero, this "other" place was the urban space in which he functioned, constituting an expression of his civil sovereignty over his homeland, while Philo's other place was a faraway focus of religious yearning. Cicero was representative of a political imagination that was in the process of vanishing, whereas Philo was articulating a new religious imagination that would take shape in the centuries to come.

As the ancient Greek cities were dear to the Hellenic settlers in the colonies, the city of Jerusalem, which was even more holy than the land, was understood to be dear to all faithful Jews in the world, who would not forget its status as the fount of Judaism. It was not, however, their homeland, and devout Jews never dreamed of settling there.

Philo lived his entire life in Alexandria, Egypt, just a short distance away from the yearned-for Holy Land. He may have even made a pilgrimage to Jerusalem, although we have no way of confirming this. Having lived prior to the destruction of the Temple, he could have dwelled in its midst, in its metropolis, had he chosen to do so. At the time, the kingdom of Judea was under Roman rule, as was Egypt, and travel between the two lands was free and safe. However, just as hundreds of thousands of other Jews in the land of the Nile never dreamed of migrating to the nearby Holy Land, the philosopher from Alexandria also chose to live and die in his original homeland.

---

30   See *Flaccus*, 46, in Pieter Willem Van Der Horst, *Philo's Flaccus: The First Pogrom*, Leiden: Brill, 2003, 62. In *The Special Laws*, 68, Philo also describes a pilgrim to Jerusalem as a man suffering because he had been forced "to quit his country, and his friends, and relations, and emigrate into a distant land." See also Yehoshua Amir, "Philo's Version of Pilgrimage to Jerusalem," in Aharon Oppenheimer et al. (eds.), *Jerusalem in the Second Temple Period*, Jerusalem: Yad Ben-Zvi, 1980, 155–6 (in Hebrew).

Philo may have been the first to keenly formulate the faithful Jew's link not only with his land but also with the holy city of Jerusalem. He would be followed by many others who would deepen and expand his approach and introduce new elements into this sense of connection. But the core of the relationship would not change much: the holy place would never become a homeland for the Jews or for the masses of Jewish converts who would join them, expanding the ranks of the "chosen people" into the hundreds of thousands.

In the far future, another aspect of Philo's conception of Jerusalem and the land of Judea would emerge in Christianity, which, unlike Judaism, adopted and preserved the writings of Philo Judaeus. For him, as we have noted, the place was much more than a piece of land; it was a spiritual capital for whose holiness yearned Jews the world over. But his religious imagination took him even further, leading him to argue that the eternal divine city was neither located on the ground nor made of "wood or stone."[31] This surprising assertion was consistent with his view that the true homeland of unusually wise souls was the "heavenly country," and that their material "earthly abode" was no more than a place "in which they dwell for a while as in a foreign land."[32] As discussed in the previous chapter, it was Augustine who, four centuries later, would transform this heavenly country from the spiritual heritage of a select group of educated people into the homeland of all believers.

Zionist historiography did everything in its power to portray Philo the philosopher as a Jewish patriot.[33] But it was much more difficult to do the same for Flavius Josephus, because of the fact that the great Jewish historian had betrayed his comrades-in-arms, crossed enemy lines, and joined the Roman camp. At the same time, however, Zionist historiography made maximum use of Josephus's major work in order to depict the uprising of the year 66 CE as a "great national revolt." This uprising, and the siege of Masada with which it came to an end, subsequently emerged as a historic

---

31   Philo, *On Dreams, That They Are God-Sent* 2.38, 250.

32   Philo, *On the Confusion of Tongues* 17.77–8.

33   For example, see Aryeh Kasher, "Jerusalem as a 'Metropolis' in Philo's National Consciousness," *Cathedra* 11 (1979), 45–56 (in Hebrew), which, although interesting and scholarly, goes to great lengths to portray Philo as a patriotic philosopher. For a slightly less nationalist and more "community"-oriented approach, see Mireille Hadas-Lebel, *Philon d'Alexandrie: Un penseur en diaspora*, Paris: Fayard, 2003.

milestone in the modern aspiration for a Jewish uprising and an inexhaustible source of Zionist pride.

The fact that the heterogeneous population in ancient Judea spoke a mixture of languages and had no understanding of the concepts of citizenship, sovereignty, and national territory was of no interest to the Zionist agents of memory. For years, Israeli schoolchildren have memorized the slogan "Masada will not fall again," and when they come of age they are expected to willingly sacrifice their lives in accordance with this national call to duty. In their youth, they are taken to view the son et lumière at the remains of the fortified walls built by Herod out of concern about an uprising among his subjects. After their induction as soldiers of the State of Israel, they swear allegiance on the Bible at the center of the mountain's summit, where the pleasure palace and Roman bathhouse of the uninhibited Jewish Edomite king once stood.

Neither the Israeli schoolchildren nor the soldiers were aware that, for many centuries, their true forefathers did not even know the name Masada. Unlike the narrative of the destruction of the Temple, which was ingrained deep in the collective memory of communities that followed the Jewish religion, the books of Josephus and thus the events they narrated remained unrecognized by the rabbinical heritage. Yet it was through these works alone that the proponents of modern nationalism learned of the collective murders and suicides perpetrated by Eleazar Ben-Yair and his fellow Sicariis. It is doubtful whether these senseless acts ever took place, but under no circumstances was Masada meant to serve as a model to emulate in Jewish tradition, as it was not undertaken for the sanctification of God's name.[34]

Josephus lived one or two generations after Philo and was a native-born Jerusalemite. He lived in the city but never returned after it was devastated. As he is the main and virtually exclusive source of our knowledge regarding the revolt of 66 CE, his view of his homeland is of particular importance. Of course, we must always remember that he

---

34   See also the shortened, distorted Jewish version of Josephus's works composed under the title *Josiphon or Josippon* (H. Hominer [ed.], Jerusalem: Hominer, 1967), which omits the suicide, changes the names of the protagonists, and has them killed in battle. See Pierre Vidal-Naquet, "Flavius Josèphe et Massada," in *Les Juifs, la mémoire et le présent*, Paris: Maspero, 1981, 43–72. Masada is an extreme example of the construction of national memory with no basis in traditional collective memory.

wrote his books as a Jew who lived comfortably in Rome, not as a Jew who played an active role in the revolt.

If we proceed in reverse chronological order and begin by reading the tragic end of Josephus's *History of the Jewish War against the Romans*, we find an unexpected, patriotic-sounding speech that the author attributes to Eleazar Ben-Yair, the suicide Sicarii from Masada. In his effort to convince his companions to kill their wives and children and then take their own lives, Eleazar invokes a war of freedom and a willingness to die, not for the sake of the heavens, but in order to avoid being taken prisoner by the Romans.[35] At the same time, Josephus does not forget to mention that prior to ascending to Masada, the Sicariis had unhesitatingly killed seven hundred Jewish men, women, and children from Ein Gedi.

In his enumeration of the reasons for the revolt and his analysis of its course and its leaders, Josephus does not regard the events he describes as a national uprising. Even if the terminology he employs includes expressions of the Hellenistic legacy, such as "homeland" or "ancestral land," and even if (aristocratic) freedom is dear to his heart, he views the rebels as the last of the "patriots."

The first reason for the revolt was the tension between the Jewish believers and their pagan "Syrian" neighbors in the mixed towns. The Hasmonean kings had already forcefully converted the majority of the population they had conquered. However, no sooner had they begun forceful conversion of the idolatrous, culturally Hellenistic inhabitants of the cities, than great difficulties began to present themselves. The second reason for the uprising was that, unlike in the past, the Roman governors now employed a destructive, irresponsible policy toward the Jewish faith and seriously compromised the sacredness of the Temple. Furthermore, stringent taxation policy was also causing social grievances and class unrest. The combination of these objective social conditions created an opportunity for messianic and extremist religious groups to sow unrest among some of the poor farmers and, with their help, to take control of Jerusalem.

Although Josephus himself initially took part in the revolt, he came to oppose and revile the rebels and to regard them as

---

35   Flavius Josephus, *The Wars of the Jews: History of the Destruction of Jerusalem* 7.8.6–7, Forgotten Books, 2008, 534–40.

responsible for loss of the homeland.³⁶ He refers to them as thieves and villains who instilled terror in their surroundings, wherever they were, and killed a significant number of their fellow Jews. As he saw it, figures such as Simon bar Giora and John of Giscala had desecrated the commandments of the Bible and damaged their ancestral heritage.³⁷ The fall of Jerusalem and the destruction of the Temple were not caused by "betrayal" of the Jewish population's traditional leadership, which tried with all its might to appease the "foreign" rulers, but rather by the uncompromising, hot-tempered, extremist religious zealots.

In a different text and a somewhat different tone, he also found it necessary—while defending observance of the Sabbath, which, according to critics, had resulted in the fall of Jerusalem—to emphasize that the faithful Jews would "constantly prefer the observation of their laws, and their religion toward God, before the preservation of themselves and their country."³⁸

Josephus regarded Judea as his land, which was dear to him; moreover, he regarded Jerusalem as the city of his ancestors. Nonetheless, we must also recognize that, in his description of the territory in which the events of the revolt took place, he divides them into three distinct lands: the Galilee, Samaria, and Judea.³⁹ From his perspective, these three regions did not constitute a single territorial unit, and his writings make no reference to the concept of the "Land of Israel."

Moreover, in his second major work, *The Antiquities of the Jews*, in which he attempts to reconstruct the history of the Hebrews since God's promise to Abraham, he occasionally "corrects" the authors of the Bible and makes additions based on his own imagination. "I give the domination of all the land," he declares in the name of God, "and their posterity shall fill the entire earth and sea, so far as the sun beholds them." And he continues:

> O blessed army, wonder that you are become so many from one father: and truly, the land of Canaan can now hold you, as being yet comparatively few; but know ye that the whole world is proposed to

36   Ibid., 4.5.3, 332.
37   Ibid., 7.8.1, 528–30.
38   Flavius Josephus, *Against Apion* 1.22.21.
39   Flavius Josephus, *The Wars of the Jews* 3.3, Digireads, 2010, 136–7.

be your place of habitation forever. The multitude of your posterity also shall live as well in the islands and on the continent, and that more in number than are the stars of heaven.[40]

With these words, Josephus articulates a view similar to Philo of Alexandria's cosmopolitan religious conception, although he wrote slightly later, during a period when the presence of Jews and Jewish converts throughout the Mediterranean basin and in Mesopotamia had reached a high point. Shortly before its decline, the spatial conception of Jewish existence acquired a new dimension. The land of the Jews was by no means a small and limited territory but rather a land encompassing the entire world. Believers in the Jewish faith could be found everywhere, and not as the result of punishment. Josephus knew full well that, despite the great downfall they had suffered, the Judaic population had not been exiled but had rather been designated by God from the outset to fill this role.

According to the vision of Josephus, a descendant of priests who had migrated to Rome, the heavenly redemption would certainly involve a return to Zion but not an ingathering of Jews within a national territory. His was an eschatological vision of the building of a new temple. Thus, despite the intellectual and mental distance between him and the authors of the Mishnah and the Talmud, who at about the same time began to cultivate their oral law in Judea and Babylonia, he shared their deep belief in salvation.

However, despite his thorough exploration of the Zealot revolt and the fact that, notwithstanding its ideological, theological, and literary nuances, his book exemplified historiographical writing at its best, Josephus clearly did not yet possess a broad historical perspective within which to contextualize the uprising of 66 CE. Only after the crushing failure of the next two major revolts did it become possible to assess the true significance of the messianic monotheistic unrest that swept the southern shores of the Mediterranean basin during the first few centuries CE. What is surprising is that, up to the present day, Zionist academic scholarship has refused to understand the three revolts, all of which took place within just seven decades, as part of a single phenomenon: monotheism's struggle against paganism.

---

40   Flavius Josephus, *Jewish Antiquities* 1, 4, Hertfordshire: Wordsworth Editions Limited, 2006, 37, 145–6.

The increasing strength of Judaism that resulted from mass conversion intensified the religious tension between the Jewish Hellenists and their idol-worshipping neighbors in the main cities throughout the Roman Empire. From Antioch to Cyrenaica, via Caesarea and Alexandria, the friction continued to intensify until its first explosion in the land of Judea between 66 and 73 CE. But the suppression of the revolt in Jerusalem was only a prelude to a larger bloody uprising that took place between 115 and 117 CE.

The vibrant and expanding Jewish religion would again try to confront Roman paganism in North Africa, Egypt, and Cyprus without a trace of the "patriotic" sentiment that supposedly existed in Judea. In the uprising of the Jewish communities, which Zionist historiography refers to as "the revolt of the Diaspora" in order to emphasize its imagined "national" focus, we find no longing for a return to an ancestral land, no trace of loyalty or connection to a faraway land of origin. The mutual killing and slaughter, and the systematic destruction of temples and synagogues, that took place during this unrelenting rebellion are indicative of the intensity of the community's belief in a single God as well as its fanaticism and yearning for the Messiah. They also indicate the intense labor pains of monotheism just before its emergence as a worldwide phenomenon.

The Bar Kokhba revolt that took place in Judea between 132 and 135 CE marked the conclusion of the desperate messianic effort to confront paganism through the power of the sword. The total defeat of this uprising would accelerate the decline and fall of Hellenistic Judaism around the Mediterranean Sea and its replacement with its younger, postmessianic sibling—Christianity—which would adopt different weaponry but retain the enticing and mobilizing monotheistic view of the unidimensional nature of the heavens.

From Jerusalem eastward, however, Christianity was less successful, and the religion's armed defeat resulted in the flourishing of pacifistic rabbinical Judaism. The Mishnah, the most important Jewish text since the Bible that was still written in Hebrew, was compiled and completed, apparently in the Galilee, in the early third century CE. The Jerusalem Talmud and the Babylonian Talmud were composed between the late third century and late fifth century CE (and the latter was most likely finally edited even later) in the area between Zion and Babylon, which, not coincidentally, were areas in which Greek languages and cultures were less dominant.

We now turn to a discussion of the attitude of major rabbinical texts toward the territory which until then had been referred to as Provincia Judea, the land of Judea, and which, after the imperial Roman edict issued in the wake of the Bar Kokhba revolt, would come to be known as Provincia Syria Palaestina.

THE LAND OF ISRAEL IN JEWISH RELIGIOUS LEGAL LITERATURE

The Mishnah, the two Talmuds, and the Midrash, like all other texts of Jewish religious law, contain no use of the term "homeland." This term, with its meaning based on the Greco-Roman tradition, made its way to Europe by means of Christianity, but made no inroads into rabbinical monotheism. Just like their predecessors, the authors of the Bible and the scholars of the Mishnah and Talmud were never patriots. Those living in Babylon, like the millions of Jews and other converts to Judaism who lived throughout the Mediterranean basin, did not find it necessary to migrate to the land of the Bible, despite its close proximity. But even if the Jewish legal literature, in contrast to the Hellenistic Jewish literature, does not include the concept of homeland, it does feature the debut of the term "Land of Israel."[41]

The elder Hillel, who helped lay the foundation for interpretative Judaism, migrated from Babylon to Jerusalem in the first century BCE. From the second century onward, however, movement flowed primarily in the opposite direction. The "people of the Land" still remained on its land, but the migration of scholars, apparently as a result of the widespread Christianization under way, was of great concern to the centers of religion in Judea and the Galilee, which resulted, among other things, in the birth of the rabbinical "Land of Israel."

It is difficult to determine precisely when the term was invented or the immediate reason for its introduction. Initially its use may have stemmed from the Roman revocation of the name Provincia Judea after the Bar Kokhba revolt, and their use, along with that of many others, of the ancient name Palestine. And because it was not customary to regard the Galilee as an immanent part of Judea, local rabbis

41   Alongside other names, of course. On this subject, see Yichiel Michel Guttman, *The Land of Israel in the Midrash and the Talmud*, Berlin: Reuven Mas, 1929, 9–10 (in Hebrew).

began to integrate the term into their teachings. It may have also been introduced to bolster the status of the centers of study in the Galilee, which, despite the Hasmonean conquest, was never truly incorporated into the land of Judea. It is most likely that the destruction of Jerusalem and the prohibition against the entry of Jews into the city increased the term's prominence immeasurably.

Isaiah Gafni, a leading historian of Judaism during the Talmudic period, has suggested that the centrality of the "Land" in Jewish religious legal literature may have been a relatively late phenomenon:

> [T]he degree to which these issues surrounding the Land were even taken up in statements attributed to the early tannaim, up to and including the Bar-Kokhba war (132–135 CE), is minimal. A review of the hundreds of statements attributed to sages such as Rabban Yohanan ben Zakai, R. Joshua, R. Eliezer, R. Eleazar b. Azariah, and even R. Akiva, reveals a striking paucity of allusions to the *character* and supernatural attributes of the Land, and similarly there is minimal allusion to the Land's centrality vis-à-vis the diaspora and the consequently required commitment of Jews towards the Land.
>
> All this is striking precisely in light of the numerous statements attributed to these very same rabbis regarding the "commandments pertaining to the Land" . . .[42]

According to Gafni, the situation began to change after the Bar Kokhba revolt in 135 CE. Although he does not explicitly advance the assertion, we can conclude from his words that from this period onward, the unique new term "Land of Israel" emerged as a customary name for the region, alongside established names such as Land of Judea and Land of Canaan.

Gafni also takes care to emphasize that because of the rising status of the Babylonian community and the threat it posed to the hegemony status of the rabbis in Judea, hitherto unknown superlatives began to be ascribed to the Land of Israel. Indeed, in the Mishnah, we already find statements such as "the Land of Israel is holier than all other lands" (Taharoth, Kelim 1:6) and "The Land of Israel is clean and its

---

42   Isaiah Gafni, *Land, Center, and Diaspora: Jewish Constructs in Late Antiquity*, Sheffield: Sheffield Academic Press Ltd., 1997, 62–3.

ritual baths are clean" (Taharoth, Mikvaoth 8:1).[43] The Jerusalem Talmud confirms these assertions (Order Moed, Tractate Sheqalim, 15:4) and adds more.

The Babylonian Talmud intensifies the rituals pertaining to the Holy Land and offers new assertions, such as "the Temple was higher than all of the Land of Israel, while the Land of Israel is higher than all other countries" (Order Kodashim, Tractate Zebahim 54:2); "ten kabs of wisdom descended to the world: nine were taken by the Land of Israel, one by the rest of the world" (Order Nashim, Tractate Kiddushin 49:2); and so forth.

Alongside these statements in the Babylonian Talmud, however, we also find commentators taking a different tone, for example: "As it is forbidden to leave the Land of Israel for Babylon, so it is forbidden to leave Babylon for other countries" (Order Nashim, Tractate Ketubot 111:1). The source even contains an original interpretation of the exile of the sixth century BCE, which reads as follows: "Why were the Israelites exiled to Babylon more than all other lands? Because just as a husband returns his damaged wife to the home of her father, it was from there that Abraham their father was descended" (Tosefta, Bava Kama 7:2). Comparing the "people of Israel" to a divorced wife being made to return to the home of her parents is hardly consistent with the image of exile and suffering in an unfamiliar foreign land.

We can identify a significant number of contradictions in the texts of the Talmud and the Midrash; as with other sacred texts throughout history, these contradictions become a source of power for the rabbinate. Because this diverse literature constitutes the most ahistorical collection of texts imaginable, it is difficult to determine exactly when each statement was written or during which period the rabbi who raised it for discussion lived and worked. Even so, we can cautiously assume that the weakening influence of the Jewish religion in the land of Judea and its displacement by Christianity, particularly in the fourth century CE, intensified the importance of the sacred center and increased the intensity of its spiritual worship. After all, it was there that the holy books were finally compiled and the major prophecies delivered.

---

43   Philip Blackman, *Mishnayoth, vol. 6: Order Taharoth*, London: Mishna Press, 1955, 32, 572.

In addition, the actual size of the area in question was not always clear, though typically it extended from the edges of Acre in the north to the outskirts of Ashkelon in the south—two pagan cities. Many parts of the biblical land of Canaan were not incorporated into the sacred Land, according to Jewish law. For example, neither Beit She'an nor Caesarea, nor the surrounding areas of either locality, were considered part of it, owing to the presence of too many people from Acre in those regions.[44] Biblical and Talmud scholar Moshe Weinfeld claims that "the willingness to forgo areas of the Land of Israel in order to fulfill the commandment of giving gifts to the poor [who could have received some of the crop had it not been sacred land] reflects an attitude that the land is a means to an end, and not an end in itself."[45]

At the same time, in the eyes of the authors of the Bible, the Land of Israel remained a territory in which special Land-dependent commandments were observed, including the special supervision of the laws of impurity, the allocation of sacred gifts, and the observance of the laws of Shmita (the sabbatical year, or the seventh year of a seven-year agricultural cycle). For Jewish farmers of the period, it was particularly difficult to cultivate and make a livelihood from land that was considered to be part of the Land of Israel. During the third century CE we also see the beginning of the transfer of Jewish bodies to the holy Land for burial. According to the Bible, the bodies of Jacob and Joseph were brought from Egypt, and burial in the Land of Israel was considered desirable, a means of hastening the deceased's entry into the world to come. As a result, heads of yeshivas and community notables who could afford the financial expense were brought for burial to Beit She'arim and, later, to Tiberias in the Galilee.[46]

If a yearning of any kind should come to exist, it would focus far more on the city of Jerusalem than on the territory as a whole. As we

---

44   On the boundaries of the Land of Israel in Jewish law, see Yaakov Sussman, "The Boundaries of Eretz Israel," *Tarbitz* 45:3 (1976), 213–57 (in Hebrew).

45   Moshe Weinfeld, *The Promise of the Land: The Inheritance of the Land of Canaan by the Israelites*, Berkeley: University of California Press, 1993, 75.

46   For example, see the Babylonian Talmud's account of the burial of Rabbi Huna (Moed Katan 3.25a), as well as Isaiah Gafni, "The Bringing Up of the Dead for Burial in the Land—Outlines of the Origin and Development of a Custom," *Cathedra* 4 (1977), 113–20 (in Hebrew). During the same period, belief was evolving in the concept of *gilgul hamekhilot*, which held that at the time of the resurrection of the dead, the bones of the righteous would roll through underground tunnels to the Land of Israel.

saw earlier in the case of Philo, the authors of the Mishnah and Talmud would incorporate references to Jerusalem and Zion into hundreds of adages and interpretations. They occur much more frequently than references to the territorial area, which is addressed primarily in the context of ritual agricultural laws. Moshe Weinfeld, who is mentioned above, emphasized that even if, in contrast to Christianity, Judaism preserved the Land as an important physical element,

> Towards the end of the Second Temple period the concept of the land underwent a process of spiritualization, as did Jerusalem. Jerusalem was interpreted in the ideal sense as "the kingdom of heaven" and "the celestial Jerusalem," and inheriting the land was similarly interpreted as receiving a place in the world to come.[47]

Because the Babylonian Talmud became a binding, hegemonic text in most Jewish communities, it also served as the main object of study in yeshivas. As a result, there developed in many Jewish circles a connection to the Land based much more on the Talmudic interpretation of the Bible than on the reading of the Bible itself. Every statement in it became sacred, and every judgment became binding. The concepts of exile and redemption, wages and punishment, sin and penance were rooted in the Bible but assigned a variety of interpretations.

Whereas the Tosefta contains the important pronouncement that "one should always live in the Land of Israel, even in a city where the majority are idol worshippers, and not outside of the Land, in a city where the majority are Jews" (Order Nezikin, Tractate Avoda Zarah 5:2), a very different but no less significant warning was implanted in Jewish law with regard to believers' attitudes toward the sacred land. In the Order of Ketubot in the Babylonian Talmud, we find the following text:

> What was the purpose of those three adjurations? One, that Israel shall not go up by a wall [collective migration to the Land]; one by

---

47　Weinfeld, *Promise of the Land*, 221. In this context, prominent Jewish historian Simon Dubnow asked: "How could a land that was the center of the Christian religion, that was sacred in the Gospel, and that was filled with churches and monasteries and pilgrims and monks, be the center of the activity of *amoraim* and princes and remain the kingdom of Israel in spirit?" Simon Dubnow, *Chronicles of the Eternal People* III, Tel Aviv: Dvir, 1962, 140–1 (in Hebrew).

which the Holy One, blessed be He, adjured Israel not to rebel against the nations of the world; and one by which the Holy One, blessed be He, adjured the idolaters [the nations of the world] that they not oppress Israel too much. (Ketubot 13:111)

These adjurations relate to three verses that repeat themselves in the Song of Songs: "I adjure you, O daughters of Jerusalem, by the gazelles or the doe of the field, that you not stir up and awaken love until it pleases" (Song of Sol. 2:7). In both theory and practice, the adjurations are divine decrees. The first prohibited faithful Jews from migrating to the holy center until the coming of the Messiah. The second was the historical lesson learned from Judaism's three failed revolts against the idolaters. The third was an order to the rulers of the nations of the world to show mercy to the Jews and to spare their lives.[48]

Until the birth of modern nationalism, few dared disregard this commandment. This "anti-Zionist" position of rabbinical Judaism would live a long life and emerge prominently at every major crossroads in the history of Jewish communities. It would not be the reason for the consistent refusal to migrate to the Holy Land, but it would serve as one of the preferred theological excuses.

"DIASPORA" AND YEARNING FOR THE HOLY LAND

As was pointed out in the introduction to this book, the fact that the Jews were not forcibly exiled from Judea after the destruction of the Temple means that they also made no effort to "return." Faithful Jews who adhered to the Torah of Moses had multiplied and spread across the Hellenistic and Mesopotamian world even before the destruction of the Temple, which is how they disseminated their religion with relative success. The connection of the masses of Jewish converts to the land of the Bible could of course not be based on yearnings for a homeland, as it represented a land of origin neither for them nor for their ancestors. The state of spiritual "exile" in which they lived, all the

---

48   On the role of these three adjurations in Jewish tradition, see Aviezer Ravitzky's informative *Messianism, Zionism and Jewish Religious Radicalism*, Tel Aviv: Am Oved, 1993, 277–305 (in Hebrew). See also Mordechai Breuer, "The Discussion Concerning the Three Oaths in Recent Generations," in *Geulah Umedina*, Jerusalem: Ministry of Education, 1979, 49–57 (in Hebrew).

while maintaining regular contact with their culture and actual places of birth, did not weaken their connection to the "place" as a focus of longing; in some ways, it actually strengthened the Land's significance and preserved it as a Jewish site.[49]

The increasing importance of this place in Judaism was the result of centrifugal movement. As the connection became increasingly symbolic and distant, it was freed from complete dependence on the corporeality of the center. The need for a holy place in which perfect cosmic order existed never equated to a human desire to actually live in it or to be always in close proximity to it.[50] The tension surrounding place in the case of Judaism is more intense because, as the exilic experience is not a state from which Jews can free themselves on their own, all thoughts of striving to return to the holy place are inherently inacceptable.

This dialectic state is completely different from the Christian connection to the Holy Land, which was much more direct and much less problematic. Its uniqueness stemmed from the Jewish metaphysical refusal to recognize that redemption had already come to the world. This spiritual experience originally emerged from interpretative Judaism's opposition to the descent of Christian grace to the Land in the form of Jesus, the Son of God, but ultimately developed into an unequivocal existential position on the complex relations between heaven and earth.

The imperative "that Israel shall not go up by a wall" expressed the immense opposition to making the human subject an active force in history and highlighted its weakness. Almighty God was seen as a total replacement for man, who was not supposed to take part in events or bring them to completion prior to redemption. As a result of their considerable flexibility and their solid, deeply ingrained pragmatism, Judaism's two younger sisters, Christianity and Islam, proved far more successful in acquiring command and control of terrestrial forces—kingdoms, principalities, the landed aristocracy—and achieving hegemony over large parts of the globe. Although attempts at

---

49   It has already been thoroughly established that religions in general and archaic religions in particular all have "places" or a "place." See Mircea Eliade, *The Sacred and the Profane: The Nature of Religion*, San Diego: Harvest/HBJ Books, 1959, 20–65.

50   Jonathan Z. Smith, "The Wobbling Pivot," in *Map Is Not Territory: Studies in the History of Religions*, Leiden: Brill, 1978, 88–103.

Jewish sovereignty had enjoyed temporary success in a number of regions, Judaism's severe defeats at the beginning of the Christian era caused it to forge a faith identity based on the self-awareness of a "chosen people," with no basis in, and no possession of, a defined physical locality. As a result, the less realistic it became, the more its spiritual longing for the Holy Land intensified. Judaism refused to be shackled to a piece of land. With all its veneration for the Holy Land, it refused to be enslaved by it. The essence and raison d'être of rabbinical Judaism was the Bible and associated commentaries, and so from this perspective, it would be no exaggeration to characterize it as largely, fundamentally, and consistently anti-Zionist.

It is no coincidence that this rebellion within Judaism, which occurred against the background of the ninth-century CE refusal to accept the Talmud in particular and the oral law in general, resulted in mass migration to Palestine. For the Karaite Mourners of Zion, the Land could not be considered sacred if it was not populated by people who believed in it. They therefore preached love of the City of David and articulated this love and their intense mourning for the destruction of the Temple by actually settling in Jerusalem. By thus taking their fate into their own hands, they apparently came to account for the majority of the city's population in the tenth century CE. Had it not been for the Crusaders' conquest of 1099, which permanently wiped out this community, its members might have become the first faithful guardians of the holy city.

With justification, the Karaites regarded rabbinical literature as antiterritorial meditation aimed at sanctifying the exile and distancing faithful Jews from the land of the Bible. Daniel ben Moses al-Kumisi, one of the most prominent leaders of the Karaites, migrated to Jerusalem in the later ninth century and called on his followers to follow in his footsteps. He scorned the rabbinical Jews' position on residing in the holy city:

> Know, then, that the scoundrels who are among Israel say one to another "It is not our duty to go to Jerusalem until He shall gather us together, just as it was He who had cast us abroad" . . . Therefore it is incumbent upon you who fear the Lord to come to Jerusalem and to dwell in it, in order to hold vigils before the Lord until the day when Jerusalem shall be restored . . . blessed is the man who places his confidence in God . . . who does not say "How shall I go to Jerusalem,

seeing that I am in fear of robbers and thieves on the road? And how shall I find a way to earn a living in Jerusalem? . . . Now you, our brethren in Israel, do not act this way. Hearken to the Lord, arise and come to Jerusalem, so that we may return to the Lord.[51]

Sahl Ben Matzliah HaCohen, another Karaite leader, also issued an impassioned appeal to the Jews of the world:

> Brothers of Israel, put your trust in our Lord and come to his temple which he consecrated for ever and ever, because it is a commandment unto you . . . congregate in the holy city and bring together your brothers because until now you have been a nation that no longer yearns for the house of its Father in Heaven.[52]

However, not only did the call of the Karaites go unanswered, even though the Jews were permitted to reside in Jerusalem under Islamic rule, but the established rabbinate did everything in its power to silence and suppress the heretical voices of the rebellious Mourners of Zion.

It is worth noting that the most prominent opponent of the Karaites was the Jewish scholar Saadia Gaon, who translated the Bible into Arabic and can be regarded as the first great rabbinical commentator after the completion of the Talmud. This prominent, well-read figure of the tenth century CE was born and raised in Egypt, and subsequently immigrated to the town of Tiberias, where he lived and worked for a number of years. Like many others, though, in an effort to advance his career he took the earliest opportunity to move to the lively, enticing centers of Babylonia. Therefore, when he was offered to head the acclaimed Sura Yeshivah in Babylon, he gave up the Land of Israel without hesitation, disregarding the explicit commandment to reside there. His reluctance to remain in the Holy Land may also have stemmed from the extensive Islamization of the land's Jewish inhabitants, a development that the rabbi, in fear of the Muslim rulers, lamented surreptitiously.[53]

---

51   Daniel al-Kumisi, "Appeal to the Karaites of the Dispersion to Come and Settle in Jerusalem," in Leon Nemoy (ed.), *Karaite Anthology*, New Haven: Yale University Press, 1952, 35–8.

52   Yoram Erder, "The Mourners of Zion," in Meira Polliack (ed.), *Karaite Judaism: A Guide to Its History and Literary Sources*, Leiden: Brill, 2003, 218.

53   On this subject, see Abraham Polak, "The Origin of the Arabs of the

Besides harboring hostility toward the Zionist Karaites, Saadia Gaon fought tirelessly against the attempt of rabbis from the Land of Israel to question the Babylonian hegemony over determining the leap year and the Jewish calendar. He achieved considerable success on both fronts and remained active in greater Mesopotamia for the rest of his life. Saadia Gaon's thinking included no nostalgic memories of or yearnings for his sacred land, perhaps because he had had firsthand experience of it, nor does his biography reflect a desire to live there.

Saadia Gaon's most prominent successor was Rabbi Moses ben Maimon—known as Maimonides or the "Rambam"—who lived two and a half centuries later and also spent time in the Galilee. Unlike his predecessor, Maimonides lived in the city of Acre for only a few months, early in life. His parents arrived in the region from Cordoba via Morocco, fleeing the strict and intolerant *al-Muwahhidun*, but failed to acclimatize to the Galilee and quickly moved on to Egypt. It was there that the young philosopher achieved greatness, becoming the most highly respected commentator and adjudicator in the history of medieval Judaism and perhaps of all time. Although we have only snippets of information regarding the time he spent in the Holy Land, it is evident that, like Philo of Alexandria, he never returned there to live, despite its short distance from his place of residence. Although Maimonides was still alive when Saladin reconquered Jerusalem and permitted Jews to settle there, and although, as a doctor, he knew the Muslim leader personally, there is no mention of this significant event in his texts. Nevertheless, the appearance of the "Land of Israel" on the margins of his many writings remains an intriguing phenomenon.

Because the Rambam is considered to have been one of the great Jewish philosophers of the medieval period—the epitaph on his gravestone reads, "From Moses to Moses there was none like Moses"— Zionist historians have tried to nationalize him somewhat and turn him into a reticent proto-Zionist, as they have done to numerous other figures from the Jewish tradition.[54] Since all complex thinking lends itself to varied interpretations, the writings of the Rambam have also been interpreted in varied and sometimes contradictory ways;

Country," *Molad* 213 (1967), 303–4 (in Hebrew).

54   For example, see Shalom Rosenberg, "The Connection to the Land of Israel in Jewish Thought: A Struggle of Outlooks," *Cathedra* 4 (1977), 153–4 (in Hebrew).

his attitude toward the Land of Israel, however, created an especially difficult problem. In his discussion of the obligatory commandments, the meticulous Maimonides made absolutely no mention of the obligation to live in the Land, even after the coming of redemption. He was much more concerned with the Bible, the commandments, the Temple, and its role in future ritual.[55]

To the Zionists' great disappointment, the Rambam was quite consistent in his position on the place of the Land of Israel in the spiritual world of Judaism. Not only was it not incumbent on faithful Jews to uproot themselves and immigrate to the Land, he maintained, but the Land itself was not characterized by all the advantages attributed to it by various impulsive rabbis. Despite his belief in the "doctrine of climates" (which he shared with many other medieval thinkers), he did not find the land of Judea in any way extraordinary in comparison to other countries, although he did find it relatively comfortable.[56] And unlike other commentators, he also did not regard the ability to prophesy as conditional on residing in the Land of Israel or the demise of this ability as stemming from residence elsewhere. Rather, he viewed the ability to prophesy as conditional on the spiritual state of people themselves, and in order to avoid too significant a divergence from the Talmudic framework, he explained that because exile caused despair and made people lazy, this significant ability went no further than the people of Israel.[57] Being a sophisticated thinker, he appears to have been unable to ignore the fact that Moses, the first prophet, had prophesied outside the land of Canaan, whereas the Jewish presence in Judea between the Maccabean revolt and resultant achievement of sovereignty and the destruction of the Temple had resulted in no new prophets.

Furthermore, in his well-known *Epistle Concerning Yemen* from the year 1172 CE, the Rambam adjures the Jews of Yemen, despite their troubles, to refrain from believing in false prophets and warns that they must not, under any circumstances, force the premature conclusion of

55   See Moses ben Maimon, "Positive Commandments," *Book of Commandments*, trans. Joseph Kafah (Arabic to Hebrew).

56   See Abraham Melamed, "The Land of Israel and Climatology in Jewish Thought," in Moshe Hallamish and Aviezer Ravitzky (eds.), *The Land of Israel in Medieval Jewish Thought*, Jerusalem: Yad Izhak Ben-Zvi, 1991, 58–9 (in Hebrew).

57   Moses ben Maimon, *The Guide for the Perplexed* 2.36, Tel Aviv: University of Tel Aviv, 2002.

exile. At the end of this important text, he also makes explicit reference to the three Talmudic adjurations that warned against collective
immigration to the Holy Land.[58] Perhaps even more decisive in the
Rambam's doctrine was the fact that he did not link the coming of the
Messiah to the deeds of the Jews. In his thinking, redemption would
come regardless of repentance or the observance of the commandments; it would be a divine miracle, independent of human desire,
and would necessarily encompass the resurrection of the dead.[59]

Maimonides' position on this point preserved him from being
exploited by the impassioned, nationalized rabbinate of the second
half of the twentieth century. The Zionization of the Jewish religion
ultimately resulted in the reintroduction to its belief system of the
human subject, whose nation-based actions could, and were meant
to, hasten the coming of the Messiah. The modern revisionist distinction between the process of redemption and its final coming heralded
the beginning of the end of historic Judaism and its transformation
into a Jewish nationalism aimed at settling in the Land of Israel in
order to lay the foundations for divine redemption.

Unlike the Rambam, to whom one attributes patriotic aims only
with difficulty, two other medieval Jewish thinkers ended up effectively serving the interests of the twentieth-century nationalist
revolution in religious Judaism. These two superstars representing the
Jewish connection with the Land of Israel were Rabbi Yehudah Halevi
(the "Rihal"), who preceded Maimonides, and Rabbi Moses ben
Nachman (Nachmanides, or the "Ramban") who was active immediately after him. These two thinkers were considerably less important
in the world of rabbinical Judaism than Maimonides the "Great Eagle,"
but not so in the realm of Zionism. Both the Rihal and the Ramban
were engraved in the Western Wall of religious Zionist consciousness
and eternalized in secular Zionist pedagogy. Halevi's well-known
work *The Kuzari* was studied in Israeli schools long after the Khazars
were swept under the rug of national memory, and Nachmanides'

---

58   See Moses ben Maimon, *Epistle Concerning Yemen*, Lipsia Publications (in
Hebrew).

59   On this subject, see Gershom Scholem, who emphasizes that "nowhere did
the Rambam recognize the causal relationship between the coming of the Messiah and
human behavior. Redemption would not be brought about by the repentance of Israel."
Scholem, *Explications and Implications: Writings on Jewish Heritage and Renaissance*,
Tel Aviv: Am Oved, 1975, 185 (in Hebrew).

residence in the Holy Land in the thirteenth century is consistently praised as an example of a pioneering nationalist act.

We do not know why Halevi, who was known by his Arabic name Abu al-Hassan al-Lawi, chose an imaginary dialogue between a religious Jew and a Khazar king as the framework around which to structure his book. Reports of the existence of a kingdom near the Caspian Sea that adopted Judaism were widespread throughout the Jewish world, and even reached the Iberian Peninsula, where Halevi lived. All important Jewish scholars were familiar with the tenth-century CE correspondence between Hasdai ben Yitzhak ibn Shaprut, an influential Jewish dignitary from Córdoba in service of the Arab caliph, and the king of the Khazars. And, if we are to believe the testimony of the "Rabad" (Abraham ben David), Khazar students of the sages were also present in Toledo, Halevi's hometown.[60] However, we must also remember that Halevi wrote his text in the 1140s, after the Jewish kingdom in the East had already moved onto the sidelines of history.

The significant hardships suffered by the Jews during the Christian Reconquista greatly affected Halevi, who was also a gifted poet. As a result, he developed a strong yearning for a Jewish sovereign in the form of an all-powerful monarch and for the faraway majestic Holy Land. In *The Kuzari*, or, as it was originally titled in Arabic, *The Book of Refutation and Proof on Behalf of the Despised Religion*, Halevi attempted to forge a link between these two longings.

In this work, the poet highlighted the virtues and the place of the land of Canaan, or the Land of Israel (he used both these terms); the outcome is that by the end of the dialogue, the Jewish protagonist decides to strive to go to the Land from distant Khazaria. According to Halevi, the Holy Land possessed all necessary climatic and geographic virtues and was the only place in which believers could achieve intellectual and spiritual perfection.

At the same time, Halevi refrained from denigrating the exile and certainly did not intend to hasten the redemption or initiate collective action based on Jewish longing for it, as Zionist scholars contend.[61]

---

60 "The Book of the Kabbalah of Abraham ben David," in *The Order of the Sages and the History*, Oxford: Clarendon, 1967, 78–9 (in Hebrew).

61 See, for example, Eliezer Schweid, *Homeland and a Land of Promise*, Tel Aviv: Am Oved, 1979, 67 (in Hebrew).

The poet himself felt a personal need to go to Jerusalem for the sake of atonement and spiritual and religious purification, which he expressed in both his poems and in *The Kuzari*. He knew very well that the Jews were in no hurry to immigrate to Canaan and therefore did not hesitate to stress that their prayers on the subject were insincere and resembled "the warble of a parrot."[62]

Yehudah Halevi's great curiosity regarding the Land of Israel may have also been the product of Christian enthusiasm for the Crusades that was then spreading throughout Europe; unfortunately, he died before reaching Jerusalem, apparently during his trip to the holy city. In contrast, Moses ben Nachman, who also lived in Christian Catalonia and was closely associated with the Kabbalistic stream, was forced to immigrate to the Land of Israel at an advanced age because of persecution and oppression at the hands of the local church. Nachmanides also voiced warm sentiments regarding the Holy Land and heaped even more praises on it than was customary—even more than Halevi. Although we have no text by Nachmanides that sums up this sense of connection with the Land, his writings repeatedly articulate related thoughts in a manner that cannot be ignored.

In the section titled "Commandments Forgotten by the Rabbi" in his interpretation of Maimonides' *Book of Commandments*, Nachmanides does all he can to reinstate the obligation to settle in the Land of Israel. To this end, he reminds his readers of the biblical commandment "to destroy" the original inhabitants, "as it is written, to smite them out," and continues: "We were commanded to conquer the land in all generations . . . We were commanded to inherit the land and to dwell in it. In that case, a commandment for all generations obligates every one of us, even during exile."[63] This is an exceptionally radical position for a medieval Jewish thinker to adopt; similar examples are rare.

Nachmanides regarded life in the Holy Land as a more elevated spiritual existence than life elsewhere, even prior to the coming of the Messiah, and attributed a mythical dimension to this existence. However, if he appears at times to overlap with the Karaites, both in

---

62   Yehudah Halevi, *The Kuzari* 2, Jerusalem: Jason Aronson, 1998, 81 (in Hebrew).

63   See the fourth positive commandment in *The Rambam's Book of Commandments with the Ramban's Critical Comments*, Jerusalem: Harav Kook, 1981, 245–6 (in Hebrew).

his statements and in his having settled in Jerusalem, it is important to remember that he remained loyal to the rabbinical Talmud and never dreamed that the Jews would immigrate en masse to the Land of Israel prior to the redemption. Indeed, as explained by Michael Nehorai, the Ramban exercised even greater caution than did the Rambam "to not cause his readership to believe in the possibility of actualizing messianic hopes under the given circumstances."[64]

The Ramban was closely associated with the mystical Kabbalistic tradition, which also articulated positions on Jews' connection with the Holy Land. The literature has already addressed the significant sexual aspects of the Shekhinah's relation to the Land, and, consequently, to the ancient land of Canaan. Nonetheless, there is no consensus among Kabbalists regarding the nature of the redemption and the centrality of the sacred space in the final days. According to *The Zohar*, to settle in the Land of Israel is of ritualistic and mystical value in its own right; on this point it is consistent with the view of the Ramban. Some Kabbalists, however, thought otherwise. For example, Abraham bar Hiyya, an early-twelfth-century scholar who lived on the Iberian Peninsula, believed that the inhabitants of the Land of Israel stood farther from redemption than those living in the Diaspora, and that settling in the Land was therefore a step in the wrong direction. And despite his clear messianic tendencies, the thirteenth-century commentator Abraham ben Samuel Abulafia also did not regard the Land of Israel as the primary destination for the redeemer's miraculous arrival. As we have noted, Kabbalistic interpretation maintained that prophecy could appear only in the Land of Israel. Abulafia, however, regarded prophecy as a phenomenon completely dependent on the human body and not on a defined geographic place. In this way, and this alone, the approach of Abulafia the Kabbalist was not so different from that of Maimonides the rationalist.

According to Moshe Idel, a scholar of the Kabbalah: "The mystical conceptions regarding the Land of Israel succeeded in terminating, or at least in reducing, the centrality of the Land in its geographic sense, which was something that none of the aforementioned scholars were willing to acknowledge."[65] He goes on to say that Jewish

---

64   Michael Zvi Nehorai, "The Land of Israel in Maimonides and Nachmanides," in Hallamish and Ravitzky (eds.), *The Land of Israel in Medieval Jewish Thought*, 137.

65   Moshe Idel, "On the Land of Israel in Medieval Jewish Mysticism," in ibid., 204.

mysticism's important contribution to the traditional physical and geographic concept of aliyah (literally "ascent," used also in reference to "going up" to the Land of Israel) was "the mystical ascent of the individual, summarized in the phrase 'ascent of the soul,' whether the experience in question was one of the soul's ascent to the heavens or one of inner contemplation."[66]

In the late eighteenth century, just before the nationalist shock waves that would transform the cultural and political morphology of Europe, fewer than five thousand Jews lived in Palestine—most in Jerusalem—compared with a total population of more than 250,000 Christians and Muslims.[67] During the same period, there were approximately two and a half million Jews living around the world, primarily in Eastern Europe. The small number of Palestinian Jews, including all immigrants and pilgrims, who resided in the country for one reason or another reflects more effectively than can any written text the nature of the Jewish religion's tie to the Holy Land up to that time.

It was not objective difficulties that had prevented Jews from immigrating to Zion over the previous sixteen hundred years, even if such difficulties did exist. It was also not the three Talmudic adjurations that curbed the "authentic thirst" to live in the land of the Bible. History is much more prosaic. In contrast to the mythos so skillfully woven into the State of Israel's Declaration of Independence, such a longing to settle in the Land never truly existed. The powerful metaphysical yearning for total redemption that was linked to the place itself—as the center of the world, whence the heavens would open—bore no resemblance to human beings' desire to rouse themselves and move to a known, familiar land.[68]

---

66   Ibid., 214.

67   On the overall population of Palestine during this period, see Yehoshua Ben-Arieh, "The Population of the Land of Israel and Its Settlements on the Eve of the Zionist Settlement Enterprise," in Yehoshua Ben-Arieh, Yossi Ben-Artzi, and Haim Goren (eds.), *Historical-Geographical Studies in the Settlement of Eretz Israel*, Jerusalem: Yad Ben-Zvi, 1987, 5–6 (in Hebrew). At the beginning of the 1870s, just before the onset of Zionist colonization, the overall population of the region totaled 380,000, with Jews accounting for 18,000.

68   Despite the Israeli education system, many Israelis are well aware that Jews never aspired to emigrate to the Holy Land. See, for example, Abraham B. Yehoshua, *Homeland Grasp*, Tel Aviv: Hakibbutz Hameuchad, 2008 (in Hebrew), in which the prominent Israeli author characterizes the Jews' preference for living in the "Diaspora" as a "neurotic choice" (53).

We should therefore not be asking why Jews did not aspire to immigrate to the Land of Israel, but rather why they should have wanted to do so in the first place. Religious people typically prefer not to live in holy centers, inasmuch as the place where they work, have sexual relations, produce offspring, eat, fall ill, and pollute the environment is not supposed to be precisely the same place where the gates of heaven open upon the coming of redemption.

Despite the hardships they faced, and despite being a religious minority in frequently oppressive societies that were controlled by foreign religion, Jews, just like their neighbors, felt strong ties to their everyday lives in their countries of birth. Like Philo of Alexandria and Josephus of Rome, the Babylonian Talmudic scholars, Saadia Gaon of Mesopotamia, Maimonides of Egypt, and tens of thousands of others, the world's "simple" uneducated Jews always preferred to continue living where they lived, grew up, worked, and spoke the language. And while it is true that not until modern times did their places of residence constitute a political homeland for them, we must not forget that during the long medieval era, no one had a national territory of their own.

But if Jews did not aspire to immigrate to and settle in the land of the Bible, did they have a religious need, like that of the Christians, to visit the Holy Land for the sake of purification, penance, the offering of sacrifices, and other such activities? After the destruction of the Temple, did Jewish pilgrimage supersede immigration to the Land?

CHAPTER THREE

Toward a Christian Zionism: And Balfour Promised the Land

Just as those understand Greek history better who have visited Athens . . . so also will he have a clearer perception of the sense of holy Writ who gazes on Judea with his own eyes and recalled at their own sites the stories of its ancient cities, whose names are either still the same or have changed.

—Jerome, Preface to Chronicles, ca. 400 CE

For in Palestine we do not propose even to go through the form of consulting the wishes of the present inhabitants of the country . . . Zionism, be it right or wrong, good or bad, is rooted in age-long traditions, in present needs, in future hopes, of far profounder import than the desires and prejudices of the 700,000 Arabs who now inhabit that ancient land.

—Lord Arthur James Balfour, Memorandum, August 11, 1919

In the year 70 CE, Titus destroyed the Temple in Jerusalem in hopes of putting an end to monotheism's defiant challenge to the idolatrous regime in Rome. He and his associates "maintained that the Temple must be destroyed without delay in order to completely eradicate the Jewish and Christian religions."[1] In both the short term and the long term, the future emperor and his advisers had been mistaken. The two subsequent revolts—that of the Jewish communities throughout the southern Mediterranean Basin in the years 115–17 CE, and that of Bar Kokhba in Judea in the years 132–5—reflect that the power of young monotheism did not subside immediately after the demolition of the Temple. Rather, the momentum with which Christianity spread following the severe suppression of the latter uprising indicated that

---

1 According to Tacitus, as quoted by Sulpicius Severus in Menahem Stern (ed.), *Greek and Latin Authors on Jews and Judaism* 2, Jerusalem: The Israel Academy of Sciences and Humanities, 1980, 64.

the thirst for a single, abstract God could not be wiped out simply by the physical destruction of a place of worship.

We do not know precisely when the place of worship known in Hebrew tradition as the Second Temple was built. Unfortunately, we have no archaeological evidence of the existence of a First Temple, although we can assume it was located on the site of an ancient house of worship that existed prior to the crystallization of Yahwistic mono-theism. According to tradition, a Foundation Stone (*even hashtiya*) that was thought to be the cornerstone of the universe stood at its center. It was this stone, among other things, that imbued the site with its sanctity. But although the Temple is mentioned in the Bible, its authors virtually forget to tell us if the commandment of regular pilgrimage to the site was observed.[2] We may therefore conclude that only the Second Temple became a true site of pilgrimage, initially for the inhabitants of the land of Judea and later for the increasing numbers of Jews living elsewhere.

In the year 19 BCE, King Herod turned the Temple into a massive, magnificent structure that attracted great masses of worshippers. Judaism was then at its height, and hundreds of thousands of Jews and converts to Judaism sent contributions from afar. The Pax Romana that was increasingly taking root around the Mediterranean enabled large numbers of people to travel the roads throughout the empire in moderate security. This period of relative peace facilitated the dissem-ination of Judaism and, later, Christianity. However, it also resulted in a material infrastructure that encouraged pilgrimages to Jerusalem. For a period of almost ninety years, until 70 CE, the "house of God"— meeting point of the heavens, the earth, and the abyss—served as the center of the increasingly powerful Jewish religion.

The commandment of pilgrimage was applicable to men but not to women. Pilgrimages were regularly conducted on three holidays (*regalim*) during the year: Pesach (Passover), Shavuoth, and Sukkoth. In addition to the testimony of Philo of Alexandria and the descrip-tion provided by Flavius Josephus, the rabbinical Jewish legal texts are replete with references to this magnificent period, in which accounts of the ritual practices surrounding the Temple appear again and again.

---

2 Evidence of such a practice "prior to the Second Temple" is limited to two vague, almost identical sentences in the book of Exodus: "Three times in the year shall all your males appear before the Lord God" (23:17 and 34:23).

In addition to the generous contributions and tithes bestowed upon the priests, pilgrims would bring with them to Jerusalem both required and voluntary sacrifices. It was a mass religious celebration that strengthened the kingdom and the priesthood, which administered and controlled the event.[3]

The destruction of the Jewish Temple put an end to the obligation of pilgrimage and significantly impacted the morphological transformation of Judaism. From then on, the role of the Temple priests was increasingly filled by synagogue rabbis of the interpretive stream. The destruction of the Jerusalem ritual site, the holy center, increased the importance of small, lively meeting places within Jewish communities, which had already contributed to the flourishing and expansion of the Jewish population. Jerusalem would not be forgotten and would remain in the hearts of faithful Jews until the end of days. However, just as the Temple was replaced in practice by the synagogue, and just as sacrificial offerings were replaced by prayer, so, too, was the actual land—the ground itself—replaced by the oral tradition.

PILGRIMAGE AFTER THE DESTRUCTION: A JEWISH RITUAL?

If there were additional inert pilgrimages of mourning during the years following 70 CE, they disappeared almost completely after the suppression of the Bar Kokhba revolt in 135.[4] As we know, the Romans brutally razed Jewish Jerusalem and established on its ruins the idolatrous city of Aelia Capitolina. The circumcised were forbidden to enter the city, and so until the Christianization of the empire in the early fourth century CE, the focal point of the Jewish faith remained for the most part off-limits to Jews. The situation did not improve much after the triumph of Christianity throughout the empire. Now, Jerusalem became a sanctified Christian city with many churches, and

---

3   See Jackie Feldman, "The Experience of Communality and the Legitimation of Authority in Second Temple Pilgrimage," in Ora Limor and Elchanan Reiner (eds.), *Pilgrimage: Jews, Christians, Moslems*, Raanana: Open University Press, 2005, 88–109 (in Hebrew).

4   Shmuel Safrai has attempted to prove that isolated pilgrimages still took place from time to time. See his "Pilgrimage to Jerusalem at the Time of the Second Temple," in A. Oppenheimer, U. Rappaport, and. M. Stern, *Chapters in the History of Jerusalem in the Time of the Second Temple*, Jerusalem: Yad Ben-Zvi, 1980, 376–93 (in Hebrew).

it was not until the arrival of the armies of Islam in the early seventh century that Jews were finally allowed to freely enter and reside in their ancient holy city.

However, the Arab conquest also resulted in the construction of two Muslim houses of worship of monumental scale—in the exact location where, in the distant past, the Jewish temple had stood. In light of the symbiotic relationship between Judaism and Christianity, it is no wonder that it was two converted Jews who, according to legend, showed the victors the exact location of the Temple among the heaps of garbage that had been piled there during the Christian era. We also propose that, as a result of the physical transformations it underwent, the Temple Mount became less and less attractive to Jewish believers from the rabbinical stream who adhered to the oral tradition. As seen in the previous chapter, it was the Karaites—the "Protestants" of the Jewish religion, who rejected Jewish religious law and called for a return to the ancient sources and the Holy Land— who settled in Jerusalem and made pilgrimages thence.[5]

Islam selected Jerusalem as its third most important holy center, after Mecca and Medina. As a religion that drew on Judaism for some of its sources, the holy city located in the heart of Palestine was initially the main site toward which worshippers directed their prayers. It was from there that Muhammad ascended to the heavens. Although the Haj—the Islamic commandment of pilgrimage—focused on Mecca, a significant number of pilgrims also visited Jerusalem. Mystics from various streams who regarded immigration and pilgrimage to Bilad ash-Sham, the Holy Land, as being of utmost religious importance continued to make their way there for many years.[6]

---

5   The Karaites continued to make pilgrimages to Jerusalem alone and staunchly opposed pilgrimage to the saintly graves that became increasingly popular within rabbinical Judaism. On this subject, see Joshua Prawer, "Hebrew Travel Accounts in the Land of Israel in the Crusader Period," in J. Prawer (ed.), *History of the Jews in the Crusaders' Kingdom*, Jerusalem: Yad Ben-Zvi, 2000, 177 (in Hebrew).

6   See Shelomo Dov Goitein, "The Sanctity of Palestine in Muslim Piety," *Bulletin of the Jewish Palestine Exploration Society* 12 (1945–6), 120–6 (in Hebrew). In this article from the 1940s, Goitein discusses the use of the term "Sham" alongside the "Holy Land," which already appears in the Koran. The Muslim conquest also inherited the term "Palestine" from the Byzantines and applied it to the entire region surrounding Jerusalem (ibid., 121). We also find the term "Palestine" employed in the writings of authors ranging from Ibn al-Kalbi the historian to Ibn'Asakir to al-Idrisi the geographer. See also Yosef Drori, "A Muslim Scholar Describes Frankish

In contrast, during the millennium between the end of the Bar Kokhba revolt in 135 CE, during which the rebels sought to rebuild the Temple, and the Crusaders' conquest of Jerusalem in 1099, we know of no attempts by the followers of rabbinical Judaism to make pilgrimages to the holy city. As already noted, the Jews did not "forget" Jerusalem, for a major facet of Judaism was its connection to this holy center. This bond, however, did not translate into an urge to connect concretely with the Land—to tread upon its soil, to travel within it, or to learn its geography.

Although Jewish commentators engage in lengthy discussion of the laws concerning the rituals of the Temple during its existence, they say little about pilgrimage to Jerusalem after its destruction. Although the Mishnah, the Talmud, and the Midrash—three texts devoted entirely to positive and negative commandments—include eschatological instructions regarding the resumption of Temple rituals at the coming of redemption, they provide no indication of the religious importance of pilgrimage beforehand. Unlike Christianity, Judaism does not regard the pilgrimage to Jerusalem as an act of penance for transgressions or an act that can purify the believer, and we therefore find no recommendation that it be implemented. Ultimately, this difficult historical reality fragmented the physical relationship with the holy center for a period of time, leaving in its wake powerful ties that were primarily spiritual and metaphysical in nature.

Jewish pilgrimage to Jerusalem in particular and to the Holy Land in general appears to have recommenced only after the conquest by the Crusaders. Elchanan Reiner, a scholar of Jewish pilgrimages, has addressed this subject at length:

> The institution of pilgrimage, as it took form in Jewish society during the medieval period, appears to have evolved in particularly close proximity to the institution of pilgrimage that took form in the Crusaders' countries of origin, either under the influence of or in response to the Crusader challenge. Prior to the Crusader period, institutionalized pilgrimage did not exist among the Jews of the countries of the Latin Church, not to mention a crystallized ritual of

Palestine," in Benjamin Z. Kedar, *The Crusaders in their Kingdom, 1099–1291,* Jerusalem: Yad Ben-Zvi, 1987, 127 (in Hebrew).

pilgrimage to the Land of Israel. The institution of pilgrimage took its first steps within the Jewish communities of Catholic Europe during the twelfth century and the beginning of the thirteenth century as the result of the third Crusade, coming to occupy its deserved place in the religious world of the Jews of France, Spain, and finally Ashkenaz.[7]

Why did the Crusader awakening and Christian attention to the Holy Land "influence" the Jewish communities of Europe? Reiner advances the hypothesis that Jewish interest in pilgrimage was the product of competition over the Land. That is to say, Christianity's claim to be the true heir of the Old Testament and therefore entitled to control the territorial assets it describes aroused concerns among Jews, sparking a mass movement of pilgrims to Jerusalem.[8]

This argument is far from satisfactory. Even if in Christian literature we find arguments contending that, as a result of Jesus' suffering, the Holy Land was promised a second time, this time to his followers, we find no substantial Jewish counterargument claiming collective human ownership of the place. Unfortunately, Reiner's analysis does not explain why Jewish pilgrimage did not begin to flourish earlier, in the fourth century CE. After all, it was then that Christianity began to assert its tie to and control over the Holy Land through the establishment of numerous churches and commemorative sites. The analysis also fails to clarify why this Jewish jealousy of "ownership" did not result in the onset of alarmed pilgrimages from large nearby communities in Egypt and Mesopotamia following the Muslim conquest of Jerusalem and the construction of their impressive houses of worship in the city. As early as the ninth century, Karaite Daniel al-Kumisi expressed his amazement at the rabbinical Jews' refusal to visit Zion:

Do not nations other than Israel come from the four corners of the earth to Jerusalem every month and every year in the awe of God? What, then, is the matter with you, our brethren in Israel, that you

---

7   Elchanan Reiner, "Overt Falsehood and Covert Truth: Christians, Jews, and Holy Places in Twelfth-Century Palestine," *Zion* 63:2 (1998), 159 (in Hebrew).

8   On the concept of Christian "ownership" of the *terra sancta*, see Robert Louis Wilken, *The Land Called Holy: Palestine in Christian History and Thought*, New Haven: Yale University Press, 1992.

are not doing even as much as is the custom of the Gentiles in coming to Jerusalem and praying there?[9]

During this period, no one prevented Jews from visiting or residing in Jerusalem as they pleased. Interpretations that attribute a sense of ownership over the Land of Israel to Jews from the rabbinical stream appear to be largely anachronistic in nature. In fact, such interpretations serve primarily to reproduce a modern Zionist sense of ownership over the traditional Jewish spiritual world, whose connection to the place was typically characterized by premodern and apolitical psychological attributes.

The truth is, we do not know for certain why Jewish pilgrimages came to a complete halt and only gradually reemerged so much later. All we can do is offer conjectures. It should be remembered that, for Judeans and converts prior to the destruction of the Temple, pilgrimage was not made to the holy places in the land of Judea but rather was directed entirely toward Jerusalem, not at one's personal initiative but on dates determined by the Bible. The destruction of the Temple and a portion of the Jewish city in the wake of the great messianic revolt thoroughly eradicated the reason for this practice and, as already noted, profoundly changed the nature of the Jewish faith. The geophysical Jerusalem faded in the consciousness of the faithful and the heavenly Jerusalem came forth, emerging as the imagined Jewish center.

The encounter between Christian and, later, Muslim converts—who had only recently been Jews—and the Land itself may also have deterred those who continued their adherence to the religion of Moses. Whereas the Christianization of the Jews of Palestine had been relatively moderate until the arrival of the Arab armies, the initially slow and not necessarily conscious process of Islamicization that began in the early seventh century appears to have eventually become thorough and sweeping. Indeed, it would take a significant period of time before this mass conversion of the people of the Land, which occurred over a number of generations, could be altogether forgotten, enabling Jews once again to explore the Holy Land without

---

9   Daniel al-Kumisi, "Appeal to the Karaites of the Dispersion to Come and Settle in Jerusalem," in Leon Nemoy (ed.), *Karaite Anthology*, New Haven: Yale University Press, 1952, 37.

encountering masses of converts and their offspring. These inhabitants, it can be assumed, would have attempted to convince Jewish
travelers to adopt their victorious rituals and their conquering faith.

We must also not forget that for the individual Jewish pilgrim, the
journey from Europe to the Land of Israel was virtually impossible
because of the danger of nonobservance of the commandments. As
far as we know, there were no hostels or way stations meant for Jews.
Potential travelers would probably have been discouraged from
embarking on this long and dangerous journey by the risk of desecrating the Sabbath because of the need to travel nonstop on
unfamiliar roads, the inability to pray with a minyan (the quorum of
ten Jews required for certain religious obligations), and the difficulty
of observing kosher dietary laws while traveling.[10] All in all, in order
to make a trip to the Holy Land, an extremely devout Jew would be
forced to become slightly less devout.

Jewish pilgrimage emerged as an afterthought to Christian
pilgrimage. It never reached comparable dimensions and so perhaps
cannot be considered an institutionalized practice. Few Jewish
pilgrims set out to the Holy Land between the twelfth century and the
end of the eighteenth century CE, by comparison to the tens of thousands of Christian pilgrims who made the trip during the same
period. Although by this time there were certainly fewer Jews than
Christians in the world, the degree to which the Land of Israel did not
attract the "original children of Israel" is nonetheless astounding.
Despite Zionist historiography's efforts over many years to collect
every shred of information reflecting the Jews' concrete connection to
their "homeland," it achieved only minimal success in this endeavor.

To the best of our knowledge, the poet and thinker Rabbi Yehu-
dah Halevi was the first to decide to travel to the Holy Land, in 1140
CE, although he never completed his trip, apparently dying en route.
Not long afterward, in 1165, Maimonides and his family left Morocco
and arrived in Acre; the young philosopher visited Jerusalem and
Hebron but subsequently found little reason to return to these places

---

10   For other factors that may have prevented Jews from making the pilgrimage,
see Elchanan Reiner, "Pilgrims and Pilgrimage to Eretz Israel 1099–1517," Ph.D. diss.,
Jerusalem: Hebrew University, 1988, 108. See also Israel Ta-Shema, "The Response of an
Ashkenazic Hassid regarding Eretz Israel" and "On the Attitude of the Early Ashkenazim
to the Value of Immigrating to Eretz Israel," *Shalem: Studies in the History of the Jews in
Eretz Israel*, 1 (1974), 81–2; 6 (1992), 315–18 (in Hebrew).

once his family had settled in nearby Egypt. From the second half of the twelfth century, we also have the testimony of Yaakov Ben Natanel, who made his way to Palestine from Provence and left behind a number of texts regarding his visit. Another short text from the same period, titled "Ancestral Graves" (*Kivrei Avot*), was written by an anonymous Jew who appears to have hailed from Damascus.

The most interesting fact here is that the two most important authors to visit and provide detailed descriptions of Palestine during this period were not pilgrims. Benjamin of Tudela (Spain) and Pethahiah of Regensburg (Germany) were two traveling researchers who left their places of residence in order to acquaint themselves with the Jewish communities of the known world, and in this capacity also made their way to the Holy Land. From an anthropological perspective, their testimonies, written in Hebrew, are irreplaceable,[11] and their picturesque descriptions of Jewish life in different regions, from Gaul to the Crimean Peninsula under the Khazars, fascinating. These two narratives reflect how limited a role the Land of Israel played in the Jewish imagination of the period.

These two daring travelers were much more interested in people than in physical places. They were curious about holy sites and burial places but address ways of life and religious practices with much more original commentary. Benjamin and Pethahiah represent the most curious and alert elements of the medieval Jewish intellectual world. Undoubtedly, not everything they convey is fully accurate, as they inevitably viewed much of what presented itself to them through the prism of familiar legends and miracles and as they acquired some of their knowledge from secondhand sources rather than personal observation. Nonetheless, their reports are of rare quality.

According to the calculations of Benjamin of Tudela, the Jewish population of the area between Acre and Ashkelon was quite small compared with that of Babylon, reflecting the fact that although Jews apparently sent their dead to the Land of Israel, they did not send their living offspring. Damascus impressed him much more than Jerusalem, which he classified as no more than a small town.

---

11   Marcus Nathan Adler (ed. and trans.), *The Travel Book of Rabbi Benjamin*, Jerusalem: The Publishing House of the Students Association of the Hebrew University, 1960 (in Hebrew); Pethahiah Ben Jacob, *The Travels of Rabbi Pethahiah of Ratisbon*, Jerusalem: Greenhut, 1967 (in Hebrew).

Pethahiah, who conveyed his impressions to his students rather than writing them down himself, was amazed by the small number of Jewish communities in the country. He, too, was impressed by Damascus, with its Jewish population of ten thousand, in contrast to the mere three hundred Jewish families then living in the Land of Israel. Jerusalem's relatively minor importance in his story is surprising; according to his account, the Jews seemed to prefer the pilgrimage to Ezekiel's grave in Babylon, which was undertaken even by representatives of the converted Khazars.[12]

The period between Benjamin's and Pethahiah's visits and the end of the seventeenth century produced a small number of extant travelers' accounts of Jews who made their way to the land of the Bible, such as Shmuel Bar-Shimson's disrupted account of a group of rabbis primarily from Provence (1210); the story of Rabbi Akiva, who came to Jerusalem to collect money for his yeshivah in Paris (before 1257); the immigration of the elderly Nachmanides and his student's later account of it; the moving poems of Yehuda Alharizi, from the early thirteenth century; the stylistic testimony of Ishtori Haparchi, from the early fourteenth century; and a few other incomplete and rare narratives.

Fifteenth- and sixteenth-century arrivals in the Land of Israel included Rabbi Isaac ibn Alfara of Málaga (1441), Rabbi Meshulam of Volterra (1481), Rabbi Obadiah of Bertinoro (1489), and Rabbi Moses Basola of Pesaro (1521). Beginning in the seventeenth century, travel journals from Eastern Europe started to appear, from Moses Porit of Prague (1650), from the messianic disciples of Judah Hahasid (early 1700s), from the surprising visit of Rabbi Nachman of Breslov (1798).[13]

Jewish pilgrimage, therefore, was practiced in a limited way by wealthy educated Jews, who were typically but not always rabbis and merchants motivated by a variety of factors that were not always religious in nature. Some journeys were the fulfillment of vows, others the result of a quest for atonement, still others motivated by curiosity and a desire for adventure for its own sake. Christian pilgrimages, too, may have enticed not only religious pilgrims but also travelers,

---

12   Pethahiah, *Travels*, 47–8.
13   On Jewish visits and pilgrimages, see Avraham Yaari, *Jewish Pilgrims' Journeys to the Land of Israel*, Ramat Gan: Masada, 1976 (in Hebrew).

especially from Italy. A regular ship line between Venice and Jaffa began to operate in the fourteenth century. As a result, the number of Christian pilgrims to the Holy Land reached between four hundred and five hundred per year.[14]

Jewish travelers' interest in and sense of solidarity with other Jews is clearly reflected in almost all their narratives. Although they are not indifferent to the sight of the ancient landscapes, this is generally not the focus of their accounts. The travel reports are relatively unemotional and employ no language suggesting spiritual elevation or religious ecstasy. Also conspicuous is the absence of any hostility on the part of the "Ishmaelites"—the local Muslims—toward the Jewish travelers. Travelers' letters are filled with expressions of appreciation for the local population who, unlike the Christians in Europe, did not regard Judaism as an inferior, contemptible religion.[15] These accounts reveal nothing that prevented Jews from exploring the Holy Land, and little that prevented them from settling there. The Land received them well, even if to many it seemed to consist only of barren desert; always it remained the land of milk and honey, because, in the final analysis, the biblical texts remained much more important than what the travelers saw with their own eyes.

After taking a pilgrimage vow, Meshulam of Volterra arrived in Jerusalem and was astounded by the beauty of its buildings. However, this fragile banker's son from Tuscany was also struck by the local way of life: "The Ishmaelites and the local Jews are like pigs when they eat, as everyone eats with their fingers from the same dish without a tablecloth, like in Egypt. Their garments, however, are clean."[16] Moses Basola, by contrast, took a much greater interest in graves and provides his future readers with a complete list, enabling other believers to follow his footsteps to the sites with ease.[17]

---

14   Jacob Rosenthal, "The Pilgrimage to the Holy Land of Hans Tucher, Patrician of Nuremberg, in 1479," *Cathedra* 137 (2010), 64 (in Hebrew).

15   See Avraham Yaari (ed.), *Letters from the Land of Israel*, Ramat Gan: Masada, 1971, 18–20 (in Hebrew).

16   Avraham Yaari (ed.), *Meshulam of Volterra's Travels in the Land of Israel, 1481,* Jerusalem: Mosad Bialik, 1948, 75. Despite the book's title, the text itself makes no mention of the "Land of Israel."

17   Yitzhak Ben-Zvi (ed.), *A Pilgrimage to Palestine by Rabbi Moshe Basola of Ancona,* Jerusalem: Jewish Palestine Exploration Society, 1939, 79–82 (in Hebrew). According to Ben-Zvi, who edited this volume and would later serve as president of the State of Israel, the traveler was infused with "a great affinity for the homeland" (15).

Indeed, most other Jewish travelers would visit and prostrate themselves on saintly graves. From the ancestral graves at the Cave of Machpela, to Joseph's Tomb in Nablus and the graves of Shimon Bar-Yochai and Hillel Shammai at Mount Meron, pilgrimage sites multiplied. Moses Porit, who wrote in Yiddish, informs us that Jews were already praying in close proximity to the Western Wall during the seventeenth century:

> Jews are forbidden to enter into the place where the Temple stood. The Western Wall is located at the same place, and Jews are permitted to visit it from its external face, not its internal face. In any event, we stand and pray some distance away from the Western Wall and do not come close to it because of its sanctity.[18]

By contrast, the travel journal of Moshe Haim Capsutto, who traveled from Firenze to Jerusalem in 1734, emphasizes that

> the Jews have no ghetto, and they can live wherever they wish; they are approximately two thousand in number [out of a total population of fifty thousand, according to his calculations], including a relatively large number of women who came to Jerusalem from different places as widows in order to enjoy what remains of their lives in heavenly reverence.[19]

Without a doubt, many more Jews made pilgrimages to Jerusalem without leaving a literary mark. A significant number of pilgrims did not know how to read or write. It is also safe to assume that many testimonies were lost over the years. Nevertheless, it is evident that journeying to the Land of Israel was no more than a marginal practice in the life of the Jewish communities. All comparisons between the numbers of Christian and Jewish pilgrims reflect that Jewish trips to the Holy Land were a drop in the ocean. We know of approximately thirty texts that provide accounts of Jewish pilgrimage during the seventeen hundred years between 135 CE and the mid-nineteenth century. By contrast, for the fifteen hundred years between 333 CE

18   Yaari, *Jewish Pilgrims' Journeys*, 284.
19   Moshe Haim Capsutto, *The Journal of a Journey to the Land of Israel, 1734*, Jerusalem: Kedem, 1984, 44 (in Hebrew).

and 1878, we have some 3,500 reports of Christian pilgrimages to the Holy Land.[20]

The "children of Israel" had many reasons for their relative indifference and physical reluctance to engage in pilgrimage to the Land of Israel. For one, within Judaism there was a deep fear of messianic streams with the potential to arouse the community and endanger the fragile Jewish existence, the security of which depended on the grace of other ruling religions. The work of sociologist Victor Turner teaches us that unsupervised, uncontrolled pilgrimage can destabilize the social order of any religious institution. Conservative communities, which at times are concerned primarily with their own existence, cannot welcome the spontaneous and sometimes anarchistic project of making private or group journeys to holy places, or the "antistructure" that may develop from participating in such experiences.[21] In contrast to the power of the Church, which was able to direct and channel pilgrimage to its benefit, Jewish community institutions were too weak to organize guided, controlled pilgrimages that would serve its interests. For this reason, except for a few exceptional cases, we find no Jewish community encouragement of journeys to the Holy Land. We also know of explicit opposition to pilgrimages when they were popular, particularly among the Jews of Ashkenaz.[22]

Every Karaite who made the pilgrimage to his holy city received the honorable title of Jerusalemite, which remained with him for the rest of his life. In the rabbinical tradition, however, there is neither record nor trace of such a classification. Unlike Christian pilgrims, Jewish pilgrims were not provided with the prestige or indulgences (*indulgentia*) that the organized Church generously granted to the faithful of the city where Jesus was crucified, as well as to other pilgrims. Moreover, unlike Muslim pilgrims to Mecca, one could continue being a perfectly good Jew without ever paying a visit to the earthly Jerusalem.

---

20   On this subject, see the impressive collection compiled by German Crusader historian Reinhold Röhricht in his *Bibliotheca Geographica Palaestinae. Cronologisches Verzeichnis der von 333 bis 1878 verfassten Literatur über das Heilige Land* (1890), Jerusalem: Universitas Booksellers of Jerusalem, 1963.

21   Victor Turner, "Pilgrimages as Social Processes," in *Dramas, Fields and Metaphors: Symbolic Action in Human Society*, Ithaca: Cornell University Press, 1974, 166–230.

22   See Reiner, *Pilgrims and Pilgrimage*, 99ff.

Of course, this was true only as long as the Jew did not forget the holy city's destruction, in which case his right hand would "forget its cunning" (Pss. 137:5–6). "Next year in Jerusalem," exclaimed every Jew on Yom Kippur and at the Passover Seder, in what amounted to a prayer for the coming redemption rather than a call to action. For Jews, the holy city was a precious region of memory, a constant source of sustenance for faith, and not necessarily a curious geographic site to which a visit could delay or prevent the coming of salvation. Ultimately, Jewish thinking focused much more on prayer and the diligent study of Jewish religious law than on pilgrimage to an unknown territory.

SACRED GEOGRAPHY AND JOURNEYS IN THE LAND OF JESUS

Despite the mythos of Jesus' pilgrimage to Jerusalem on the holiday of Passover, the idea of one or multiple holy centers was not part of Christianity at its beginnings. Although the authors of the Bible attributed to God the words "And let them make me a sanctuary, that I may dwell in their midst" (Exod. 25:8), Paul's rebellious statement in the New Testament asserts precisely the opposite: "The God who made the world and everything in it, being Lord of heaven and earth, does not live in temples made by man" (Acts 17:24). However, as has been the case with other religions, the generations of Christians that would follow the founder would subordinate this message to changing psychological needs. Christian faith in Jesus' having worked, walked, and been crucified in Judea was so strong and present that it simply could not have not been fashioned into an ethos of a central holy place.[23]

As we have seen, following the three Jewish revolts the Romans attempted to topple Jerusalem as a center of monotheism and to erase the aura of sanctity that enveloped it. However, even before Christianity became the official religion of the Roman Empire, a number of Christian pilgrims arrived in the troubled city. The first was Melito, the bishop of Sardis, who made his way to Jerusalem in

---

23   The term "Holy Land" itself became widespread in Christianity only after the Crusades. For more on this, see C. H. J. de Geus, "The Fascination for the Holy Land during the Centuries," in Jacques van Ruiten and J. Cornelis de Vos (eds.), *The Land of Israel in Bible, History, and Theology*, Leiden: Brill, 2009, 405.

the second century CE and was followed by many others. We also know of pioneering pilgrims who, during the same period, visited Bethlehem, the birthplace of the son of God, and Golgotha, the site of his crucifixion.

But it was the pilgrimage to Palestine in 326 CE of Helena—the mother of Emperor Constantine I, who converted to Christianity before her son did—that truly inaugurated the era of Christian sanctification of the city. Similar to a different Helena, the Jewish converted mother of Izates and Monobaz II, kings of Adiabene, who visited Jerusalem during the early decades of the first century CE and added splendor to the Temple, the later Helena built the first churches that became pilgrimage sites. The visit of Empress Helena began a centuries-long tradition that became an integral part of the life of the Christian Church.

Although the institution of pilgrimage exists in most religions, its role and relative importance varies from faith to faith. From the outset, the journeys of Christian pilgrimage differed from the festive pilgrimages to the Jewish Temple and from the annual Muslim pilgrimage to Mecca that developed much later. Unlike its Jewish and Muslim counterparts, the Christian pilgrimage was not related to an explicit commandment, and its theoretical basis was purely voluntary. It also differed in that it was not conducted within a formal collective framework and did not take place on set dates during the year.

Edward David Hunt has conjectured that it was the Hellenistic and Roman tradition of the research expedition, more than the ancient Jewish pilgrimage, that provided the cultural foundations for the evolution of the Christian pilgrimage.[24] The erudite tourism of the Pax Romana stemmed from curiosity and a desire to investigate, in the tradition of Herodotus. The excitement of a firsthand encounter with places mentioned in the literature of the past resulted in a wave of visits, and the journeys there shaped the later practices of religious pilgrimage. It was wholly intellectual activity, and most who engaged in it were well educated, well read, and well-to-do, as were their heirs, the new monotheists.

---

24   Edward David Hunt, *Holy Land Pilgrimage in the Later Roman Empire, A.D. 312–460*, Oxford: Clarendon Press, 1982. See also Hunt, "Travel, Tourism and Piety in the Roman Empire: A Context for the Beginnings of Christian Pilgrimage," *Echos du Monde Classique* 28 (1984), 391–417.

The deep sense of universalism ingrained in the new religion served as an additional stimulus for Christian pilgrimage. The new believers thirsted for knowledge regarding the practices of others from foreign places who shared their faith, and they set out to see for themselves. Their first destination was the capital city of Rome, which offered the finest intellects and the cultural and religious treasures of the ancient world. For these reasons, it was only logical that this city would become the primary holy center of Christianity. The crucifixion of the apostle Peter in Rome also resulted in the construction there of the world's largest church, which would eventually be known as the Vatican.

Christian history has produced numerous pilgrimage sites, including the graves of exceptional monks and clergymen and the sites of miracles. Such places have been sanctified and often visited. But it was the land of the Bible, where prophets prophesied and where Jesus walked, that became the most popular site of all. The province of Palestine quickly became the Holy Land for all the world's Christians; tens of thousands, if not hundreds of thousands, of Christian believers visited it from the time of the pilgrimage made by the anonymous traveler from Bordeaux in 333 CE till that of Pope Benedict XVI in 2009. Whereas Judaism started out as a religion focused on a physical center, from which it was subsequently detached through a process of spiritualization, Christianity in many ways developed in the opposite direction.

The territorialization of Christian sanctity arose primarily through a vanguard of pilgrims and the mental and material resources at the Church's disposal. Even if initial Zionist scholarship attempted to appropriate the "traveler from Bordeaux" to the Jewish tradition,[25] this first true pilgrim to leave us a report was a devout Christian, who succeeded in introducing a new tradition to European consciousness. This pioneer arrived in "Palestine, which is Judea" (as he described the country)[26] during the early days of Christianity, while the first churches were being constructed there. He visited biblical and Christian sites in Caesarea, Jezreel, Scythopolis, Neapolis, and Jerusalem

25   See, for example, the father of Israeli geography Shmuel Klein, "The Travel Book: *Itinerarium Burdigalense* on the Land of Israel," *Zion* 6 (1934), 25–9.

26   See "The Journey from Bordeaux" in Ora Limor, *Holy Land Travels: Christian Pilgrims in Late Antiquity*, Jerusalem: Yad Ben-Zvi, 1998, 27 (in Hebrew).

(the Temple plaza, the pool of Siloam, the home of Caiaphas the priest, the Tower of David, Golgotha, the tombs of Isaiah the prophet and King Hezekiah, and others). From Jerusalem, he continued on to Jericho, to the home of Rahab the prostitute, and to the Jordan River, where John baptized Jesus; to Bethlehem, the location of Rachel's grave and the birthplace of Jesus; to Hebron, the burial place of Abraham and Sarah, Isaac and Rebecca, and Jacob and Leah; and from there to Diospolis, or Lydda, and then back to Caesarea.

On his way to Palestine, the pilgrim from Bordeaux stopped in Rome but had nothing to say about it. He also took no interest in the Land's inhabitants, its corporeal landscapes, its rivers, or the quality of the land in its valleys. As a child of the "true Israel," he understood the Old and New Testaments as one narrative unit, and reported only on specific sites relevant to his close reading of the Bible. In actuality, he presents us not with a diagram of a journey through a real area but rather an exact, measured, geo-theological sketch of the holy places. In his effort to capture the physical reality behind the written literature, he inadvertently created sacred geography.

The second travel journal we have at our disposal reinforces the outline of the new geo-theology. Egeria, a woman from the Iberian Peninsula, possibly an abbess, who made a pilgrimage to Jerusalem during the second half of the fourth century, recorded a description of all the holy sites in the Middle East, from the footsteps of the ancient Israelites to Jesus' final walk in Jerusalem. Not limiting herself to "Palestine, which is the land of promise,"[27] she managed to explore Abraham's dwelling-place in Mesopotamia as well as the mysterious Sinai Desert, through which the prophet Moses led the tribes of Israel. She described the Holy Land itself in minute detail, especially Jerusalem, the most precious place of all, and tried to cover every site mentioned in her Holy Bible. "Somewhat curious,"[28] according to her own testimony of her personal character (she writes in first person), she persistently adapted her geographic findings to the ancient texts. In her great enthusiasm, she added insufficiently detailed information by asking questions of local inhabitants. Yet she displayed no interest in the present, and, as was the case with the traveler from Bordeaux, she had no particular interest in the local inhabitants except when

27 Egeria, *Diary of a Pilgrimage*, Mahwah, N.J.: The Newman Press, 1970, 75.
28 Ibid., 74.

they were conducting ritual ceremonies, by which she was moved and heartened.

Egeria's rich writing reveals a new and fundamental dimension of Christian pilgrimage that intensified during the years following her visit. More than moving through space, she moved through time, making use of the distant past in order to reinforce and institutionalize the essentials of her faith. Learning about the holy places helped provide a concrete basis for a more abstract religiosity. In her writings, intense, urgent, and ascetic piety is interwoven with scholarly investigation, and it appears that geography is meant first and foremost to reinforce this "mythistory." She does not question the miracles and wonders of the Christian stories of the Bible. Instead, the physical places themselves serve to reaffirm the veracity of everything recounted: the existence of the land gives validity to divine truth and offers decisive evidence of reality.

In this way, Christian pilgrimage to the Holy Land embraced two intellectual strata: the biblical theological tradition and the Greek tradition of inquiry. Jerome, the learned priest who arrived in Bethlehem and remained there as a permanent resident, clearly and publicly illustrated this point in his writings and translations. Despite his distaste for mass pilgrimage and his reservations regarding the veneration of sites and graves for their own sake, he praises erudite travel to "the Athens of Christianity," and regards it as an important supplementary means of investigating the hidden meaning of the old and new covenants. Ultimately, Jerome proposes that topography is the anvil on which true theological understanding is forged. Every place has a name and every name conceals hidden meanings, our understanding of which brings us closer to an understanding of divine intention. When Jerome's close friend Paula, the wealthy matron from Rome, strolls through the holy sites, what she encounters is a wondrous world that is all allegory. The Palestine of Jerome and Paula is an imagined territory; visiting it becomes a textual journey of sorts, just as it was for Egeria and the Bordeaux pilgrim.[29]

---

29   See Jerome, "Jerome on the Pilgrimage of Paula," in Brett Edward Whalen (ed.), *Pilgrimage in the Middle Ages: A Reader*, Toronto: University of Toronto Press, 2011, 26–9. On Paula, see J. N. D. Kelly, *Jerome: His Life, Writings, and Controversies*, London: Duckworth, 1975, 91–103.

Travel diaries of monks and priests reflect how much Christianity needed topography, not only to reinforce the veracity of its stories, but also, and equally important, to create a bridge between the kingdom of Judea, with its ancient rulers and prophets, and the later work of Jesus and his loyal apostles. The construction of continuity between the stories of the Old Testament and the narratives of the Gospels was assisted by the creation of a sacred geographic contiguity, which, despite its application to the past, lacked a true chronology. Ancient buildings could simultaneously be attributed to different periods, and if pilgrims were to have encountered Abraham the Aramaean and John the Baptist walking hand in hand, they would certainly have been flustered and excited but perhaps not entirely surprised.

The certainty that Jesus was at once a descendant of the House of David and the spiritual heir of the biblical prophets Moses and Elijah was also achieved by identifying the series of sites depicted next to one another in the same given space. The territorial unity of the Holy Land throughout the different time periods served as additional proof of the narrative unity of all the books of the Bible.

All pilgrims who left behind written documentation added new elements, reinforcing the geographic knowledge that began to coalesce between the fourth and sixth centuries CE. It must also be remembered, however, that written documentation was not the only means of disseminating this knowledge. When pilgrims returned to their places of residence, they traveled from city to city telling listeners about their experiences, usually for payment. Sometimes they traveled in groups, other times as individuals. Although at times the Church feared them, it was typically able to channel their experiences into its continued empowerment and expansion.

Byzantine rule marked the first golden age in the administration of sacred geography for the educated members of all branches of the Church. From the British Isles and Scandinavia to Germany and Russia, medieval pilgrims organized themselves in order to get a taste of the Holy Land and smell the majestic land of Jesus. To breathe the air that the Messiah had breathed, they thronged toward the Holy Land, ready to undergo self-denial and hardship and to risk their lives. Under Muslim rule, no strong measures were taken to stop these pilgrimages, as local Arabs generally derived material benefit from the never-ending flow of visitors, most of whom arrived with cash in hand. Moreover, Islam regarded Christianity as a sister religion, despite the latter's emphatic refusal to recognize the former as such.

Toward the year 1000, the flow of pilgrims increased because of the millenarian and eschatological notions then sweeping Europe. More than ever, Jerusalem appeared to be the navel of the world, which would crack open to afford final salvation. The Christians who drew the maps during this period consistently placed the holy city at the center of the world, portraying it as the core from which everything emerged and to which everything would return. Even though the decisive year did not fulfill expectations, masses of pilgrims continued to visit Jerusalem, including dignified bishops and well-known, wealthy, revered abbots. They were joined by adventurers, merchants, and the occasional escaped criminal, whose journey resulted in a place of refuge and possibly the opportunity for a deed of penance.

Not until the fall of Jerusalem to the Seljuk Turks in 1078 and the imposition of restrictions on the freedom of worship in the Church of the Holy Sepulchre and other houses of prayer was the flow of pilgrims stemmed, though not for long. The First Crusade reopened the city gates in 1099, and the flow of visitors to Jerusalem resumed uninterrupted until modern times.

The restrictions imposed by the Seljuks and their harassment of Christian pilgrims provided the main pretext for the Crusades. But there were more important internal European political and socioeconomic reasons for this sweeping Christian eruption into the land of Jesus. Among other factors, reasons for this invasive and bloody campaign included the landless aristocracy's class-based problems, desire for control and expansion within the Catholic Church, seasoned merchants' lust for money, and uninhibited knights' search for reasons to sacrifice themselves.[30] It seems almost certain, however, that the extensive ideological cultivation of sacred geography also contributed to the extent of mobilization and the Crusaders' sense of religious and psychological empowerment. As a result of the dissemination of Crusader diaries (as a supplement to the Bible, not as a replacement), many Crusader fighters arrived in a somewhat familiar country that,

---

30   On the circumstances that caused the Catholic Church to adopt religious militarism, see Jean Flori's thorough *La Guerre Sainte: La Formation de l'Idée de Croisade dans l'Occident Chrétien*, Paris: Aubier, 2001.

to a great degree, was perceived as having always been their Holy Land. Some scholars even regard the Crusades as a type of pilgrimage—that is to say, an armed pilgrimage.[31]

It is interesting to note that in his mobilizing speech of 1095, in which he called on his followers to embark upon the First Crusade, the militant pope Urban II praised the "children of Israel's" biblical conquest of the Holy Land and implored their Christian successors to follow in their footsteps.[32] It has also been said that when the Knights of Jesus, as they called themselves, reached Jerusalem in 1099, they circled the city barefoot seven times in hopes of repeating the miracle that took place at Jericho. However, as all serious believers know, miracles do not repeat themselves, and the knights were forced to penetrate the city walls without God's direct assistance. The massacre of the city's inhabitants—Muslims, Karaites, Jews, and even Byzantine Christians alike—is reminiscent of the atrocities recounted in detail in the biblical narrative.

The Crusader kingdom held Jerusalem for eighty-eight years and, for an additional period, controlled a narrow strip along the coast of Palestine and modern-day southern Lebanon. The kingdom was finally destroyed in 1291. Its control of the holy city lasted about the same amount of time as the independent kingdom of the Maccabees, which existed from the mid-second to the mid-first century BCE. The Crusaders attempted to convince the numerous pilgrims, who saw them as brothers, to make their home in Jerusalem so as to bolster the Christian character of the city. But many pilgrims reviled the Crusaders for their crude, secular way of life and their desecration of the Holy Land, and most elected to make a quick return Europe.[33] At the height of the settlement process, Christian settlers in the city numbered 30,000, whereas the total Crusader population never exceeded 120,000. The majority of the working population—between a quarter-million and a half-million people—remained Muslim, with a Byzantine Christian minority. Despite great efforts, combined with

---

31   Alessandro Barbero, *Histoires de Croisades*, Paris: Flammarion, 2010, 12.

32   See the report of Balderic, the bishop of Dol, in August C. Krey, *The First Crusade: The Accounts of Eyewitnesses and Participants*, Princeton: Princeton University Press, 1921, 33–6.

33   For more on this, see Aryeh Grabois, "From 'Sacred Geography' to 'Writing Eretz Israel': Changes in the Descriptions of Thirteenth-Century Pilgrims," *Cathedra* 31 (1984), 44 (in Hebrew).

the logistical assistance periodically brought over from Europe, Palestine was never truly Christianized. During the thirteen hundred years preceding the second half of the twentieth century, it remained an overwhelmingly Muslim region.[34]

Yet these developments did not uproot the Holy Land from the hearts of Christians. The fact that so much Christian blood had been spilled on the soil of Jesus pushed the Land increasingly into the center of the Christian imagination. Nor did pilgrimage decline, although travel diaries did undergo significant changes. Apparently the missionary character so deeply ingrained in the religion of the Holy Trinity required a continual influx of terrestrial images that demonstrated the spiritual reality. The rhetoric of persuasion and the religion's dissemination relied primarily on the power of the grace that had already descended to earth. But this redemption had emerged not in an abstract place but rather at a specific site, and so the fresh facts that continued to arrive from the field served as an important and effective component of religious propaganda. From its inception, pilgrimage was infused with a strong missionary impulse, and the effort to reach Jerusalem became an integral part of the intense desire to make the entire world Christian.[35]

Toward the end of the medieval era, the pilgrim returned from Jerusalem—the embodiment of the courageous, authentic believer— emerged as a cultural hero, if this term can justifiably be applied to the period. His characteristic attire was known to uneducated villagers, and his image adorns many writings. It was he who brought the latest news from the Land that had been chosen by God to bear his Messiah, and it was he who informed them that the Land was being repeatedly desecrated by uncivilized foreign heretics.

Nevertheless, we should also remember that Christians' strong love for the Holy Land and the admiration of the ancient Hebrews

34   This basic demographic reality did not prevent Israeli Crusader historian Joshua Prawer from referring to the region during this period as "our Land." See, for example, his book *The Crusader Kingdom of Jerusalem*, Jerusalem: Bialik, 1947, 4 (in Hebrew). In this spirit, his later book *The Crusaders: A Colonial Society*, Jerusalem: Bialik, 1985 (in Hebrew), has no separate chapter on the Muslim inhabitants but does have a large chapter on "the Jewish community" during that period (250–329).

35   The disappearance of this missionary spirit from Jewish tradition, which stemmed not from its rejection or from a lack of desire but rather from its disruption and prohibition by the two dominant religions, was one reason for the relatively marginal role of Jewish pilgrimage.

who trod upon its soil did not counteract their hostility toward the Jewish believer who huddled in the shadows of victorious Christianity. This was periodically proven by the Crusaders, and especially by those who accompanied them, when they made their way to Jerusalem. Upon their return, the pilgrims spoke of Judas Iscariot, betrayer of Jesus[36]; in their view, the humiliated Jews were expelled from the Land because of their unworthiness, which was proven by their marginal, shameful existence in the ghettos of Europe. This point of view, widespread among both Crusaders and pilgrims, would change somewhat in the West with the onset of the Reformation.

FROM PURITAN REFORMATION TO EVANGELICALISM

The turbulence of the Reformation temporarily reduced the waves of Christian pilgrimage. The criticism leveled against Church corruption surrounding the sale of indulgences, in addition to the great doubts regarding the ritual worship of graves and sites of stone and soil, temporarily cooled—but did not end—the traditional enthusiasm for pilgrimage. In developments similar to what took place within rabbinical Judaism after the destruction of the Temple, heavenly Jerusalem came to occupy a more exalted position in the original Protestant protest that accompanied the separation from Catholicism than did the corporeal, earthly Jerusalem. According to the new purist rhetoric, spiritual redemption preceded bodily redemption, and salvation became a much more internal and personal process.

This refreshing climate did not make the Holy Land irrelevant for the new Christians. In fact, to a certain extent, it revitalized the Land and brought it even closer to their hearts. Two intertwined developments played a role in this dynamic: the printing revolution of the fifteenth and sixteenth centuries and the translation of the Bible into multiple other languages. Within the course of four decades in the sixteenth century, the complete Bible appeared in the administrative superlanguages of German, English, French, Danish, Dutch, Polish,

---

36   The pilgrims tended to ignore the Jewish inhabitants of the Holy Land, as they were extremely few in number and attracted little attention. By contrast, the pilgrimage literature reflects hatred and scorn for the local Muslims; in the pilgrims' eyes, the latter were "dogs," "idolaters," and miserable "heretics." On this subject, see Michael Ish-Shalom, *Christian Travels in the Holy Land*, Tel Aviv: Am Oved, 1965, 11–12 (in Hebrew).

and Spanish, later to become national languages. Within just a few more years, it was translated into the remaining literary languages then undergoing crystallization and standardization. The printing revolution, which from its outset completely changed the cultural morphology of Europe, transformed the Bible into history's first best seller. Of course, its readership still consisted primarily of members of the elite, but it was now possible to read aloud the theological legends and wonders to continually expanding communities, in languages with which they were more familiar.

In the regions of the Reformation, the popular Bible replaced papal authority as the source of divine truth. The sweeping move back to the scriptures, and the increasing tendency to rely solely on them and not on mediating institutions, imbued the texts with an aura of renewed authenticity. From then on, believers did not require symbolism or allegory and were authorized to interpret the written texts literally. Translations made the ancient stories seem closer and more human. And because the setting for these stories was the space where Abraham the forefather, King David, the ethical prophets, the heroic Maccabees, John the Baptist, and Jesus the son of God and his apostles all lived, this space became familiar—and yet, at the same time, wonderful and mysterious. In this way, both the Old and the New Testament became characteristically Protestant books.

In just one kingdom, however, did the renewed scriptures praise not only the Promised Land but also the "treasured people" chosen to inherit it. Late sixteenth-century England witnessed the appearance of elite educated circles that displayed the first signs of primal protonationalism.[37] The separation from Rome accomplished, the establishment of the Anglican Church contributed significantly to the construction of a more distinct local identity, which, like all future collective identities, sought models to emulate.

Models play a decisive role in the emergence of new, hesitant, and uncertain nationalisms. In the case of pioneering England, it was no simple matter to choose a historical model around which a new identity could crystallize. The English protonationalist sensibility began to

---

37   On the crystallization of this protonationalism (although I do not necessarily endorse its overall conceptualization of chronological delineation), see Liah Greenfeld, *Nationalism: Five Roads to Modernity*, Cambridge, Mass.: Harvard University Press, 1993, 29–87.

emerge prior to the eighteenth-century era of enlightenment. The buds of modern collective identity, which later grew into an overarching conceptual framework that would define political life the world over, began to sprout on the deeply religious soil of the British Isles, unfertilized by doubt. This fact would later play a decisive role in the formation of English, and subsequently British, nationalism.

For example, the first Englishmen did not have the option of regarding the Celtic queen Boudicca as the ancient mother of the English nation, as would be proposed in the nineteenth century. This tribal leader, who rebelled against the Romans in the first century CE, was a true pagan, of whom few if any in the sixteenth century had heard. Another impossibility was French identification with the ancient Roman Republic, as would be proposed during the French Revolution—impossible both because ancient Rome was polytheistic and because contemporary, papal Rome was a focus of hostility and ridicule.

The forceful conquest of a land by the tribes of Israel, fortified by the encouragement of God; the stern judges of Judea, who led the war against their neighbors; the courageous Maccabees, who set out to defend their Temple—now these and other representatives of the biblical "people" came to be seen as exalted models, worthy of emulation and identification. For this reason, in England the Old Testament was given priority over the New Testament. True, it was less universal, but it revolved to a greater degree around a message meant for a chosen, distinct people. It also did not call for turning the other cheek: its God was jealous and brawny in his uncompromising struggle against his idolatrous enemies. Thus, the England that was defending its unique church of truth and the England that had designated itself as conquerer of vast areas merged on the eve of the modern era, in the shadow of the Hebrew Bible.

Between 1538, when Henry VIII ordered that the Bible be placed in all churches throughout England, and the completion of its new translation in 1611 during the rule of James I (the King James Bible), England took the ancient children of Israel to its warm monarchical bosom. This did not mean that the Jews were immediately permitted to return to the kingdom from which they had been expelled in the year 1290; for this, they would have to wait until 1656, that is, for the Puritan Revolution and Oliver Cromwell. In the meantime, England still did not associate the proud Hebrews of the past with the despicable Jews of the present, and it was therefore not at all problematic to regard the former as noble and the latter as contemptible.[38] Moreover, the Hebrews of the Bible now began to speak in contemporary English instead of ancient, cumbersome Latin. This bypassing of Latin and distancing from Catholicism helped turn Hebrew into a pure language, to be emulated, and it became an increasingly prestigious and widespread subject of university study. Ultimately, this process gave rise to a new "philo-Semitism."[39]

Some English scholars of the period searched for roots that would link them biologically to the land of Canaan. Others conjectured that the inhabitants of the British Isles were the authentic descendants of the ten lost tribes. Almost the entire elite subscribed to this trend, and the Bible was the only thing read in many homes. The Book of Books was also made the focus of the prestigious educational framework, and many children of the aristocracy were introduced to biblical heroes even before being taught the names of England's ancient kings. Often, too, they learned the geography of the Holy Land before learning the borders of the kingdom in which they themselves were born and raised.

The establishment of the Anglican Church, then, catalyzed a new atmosphere and, at the same time, new streams of anti-conformist protest. Rebellious Puritanism, which emerged against the background of the royal house's instrumental use of the new Church, attracted many members and, at the height of this religious ferment, merged with the new political and social forces, leading to a great revolution. During the entire period, the Hebrew Bible served as the dominant ideological guide for not only the ruling Church but most of its critics as well.[40]

Among the Puritans, the rejection of all religious institutions and religious authority produced a boundless loyalty to the uninterpreted

38   At the end of the sixteenth century, the "real" Jew was still regarded in many circles throughout England as a repellent creature. For example, see Christopher Marlowe's play *The Jew of Malta* (written 1589–90) and William Shakespeare's *The Merchant of Venice* (written 1596–98). It is safe to assume that neither playwright had ever seen a Jew in person.

39   On the changing attitude toward the Jews themselves, see David S. Katz's informative *Philo-Semitism and the Readmission of the Jews to England, 1603–1655*, Oxford: Oxford University Press, 1982.

40   For more on this subject, see Christopher Hill's fascinating book *The English Bible and the Seventeenth-Century Revolution*, London: Penguin, 1994.

text. The persecuted sects preferred the original laws of Moses over the rulings of the established Church; they regarded the sword of Judah Maccabee as truer than the mission of the apostle Paul; and they embraced a moral severity that was more in line with the commandments of an angry God than with the mercy and forgiveness of Jesus. Therefore, after a few generations, we find among them more Hebrew names than traditional Christian names, and when they lost strength in England and immigrated to North America, they would compare themselves to the loyal soldiers of Joshua the conqueror, about to inherit the new land of Canaan. Oliver Cromwell, too, was known to regard himself as a biblical hero. His battalions sang psalms before going into battle and at times chose military strategies based on combat models recounted in the Bible. England became ancient Judea, and Scotland its neighbor Israel. To a great extent, the distant past was seen as a dress rehearsal for the present that was preparing the ground for the coming salvation.

This Hebraic trend also resulted in reflections on the reestablishment of the country of the Bible. And who could be more worthy than the Jews to establish this country, which was then controlled by Muslim heretics? With the outbreak of revolution, two English Baptists in exile in Holland—Johanna Cartwright and her son Ebenezer—petitioned the new government

> That this Nation of England, with the inhabitants of the Netherlands, shall be the first and readiest to transport Izraell's sons and daughters in their ships to the Land promised to their forefathers, Abraham, Isaac and Jacob for an everlasting Inheritance.[41]

Woven through not only the Cartwrights' petition but also the stance taken by the foreign secretary Lord Palmerston in the 1840s and Lord Balfour's well-known letter to Lord Rothschild in 1917 is a common thread or, to use another metaphor, a critical artery pulsating within the English (and subsequently British) body politic. Lacking this artery and the unique ideological elements it carried, it is doubtful whether the State of Israel could have ever been established.

---

41   Barbara W. Tuchman, *Bible and Sword*, London: Macmillan, 1982, 121. The main weakness of this book, which is otherwise one of the most fascinating and comprehensive studies ever undertaken on Britain's role in the birth of Zionism, is its crude Orientalism, manifested in its complete blindness and indifference to the original inhabitants of Palestine.

As noted, the relatively early rise of protonationalist sentiment in England, like the English kingdom's early separation from the pope, played a significant role in bringing about the powerful role fulfilled by the Hebrew Bible in the construction of the country's modern political identities. It is no coincidence that the first "Zionist" idea emerged not among Jews living at the boundary between Western and Eastern Europe, as would occur three centuries later, but rather in the revolutionary/religious atmosphere of the British Isles.[42]

The Puritans began reading the Bible as an historical text long before the Jewish Zionists considered doing so. They were believers who craved salvation, which they regarded as closely linked to the revival of the people of Israel in its Land. This link was not the result of any special concern for Jewish suffering, but rather stemmed from the belief that the Christian redemption of all humanity had to be preceded by the return of the children of Israel to Zion. In the course of this long-term scenario, the Jews were also supposed to convert to Christianity. Only then would the world see the second coming of Jesus.[43]

This eschatological approach penetrated deeply into the diverse Protestant streams, remaining alive into the twenty-first century. As this book is being written, there are still many Evangelical groups within the United States that support the existence of a strong, large Israel, based on their certainty that such support is essential to the hastening of Jesus' universal rule on earth—and that Jews who refrain from conversion must ultimately pay the price, i.e., to disappear and, of course, burn in hell.

In the meantime, many seventeenth-century Puritans were convinced that in order to hasten redemption, the Jews should be allowed to return to England, from which they had been expelled more than three centuries earlier. In their eyes, the Jewish dispersion had been a precondition for their subsequent ingathering in the land of Zion. As the book of Deuteronomy had prophesied:

---

42   The first to propose the idea of a Jewish restoration to the Holy Land in a published work appears to have been member of Parliament Sir Henry Finch, who did so in 1621. For more on this, see Meir Verete, "The Idea of Restoration of the Jews in English Protestant Thought, 1790–1840," *Zion* 33:3–4 (1968), 158 (in Hebrew).

43   For more on this, see Avihu Zakai, "The Poetics of History and the Destiny of Israel: The Role of the Jews in English Apocalyptic Thought during the Sixteenth and Seventeenth Centuries," *Journal of Jewish Thought and Philosophy* 5:2 (1996), 313–50.

"And the Lord will scatter you among all peoples, from one end of the earth to the other, and there you shall serve other gods" (28:64). In this way, the English kingdom's refusal to allow the settlement of the children of Israel on the western edge of Europe was seen as a factor that delayed the coming of redemption. Therefore, when various persons asked Cromwell to permit the return of the Jews to England, he acquiesced, forcing this historic authorization on Parliament.

This meaningful change in attitude toward the Jews was not completely devoid of self-interest. As in the case of Lord Balfour some 250 years later, the Hebrew Bible merged well with the world of international business familiar to Cromwell. The Lord Protector recognized the rights of Jews to return to the British Isles not only for reasons that were purely ideological in nature, but seemingly for economic and commercial reasons as well.[44] The instability that plagued Britain during the tremors of the revolution temporarily weakened the young empire's foreign trade. Britain's fiercest competitor was the Netherlands, which continued to push forward, acquiring more and more markets, particularly in the Levant. To a large extent, the most dynamic forces in the economic life of Amsterdam were Jewish. Most were descendants of *anusim* (Jews who were compelled to abandon their faith against their will) who had experience in commerce and had arrived in Amsterdam from Spain and Portugal. England was interested in drawing this human capital into its foreign trade. Indeed, the arrival of Jewish merchants would contribute somewhat to the improvement of the economy at a later stage. Devout Puritans as well had proved their mettle as skilled artisans and merchants; as we know, they and other Protestants managed to efficiently develop large parts of an entire continent, following the removal of its indigenous population.[45]

---

44   According to David Katz, the economic motivation for bringing the Jews into Puritan England was secondary and evolved somewhat later. See Katz, *Philo-Semitism*, 7.

45   On the powerful influence of the Bible and its mythoi among the Puritans and other Christians in North America, see Moshe Davis, "The Holy Land Idea in American Spiritual History," in Menahem Kaufman (ed.), *The American People and the Holy Land: Foundations of a Special Relationship*, Jerusalem: Magnes, 1997, 3-28 (in Hebrew). Many Americans gave biblical names not only to their children but to their towns, cities, and even pets. It was their practice to quote the Bible not in the past tense but in the present tense.

At the end of their revolutionary golden age, the Puritans turned to the West, while during the same period, the English kingdom itself displayed increasing interest in trade routes to the East. To be more precise, it was the kingdom's merchants who demonstrated the interest, by, as usual, setting the stage for political measures through their tireless efforts to buy and sell in regions not yet penetrated by English commerce. Their main target was the Indian subcontinent, but their route there passed through the Middle East, traversing the Ottoman Empire.

In 1581 Queen Elizabeth I awarded the London-based Levant Company a concession to trade with the Ottoman sultan Murad III. This was the first step in a long and circuitous journey that would lead Britain to rule India, penetrate the empire of China, and finally in 1918, capping the age of imperialism, replace the collapsed Ottoman power in large portions of the Middle East. The history of the late sixteenth to the mid-twentieth century created the vast British Empire "on which the sun never sets." And during that same period in Britain itself, a belief in the religious uniqueness of the Holy Land never completely disappeared.

As a result of the flourishing of commerce in the East, pilgrims were no longer alone in traveling to Palestine; now they were joined by adventurous merchants. The Land itself did not interest the merchants as a source of economic profit, but Jerusalem was on their route, and the religious cloak that enveloped the commercial drive sparked a special curiosity. The best-educated travelers among them wrote diaries of their journeys that sold well in their home countries. Less replete with descriptions of the sacred geography so crucial to the Crusaders, their accounts tell us much more about the country's economic state. However, like their ascetic counterparts, they, too, were quite uninterested in the Muslim majority population. They took note primarily of Christian inhabitants, and here and there a few Jews. True, they were forced to negotiate with the local rulers, but the rank-and-file tillers of the soil did not, in effect, exist for them. Their disregard for the Arab population, and profound contempt for people they regarded as barbarian heretics, had a direct impact on the evolution of the Orientalist gaze that would develop in Western intellectual circles.

Despite the rise of sharp revolutionary British empiricism, and notwithstanding the growing strength of philosophical skepticism and rationalism, from the deists through Hume,[46] British culture remained wrapped in millenarian beliefs. Many groups sought to establish linkages between prophetic verses in the sacred texts and contemporary political events, although the practice appeared to decline in the face of the eighteenth-century progressivism of the small intellectual elite. However, the semi-educated continued to vigorously cultivate devout Christian morality in a variety of ways. Through works such as John Bunyan's *The Pilgrim's Progress* (1678), a best seller second only to the Bible, the American William M. Thompson's popular *The Land and the Book* (1858), and George Eliot's Zionist novel *Daniel Deronda* (1876), the Holy Land found its way deep into the minds of many Anglo-Saxons, including, of course, many Americans.[47] Although the road to "Christian Zionism" was initially paved during the religious studies lessons conducted in schools for the nobility, particularly on Sundays, it was subsequently tiled with the help of popular literature. The list of authors who visited Palestine during the nineteenth century reveals the extent to which the Land fired the literary imaginations of Americans, Britons, and Europeans in general. For William Makepeace Thackeray, who visited it in 1845, for Herman Melville, who visited in 1857, and for Mark Twain, who visited in 1867 and mocked the anxiety-ridden holiness of all those who preceded him, the mysterious land of the Bible drew to it a large number of artists.[48]

Literary fiction meshed easily with the contemporary political imagination and the hesitant beginnings of the hunger for empire. After Napoleon insolently challenged British strongholds and spheres of influence across Europe and the world, a strategy began to crystallize in London that was somewhat more consistent than its policy in the Levant. In 1799, during Napoleon's campaign along the Palestinian coastline which ended with the siege on Acre, the British

---

46   Deists' negative attitude toward the churches of Christianity also incorporated sharp criticism of the Bible and Judaism. Israeli historians have characterized this as anti-Semitism. For example, see Shmuel Ettinger, "Judaism and Jews in the Eyes of the English Deists," in S. Ettinger (ed.), *Modern Anti-Semitism: Studies and Essays*, Tel Aviv: Sifriat Poalim, 1978, 57–87 (in Hebrew).

47   John Bunyan, *The Pilgrim's Progress*, Oxford: Oxford University Press, 2008; William M. Thomson, *The Land and the Book,* Whitefish: Kessinger Publishing, 2010; George Eliot, *Daniel Deronda*, London: Penguin, 2004.

48   See selected excerpts from their experiences in Yaacov Shavit (ed.), *Writers Travel in the Holy Land*, Jerusalem: Keter, 1981 (in Hebrew).

navy came to the aid of the Ottoman sultan and helped defeat the young French general.[49] By developing a favored status with the Ottomans based on commercial interests, British representatives were able to intensify their activities in the Holy Land itself.

The year 1804 marked the establishment of the Palestine Association, and 1809, the London Society for Promoting Christianity Amongst the Jews. The efforts of these two associations were relatively unsuccessful, with the former managing only to organize one failed trip, and the latter converting a small number of Jews in the land of the Bible to Christianity. The Palestine Association would, however, serve as a model for later groups. In addition, George Stanley Faber, a founder of the Society for Promoting Christianity, was an Oxford professor of theology whose books proved extremely influential and whose followers far outnumbered the society's registered membership. The primary efforts of this scholarly Anglican theologian focused on interpreting the Biblical prophecies, from Isaiah's and Daniel's predictions of the future to the visions of John. In 1809, Faber published his well-known work *A General and Connected View of the Prophecies, Relative to the Conversion, Restoration, Union and Future Glory of the Houses of Judah and Israel*, in which he predicts that in the year 1867, most of the Jews who would be returned to Palestine with the help of a great maritime nation in the West would convert to Christianity.[50] Many Evangelicals shared similar views and saw themselves as belonging to the generation whose children would live to see the redemption. All they had to do was convince the world to return the Jews to "their land."

---

49   It has been asserted that, during the siege of Acre, the young Bonaparte wrote a letter in which he ostensibly promised a state to the Jews. The letter itself did not survive and in any event appears to have been a forgery. See Henry Laurens, "Le Projet d'État Juif Attribué à Bonaparte," in *Orientales*, Paris: CNRS Éd., 2007, 123–43. On Napoleon's conception of the Jews as an integral part of the evolving French nation, and not as a separate nation, see Lilly Marcou, *Napoléon Face aux Juifs*, Paris: Pygmalion, 2006.

50   G. S. Faber, *A General and Connected View of the Prophecies, Relative to the Conversion, Restoration, Union and Future Glory of the Houses of Judah and Israel*, London: Rivington, 1809. On this figure, see Sarah Kochav, "The Evangelical Movement in England and the Restoration of the Jews to Eretz Israel," *Cathedra* 62 (1991), 18–36 (in Hebrew).

Other members of the Society for Promoting Christianity included the missionary Alexander McCaul, Faber's colleague and a professor of Hebrew at Kings College in London; Louis Way, an affluent attorney who funded a large portion of the group's work; and the well-known English Evangelical clergyman Edward Bickersteth. Bickersteth wrote books and initiated and organized a large number of performances to encourage the eastward immigration of the children of Israel. He believed that only the establishment of the kingdom of Israel would return the son of God to earth and bring about the full Christianization of the world.[51] His importance in promoting the proto-Zionist idea lay in the fact that he was a friend and close advisor of Lord Anthony Ashley Cooper, the seventh Earl of Shaftesbury. This nobleman was regarded as one of the most influential figures in Britain during the Victorian era. He was a conservative philanthropist who played an important role in legislation that limited child labor, prohibited the slave trade, and cultivated the idea of a Jewish-Christian restoration in the Holy Land.

In light of his contribution to the evolution of Christian Zionism, Shaftesbury can perhaps be thought of as the Anglican Herzl. Some scholars believe it was he who first coined the well-known phrase that characterized Palestine as "a land without a people for a people without a land," while others maintain he was only responsible for its mass dissemination.[52] This aristocratic lord viewed the "children of Israel" not simply as believers in the Jewish religion but as descendants of an ancient race that, once converted to Christianity, would again become a modern nation in natural alliance with Great Britain. It was precisely because he did not conceive of Judaism as a legitimate religion that could remain in existence alongside the true faith that he chose to regard the Jews as a people unto themselves. However, just as he did not support the right of Jews to be elected to the British parliament, he also did not believe that this rehabilitated people deserved a state of its own[53]; rather, the obedient Jews would have to make do with being the patrons of Britain's Christianity. In truth, Jewish suffering as

---

51   Edward Bickersteth, *The Restoration of the Jews to Their Own Land*, London: Seeley, 1841.

52   See Diana Muir, "A Land without a People for a People without a Land," *Middle East Quarterly* 15 (2008), 55–62.

53   See Menahem Kedem, "Mid-Nineteenth Century Anglican Eschatology on the Redemption of Israel," *Cathedra* 19 (1981), 55–71 (in Hebrew).

a result of anti-Semitism was not the primary motivation for his work, even if his sensitivity to Jewish persecution was sincere. What mostly captured the heart of this devout aristocrat was that "restoration" in the Middle East could do away with the Jewish faith, which, in turn, would lay the groundwork for the coming of redemption to the world.

As with the acquisition of new souls, one of the factors that drew pilgrims to the Holy Land, Shaftesbury's deep missionary sentiment is what caused him to develop his eschatological vision of the restoration in Zion. However, the fact that he and the Society for Promoting Christianity managed to Christianize only a small number of Jews failed to undermine his strong faith or to weaken his proto-Zionist activity.[54]

Shaftesbury's boundless devotion to the idea of a Jewish return to Zion sheds light not only on a broad array of Evangelical groups but also on prominent governing circles. The fact that he was a Tory member of Parliament did not prevent his close relationship with Lord Palmerston, the Whig foreign secretary and future prime minister, and it was he who in 1838 convinced his political acquaintance to send the first British consul to Jerusalem, a small initial step toward British entry into Palestine. One year later, he published an article in London's *Quarterly Review* in which he discussed the array of British economic interests in the Holy Land. For many British figures of the time, the incorporation of financial justifications into religious arguments was a winning combination. A short time later, Shaftesbury published an article in the *Times* under the title "The State and the Rebirth of the Jews," which also made waves and received a great deal of positive feedback, not just in Britain but also in the United States. It would be no exaggeration to say this article was to Christian Zionism what Theodor Herzl's *The Jewish State* was to Jewish Zionism in 1896.

In addition to its religious background in the awakening of the Christian Zionist idea in Britain—which can also be understood as a theoretical reaction to the shock waves caused by the French Revolution—this awakening also benefited from the immediate political

---

54   For more on this charismatic figure, see also Donald M. Lewis's comprehensive study *The Origins of Christian Zionism: Lord Shaftesbury and Evangelical Support for a Jewish Homeland*, Cambridge: Cambridge University Press, 2009. Lewis places his emphasis on the evangelical lord's philo-Semitism, not on his powerful desire to convert Jews to Christianity.

processes then under way in the Middle East. In 1831, Muhammad Ali Pasha, the former governor of Egypt, conquered Syria and Palestine. This conquest clearly highlighted for the major powers the great fragility of the Ottoman Empire and ultimately led Britain and France to support the declining Muslim entity. In 1840, the British helped the Ottomans push Muhammad Ali's army back to Egypt. To a certain extent, the competition between Britain, France, and Russia over the territorial division of the "sick man on the Bosporus" began to dictate diplomatic measures, intensifying toward the end of the nineteenth century. It is no coincidence that Palestine would slowly but surely find its way onto the international diplomatic agenda.

On August 11, 1840, Foreign Secretary Palmerston wrote the following to John Ponsonby, the British ambassador in Istanbul:

> It would be of manifest importance to the Sultan to encourage the Jews to return and to settle in Palestine because the wealth which they would bring with them would increase the resources of the Sultan's dominions; and the Jewish people, if returning under the sanction and protection and the invitation of the Sultan, would be a check upon any future evil designs of Mehemet Ali or his successor . . . I have to instruct Your Excellency strongly to recommend [the Turkish government] to hold out every just encouragement to the Jews of Europe to return to Palestine.[55]

Clearly, Shaftesbury's ideology lay behind this extremely pragmatic suggestion of Palmerston's. The foreign secretary was not overly concerned whether Jews were converted to Christianity before or after immigration. Instead, his small dream was to have a strategic asset under British imperial patronage. For Shaftesbury, however, conversion was an imperative, a precondition, and he systematically strove for the establishment of Israel, which would become Anglican at the end of days.

Britain had virtually no subjects of its own in the Middle East, causing the nature of its presence there to be thrown into question. Colonization of the region by British subjects, as had been carried out

---

55 Quoted in Tuchman, *Bible and Sword*, 175. See also Alexander Schölch, "Britain in Palestine, 1838–1882: The Roots of the Balfour Policy," *Journal of Palestine Studies* 22:1 (1992), 39–56.

in Africa and Asia, was not possible under Ottoman rule. The original Christian Zionist idea of settling Jews in Palestine presented itself as a means of bypassing this obstacle to the establishment of an imperial foothold in the Middle East. After all, the Jews were a natural ally of Britain, which was known to be the least anti-Semitic country in Europe and a long-standing admirer of the ancient Hebrews. German and French Jews could, of course, also take part in this joint European enterprise, in which the private capital of the wealthy would undoubtedly play a significant role.

The figure who served as a living example of the potential of the world's Jewry to participate in Jewish colonization was the well-known British businessman and philanthropist Moses Montefiore. A religious Jew born in Italy, Montefiore had been knighted by his friend Queen Victoria and appointed sheriff of London. He supported the idea of making Jerusalem the capital of the Jewish religion and worked hard to make this a reality. In 1827 Montefiore made his first visit to the Holy Land—a visit that profoundly influenced him—and returned in 1839, this time with the aim of helping the Jewish community of the holy city with donations and charitable projects. He even presented Muhammad Ali with a plan to purchase land in Palestine, which at the time was still under Egyptian control. Predictably, this plan completely disregarded the local cultivators. By the time Montefiore died, he had visited Jerusalem five times more and used every possible opportunity to establish autonomous Jewish settlements that would not be dependent on the financial support of philanthropists abroad. His efforts did not bear fruit, however, and he was ultimately forced to compromise with the traditional Jewish institutions in Jerusalem. Nevertheless, his dream of transforming the Holy Land into a Jewish land never faded. His political connections with British, Ottoman, and other circles of international government were of direct benefit to various Jewish communities and indirectly helped promote proto-Zionist ideas in British political culture.[56]

---

56   See Israel Bartal's article "Moses Montefiore: Nationalist before His Time or Belated Shtadlan?" *Studies in Zionism* 11:2 (1990), 111-125. For an account of his general activities, see also Abigail Green, "Rethinking Sir Moses Montefiore: Religion, Nationhood and International Philanthropy in the Nineteenth Century," *American Historical Review* 110:3 (2005), 631-658. Also highly recommended is Eliezer Halevi (ed.), *Biographies of Moses Montefiore and His Wife Judith*, Warsaw: Tushia, 1898 (in Hebrew).

Palmerston was not the only British politician to begin seriously considering the prospect of mass Jewish immigration to Palestine. Later, other figures within the British government administration came out in support of the idea as well. One was Colonel Charles Henry Churchill (a distant relative of the famed statesman), a member of the military delegation to Damascus who was drawn to the proto-Zionist vision both by Montefiore and by his own anti-Ottoman and pro-colonial beliefs. In his letters to Montefiore and in his semiautobiographical work *Mount Lebanon*, he called on Jews to settle in Palestine and, in the tradition of colonial expansion, advised Britain to station a substantial military force there to defend them.[57]

Another colonel and loyal supporter of Jewish restoration in Palestine was George Gawler, who also served for a time as the governor of South Australia. In close contact with Montefiore, with whom he toured Palestine in 1849, this imperial official outlined a plan to "restore the Jews to their land," primarily in order to create a safe buffer zone for the British between Egypt and Syria.[58] Based on his extensive experience in the successful colonization of Australia, Gawler assumed it would be possible to implement some forms of land acquisition in Palestine as well. Although in his view the Bedouin Arabs would attempt to disrupt their efforts, most of the country was wilderness that, under the care of hardworking Jews, could certainly be made to bloom. Despite attempts at obfuscation, a fertile Evangelical eschatology operated behind Gawler's practical Zionist project: from his perspective, Britain was a chosen emissary of God that would redeem Israel and the rest of the world.[59]

There were many opponents to such plans within British government, and an even larger number of people who were completely indifferent to the idea of Jewish immigration to the Holy Land. In the mid-nineteenth century, the colonial era had not yet reached its high

---

57   Charles Henry Churchill, *Mount Lebanon*, London: Saunders & Otley, 1853. See also Franz Kobler, "Charles Henry Churchill," in *Herzl Year Book* 4 (1961–2), 1–66.

58   Menahem Kedem, "The Endeavors of George Gawler to Establish Jewish Colonies in Eretz Israel," *Cathedra* 33 (1984), 93–106 (in Hebrew); Israel Bartal, "George Gawler's Plan for Jewish Settlement in the 1840s: The Geographical Perspective," in Ruth Kark (ed.), *Redemption of the Land of Eretz Israel: Ideology and Practice*, Jerusalem: Yad Ben-Zvi, 1990, 51–63 (in Hebrew).

59   For a brief and intriguing summary of British Zionist ideas, see Albert M. Hyamson, *British Projects for the Restoration of the Jews*, Leeds: British Palestine Committee, 1917.

point, and Britain had not yet completely mobilized to satisfy its ravenous hunger for control of vast areas. We now turn our attention to the figure who, more than any other, would come to symbolize the historical transition to open-ended imperialism and penetration in the Middle East, not only because of his role in the process but also because of his own Jewish associations.

PROTESTANTS AND THE COLONIZATION OF THE MIDDLE EAST

Tel Aviv, the largest city in Israel, has no street named after British prime minister Benjamin Disraeli, because at some point its city council passed a resolution prohibiting the commemoration of figures who converted from Judaism to another religion. The council did, however, commemorate another British prime minister, Lord Balfour, with a respectable road in the city center. He was also the namesake of Balfouriya, a rural Jewish settlement in the Jezreel Valley.

Like Montefiore, Benjamin Disraeli was of Italian Jewish descent. But unlike the extremely religious parents of the proto-Zionist philanthropist, Disraeli's father had a conflictual relationship with the Jewish community and converted his children to Christianity. The future Tory leader was fortunate to have become a devout Anglican, because in 1837, when he was first elected to the House of Commons at the age of thirty-two, it was still not permitted for an openly Jewish person to be elected to Parliament. Disraeli quickly emerged as a colorful figure in British politics. With graceful oration and sharp, seasoned political strategizing, he charted his ascent to the political elite and became leader of the Conservative Party. In 1868, he was appointed to serve as prime minister for a brief period, a post to which he returned between 1874 and 1880.

Also like Montefiore, Disraeli was a personal friend of Queen Victoria. As their common royal acquaintance made Montefiore a knight, so did she make Disraeli an earl, a gesture for which he would repay her in years to come when, as prime minister, he suggested adding Empress of India to her list of titles. Although a prominent politician, Disraeli never limited himself to political work; motivated by a passion for literary fiction, he wrote novels, which he began publishing at an early age and continued writing until just before his death. A number of his literary works shed light on his attitude toward both his Jewish heritage and the Holy Land.

In 1833, before entering Parliament, Disraeli published a novel about a twelfth-century Jewish messiah by the name of David Alroy, who lived between northern Mesopotamia and the Caucasus. We know very little about this historical figure, and Disraeli had no more sources at his disposal than we have today. Nonetheless, he depicts Alroy as an authentic leader and a descendant of the House of David who never forgets his Judeo-Palestinian roots and who launches a rebellion against Muslim authorities in order to redeem the world's Jews. The problem is, the other members of his "race" refrain from following him, and he ultimately fails to realize his spectacular messianic vision.[60] In the original edition of *The Wondrous Tale of Alroy*, the author includes a parallel story about a no less mysterious prince named Iskander, who is forced to convert to Islam in his youth but always remembers his Greco-Christian roots.

Throughout his life, Disraeli maneuvered between the religion into which he was born and the religion he joined. Perhaps for this reason, he regarded Christianity as the logical and improved continuation of ancient Judaism. Even if he could have been classified as a believer, he was never devout. He saw himself as a faithful Christian but, in keeping with pseudoscientific fashions of his day, conceived of himself as belonging to a distinct, race-based nation and at times proclaimed so in public.

Disraeli believed that the issue of race, not religion, was the key to understanding the history of the world. His proud position regarding the "Hebrew race" was echoed by educated Jews in Eastern and Central Europe and played a significant role in reinforcing their emerging "scientific" ethnic identity.[61] The sentimental story of David

---

60   The book was translated into Hebrew relatively quickly. See Benjamin Disraeli (Earl of Beaconsfield), *Khoter m'Geza` Ishai, o-David al-Roey*, Warsaw: Kaltar, 1883 (in Hebrew). The editor's introduction to the Hebrew edition includes the following words: "The aim of this respected story . . . is to arouse and to awaken in the hearts of its readers a love for the Holy Land, the homeland of our ancestors . . ." (1). See also Benjamin Disraeli, *The Wondrous Tale of Alroy: The Rise of Iskander*, Philadelphia: Carey, Lea and Blanchard, 1833.

61   See, for example, the proto-Zionist historian Heinrich Graetz in his debate with Heinrich von Treitschke, in *Essays-Memoirs-Letters*, Jerusalem: The Bialik Institute, 1969, 218 (in Hebrew). See also Nathan Birnbaum, who coined the term "Zionism" in his article "Nationalism and Language," quoted in Joachim Doron, *The Zionist Thinking of Nathan Birnbaum*, Jerusalem: The Zionist Library, 1988, 177 (in Hebrew).

Alroy reflects this Jewish essentialism at its best, as his mission is dictated by the blood of the Jewish Messiah. At the same time, Jerusalem is depicted in a romantic, almost mystical manner; in 1831, before becoming a Conservative politician, Disraeli traveled in the Middle East and visited the city, which left an indelible, exotic impression on him.

Another of his well-known novels reflects his intense longing for his Middle Eastern "roots." *Tancred: Or the New Crusade* was published in 1847, when Disraeli was already an established politician. Here the story revolves around the personality of a young English aristocrat who decides to follow in the footsteps of Tancred, the ancient Crusader, in order to reach the Holy Land. At first, the goal is to discover and decipher the secrets of the East. Then the protagonist reaches Mount Sinai, where he hears the voice of an angel instructing him to establish a "theocratic equality."[62] Unfortunately, in this story as well, the religious vision goes unfulfilled and the longed-for symbiosis between Jews and Christians, a product of the author's fertile imagination, remains unrealized. Still, the story reflects the Eastern analysis that then prevailed in London's cultural salons, as well as the great interest in representing the ancient territory as the arena in which both religions came into being. Even if Disraeli the author denies the reader a truly happy ending, Disraeli the statesman becomes successful, within the historical reality of his day, in making Britain a bit more "Asiatic," that is to say, colonialist and much larger.

This leader of the British Empire never became a Zionist and was certainly not a Christian Zionist. Although he belonged to the same political party as Shaftesbury, and had maintained close relations with him as early as the 1860s, cultivating a Jewish restoration in Palestine that would ultimately become a Christian society was an enterprise not particularly close to his heart.[63] In his political work, he provided unswervingly faithful service to the British upper class. But perhaps without intending to do so, he also contributed indirectly to creating

---

62   Benjamin Disraeli, *Tancred: Or the New Crusade*, London: The Echo Library, 2007, 253.

63   Jewish enthusiasm for Disraeli's self-definition as a member of the "Hebrew race" resulted in a forgery aimed at proving that he was also secretly a Zionist. On this, see Nathan Michael Gelber, *The Lord Beaconsfield's Plan for a Jewish State*, Tel Aviv: Leinman, 1947 (in Hebrew).

the diplomatic conditions that later enabled Britain to adopt the Jewish Zionist idea.

In 1875, while serving as prime minister, Disraeli approached his close friend Baron Lionel Nathan de Rothschild to solicit his help in purchasing for Britain 44 percent of the shares in the Suez Canal. This major transaction was completed successfully, representing the first stage of the empire's tangible entry into the Middle East. The route to distant Asia was now open, and the regions surrounding the maritime gateway—Egypt and Palestine—now emerged as strategic objects of utmost importance.

In 1878, in return for British support of the Ottomans, and at the expense of the brutal suppression of the Bulgarians, Disraeli turned Cyprus into a British colony. At the same time, he initiated the conquest of Afghanistan in order to ward off the Russians, and by so doing to tighten the connection between the Middle East and the Far East. As has already been noted, no other British politician contributed so greatly to making the empire "Oriental" and expansive.

The division of colonial assets toward the end of the nineteenth century, which encompassed almost every part of the globe, was not facilitated primarily by the exceptional talents of Disraeli and those like him in other countries. Rather, the process was the product of the massive industrial development of Western Europe. The gap between the societies of this region and those of elsewhere continued to increase, and was responsible for the rapid imperial expansion. Between 1875 and the end of the century, the Northwestern world had conquered some twenty-five million square kilometers, in addition to the areas they had controlled beforehand. If in 1875, 10 percent of Africa was under European rule, by 1890 whites controlled 90 percent of the Dark Continent.

This material and technological inequality was accompanied by an Orientalist discourse that became increasingly callous and barefaced. And if a significant number of thinkers in the late eighteenth century believed that all people were equal, the prevailing tone was now being set by those who were certain that this was not the case. Chinese, Indians, Native Americans, black Africans, and Middle Eastern Arabs were thought of as inferior in comparison with white Europeans. And they were, indeed, unequal: they had no thick metal cannons, no swift steamships, and no sturdy, efficient railways. They also had very few educated spokespersons. At the precise moment that political voice and the communications media were having an increasing impact on the democratization of the industrialized West, people not of European descent had almost no voice.[64]

The Arab inhabitants of Palestine also remained invisible to the Western eye. From the mid-nineteenth century onward, each new proposal for Palestine almost completely disregarded them. The renewed Western penetration of the Holy Land, though still only "scientific" and "spiritual," barely mentioned them. Despite the fact that in 1834 a group of local farmers rose up against Egyptian occupation, they were generally regarded as no more than a wild mob, in part because of uncontrollable attacks against non-Muslim inhabitants that took place during the revolt.[65]

The year 1865 witnessed the establishment of the Palestine Exploration Fund (PEF) in London. Although the PEF had anthropological aims as well, most of its work focused on the country's history, archaeology, and physical geography. The quest for sacredness rooted in the ancient past on the one hand, and colonial mapping on the other, were the engines of the enterprise, much more so than was the population living there at the time. It is therefore no wonder that Queen Victoria immediately granted the PEF her patronage, and that Montefiore and many others soon joined the project.[66]

As effectively highlighted by John James Moscrop, a historian of the fund, the organization's scholarly research was carried out in conjunction with strategic military aims, and both were animated by a feeling that Britain was about to inherit the Land.[67] The widespread

64   Whereas it is possible to debate Edward Said's assessment of the power of Orientalism up to the eighteenth century, his analysis regarding the nineteenth and twentieth centuries is accurate and difficult to refute. Said, *Orientalism*, London: Penguin Books, 2003.

65   The most intriguing book on the prevalent attitude toward the land of the Bible in Victorian Britain published to date is Eitan Bar-Yosef's *The Holy Land in English Culture 1799-1917: Palestine and the Question of Orientalism*, Oxford: Clarendon Press, 2005.

66   On British and non-British colonial cultural activity in Palestine, see Yoad Eliaz's courageous book *Land/Text*, 27–143.

67   John James Moscrop, *Measuring Jerusalem: The Palestine Exploration Fund and British Interests in the Holy Land*, London: Leicester University Press, 1999. In 1870, a similar fund was set up in the United States (96). The British demonstrated a greater interest in the plants and birds of Palestine than in its Arab inhabitants. For example, see *The Land of Israel: A Journal of Travels in Palestine* by English zoologist and clergyman Henry Baker Tristram, who also worked closely with the Fund (London: Society for Promoting Christian Knowledge, 1882).

support enjoyed by the PEF stemmed in part from Britain's colonial rivalry with France, as well as its great interest in the Suez Canal. In any event, by 1890, the fund had made an important contribution to the state of knowledge regarding the geography and topography of Palestine. Numerous associates of the fund were British intelligence personnel whose major effort, prior to their nation's control over the canal, was to learn more about the Sinai Desert. Not coincidentally, the mappers included T. E. Lawrence, who would later fall in love with the yellow sands of Arabia.

It was not only the desert that the enthusiastic British pioneers regarded as empty space. Neighboring Palestine, aside from the holy places, was also typically viewed as an abandoned area waiting impatiently for the Christian West to redeem it from generations of desolation.

In this political and conceptual climate, it is no surprise that the British public regarded the colonization of Palestine as a natural undertaking. The Holy Land, however, was still part of the fragile Ottoman Empire. But when the first Jewish settlers began to trickle into Palestine in the early 1880s as a result of the vicious pogroms in Russia, the idea of colonization found new supporters in Britain. Until that point, Shaftesbury's Christian millenarian hallucinations and Montefiore's Jewish religious dreams had been hollow, owing to the lack of human subjects to carry them out. British, French, German, and Italian Jewry were all engaged in cultural integration into their home countries and regarded as intolerable the notion of sending Jews off to "the land of their ancestors"—pushing them into the margins of the civilized world. But now, new circumstances had created the first possible basis for the fulfillment of the vision.

The rise of local protonationalism in the western areas of the Russian empire, which contained the Jewish Pale of Settlement, created increasing pressure on the large Yiddish-speaking population in the region. The religious, cultural, and linguistic differentiation of this large community provoked displays of intolerance and openly aggressive anti-Semitism. In addition, the population increase under way at the time, considering that there was no way of moving out of the Pale of Settlement, resulted in economic deterioration within the Jewish community and created unbearable living conditions. The onset of the pogroms in 1881, which continued in waves until 1905, sparked the mass immigration of Jews westward. According to some estimates, two and a half million Jews left the Russian empire by the end of the First World War. The immigrants arrived in the countries of Central and Western Europe and even reached the Americas. The rise in Judeophobia in some of the receiving countries was directly related to this large population movement, which was also responsible for the early colonization of Palestine, the emergence of the Zionist idea, and the birth of the Zionist movement.

Immigration from the Russian empire (and from Romania) raised concerns within various Jewish institutions in Central and Western Europe. Fear that the arrival of Jews from Eastern Europe would result in mounting anti-Semitism led to a search for ways to assist and/or get rid of the "foreigners." The leaders of the Jewish community in Germany used all means possible to direct them to the port in Hamburg and have them continue their journey directly to the United States. Wealthy members of the communities in France and Britain sought other ways of easing the influx of refugees. Baron Maurice de Hirsch, for example, actively assisted in the establishment of Jewish immigrant settlements in Argentina; Baron Edmond James de Roth-schild did the same in Palestine.[68] Both of these settlement enterprises faltered, and both required repeated monetary infusions. Neither had a nationalist flavor.

Of the hundreds of thousands and even millions of immigrants flocking westward, some, including a few dozen young idealists, began to make their way to Palestine in the early 1880s. This trickle of immigration was not yet significant, and some of the immigrants continued moving until they reached the countries of the West. Nonetheless, this was the beginning of a gradual, long-term process.

One of the most dynamic activists in this first attempt at settlement was another British Christian: Laurence Oliphant. A former diplomat and member of Parliament, Oliphant believed that the Judeo-Christian race was destined to rule the Holy Land and by 1880 had already published an interesting book titled *The Land of Gilead*.[69]

---

68   See Haim Avni, *Argentina and the Jews: A History of Jewish Immigration*, Tuscaloosa, AL: University of Alabama Press, 2002. See also Simon Schama, *Two Rothschilds and the Land of Israel*, which I discuss in the introduction.

69   Laurence Oliphant, *The Land of Gilead*, Edinburgh: Blackwood, 1880. For more on this curious figure, see Anne Taylor, *Laurence Oliphant*, Oxford: Oxford University Press, 1982, particularly the chapters focusing on his connections to Palestine (187–230).

Because it was difficult to purchase land west of the Jordan River, Oliphant believed it would be easier to settle Jews to its east. In order to do so, the Bedouin inhabitants of the area would have to be expelled. Arab cultivators, however, would be concentrated in reservations, as the Indians of North America had been, and they would be used as laborers in the Jewish colonies. Carrying with him a letter of recommendation from Benjamin Disraeli, Oliphant met with the Ottoman sultan, whom he failed to convince of the merits of his Transjordanian vision of Jewish settlement. In the end, his plan to mobilize British funds for the construction of a railroad line running the length of the future Jewish state remained unimplemented.

To Oliphant's credit, and in contrast to many Christian Zionists— who called for sending the Jews to the Holy Land, there to be converted to Christianity, while they themselves continued to live in civilized and comfortable Christian centers—the eccentric Oliphant immigrated to Palestine and settled in Haifa. It is an irony of history that his personal secretary in Haifa was the Jewish poet Naftali Herz Imber, whose poem "Tikvatenu" later became the basis of the lyrics for "Hatikvah," Israel's national anthem. Like a number of other immigrants of his generation, Imber left "Zion," his poem's object of nostalgia; after moving to Britain, he eventually settled permanently in the United States.

As we know, the Jewish nationalist movement itself was born only in the late 1890s. Theodor Herzl, the originator of the concept and founder of the Zionist Organization, was influenced by Viennese culture and perhaps even German nationalism; initially he tried to realize his vision not through colonization but through diplomatic means. After failed attempts to establish ties and gain the assistance of the German kaiser, the Ottoman sultan, and the prime minister of Austria-Hungary, Herzl was afforded a golden opportunity to present his daring ideas.

At the beginning of the twentieth century in Britain, there was fierce and mounting political pressure to stem the tide of immigrants arriving from Eastern Europe. The immigration was perceived to be a threatening invasion; in many ways, the reactions to it were similar to prevalent early-twenty-first-century attitudes toward Muslim immigration to Europe. A large portion of the public identified almost all Eastern Europeans as Jews, and new expressions of anti-Semitism could be heard in the working-class neighborhoods of London as well as in Parliament.[70] Indeed, between 1881 and 1905, Britain was the destination of more than a hundred thousand "Eastern" Jews, with more on the way. In this context, a royal commission was established in 1902 to address the phenomenon of unchecked immigration. The Jewish establishment in Britain, headed by the Baron Nathan Mayer Rothschild, expressed concern about the new situation and sought to prevent injury to the resident British Jewish community. Despite Rothschild's initial hesitations, Herzl was also invited to testify before the committee and to present his ideas regarding the settlement of Jews outside of Europe.

That same year, Leopold Greenberg, the extremely resourceful editor of the *Jewish Chronicle*, succeeded in orchestrating a personal meeting between Herzl and Joseph Chamberlain, the United Kingdom's all-powerful colonial secretary. Chamberlain, a colonialist through and through, was intrigued by the Zionist leader's unusual territorial program. At this historic encounter on October 22, 1902, Herzl proposed moving Jews to Cyprus or to El-Arish in the Sinai Peninsula, in order to relieve Britain of the threat of massive immigration. Both locations were close enough to Palestine so that it would be possible to expand toward it or move to it at some point in the future. In this way, Herzl hoped to neutralize the opposition of Zionists who insisted on maintaining the land of Zion as the focus of their designs at all costs, and at the same time to acquire the strategic support of the world's foremost superpower. It is important to remember that Palestine at the time was still part of the Ottoman Empire, while Cyprus and the Sinai Peninsula were under British control. In his naïveté, the Zionist leader believed that his proposal would be accepted both by governing circles in Britain and by the movement he had founded.

The problem was that although the Muslim population of Cyprus was sufficiently "anonymous," the island also had a white Christian population whom the British were obligated to support. Chamberlain was therefore forced to politely reject Cyprus, but he was willing to discuss the option of the Sinai Peninsula, on condition that Egypt be willing to accept the arrangement. British representatives in the land of the Nile (Lord Cromer for example),

---

70 On this subject, see Bernard Gainer, *The Alien Invasion: The Origins of the Aliens Act of 1905*, London: Heinemann Educational Books, 1972.

however, immediately articulated their decisive opposition. Nevertheless, the British colonial secretary, whose mandate was to do everything in his power to expand and strengthen the empire, did not give up hope, as he did not want to miss this double golden opportunity: on the one hand, to rid the country of the foreign Jews, with their strange attire and their German-sounding language, who were desperately seeking entry at the ports of the British Isles; and on the other hand, to settle potential loyal supporters of Great Britain in a thinly populated colony across the sea. At his second meeting with Herzl, on April 24, 1903, Chamberlain made a counteroffer: Uganda, a region that now belongs to modern-day Kenya but at the time was a colony in need of settlers. It could be given to the Chosen People free of charge.

This proposal was of considerable significance. It was the first time that a European power had entered into territorial negotiations with the fledgling Zionist movement. Even if the plan had been motivated by narrow colonial interests and, to an even greater extent, by a desire to prevent foreign immigration to Britain, it was nonetheless a turning point in the history of Zionism and of the British elite's complex attitude toward the descendants of the people of the Bible. Still a marginal force within the world Jewish community, Zionism had progressed from craving diplomatic legitimacy to achieving it on a major scale. For its part, Britain came to be perceived as the preferred custodian of Jewish destiny at the beginning of the twentieth century. As a result of Herzl's consistent pressure, the sixth Zionist Congress approved the Uganda scheme, albeit not without tempestuous debate and a great deal of tension. In truth, however, no one took the plan too seriously. If it had been difficult to recruit a large number of candidates to immigrate to Palestine, it would be much more problematic to find Jews willing to settle in a remote region of East Africa that lacked the mythological background necessary to the creation of a national homeland. But Herzl clearly understood that the proposal by the Foreign Office created a precedent, not necessarily of Zionist ownership over Palestine, but rather of the Jews' right to a territory of their own.

By the time the Uganda plan was proposed, the charismatic Lord Balfour had already become Britain's new prime minister. He supported Chamberlain's semi-Zionist plan, due in part to its being consistent with his own intention to enact a draconian law against foreign immigration. Balfour, a name ingrained in Zionist history as the greatest benefactor of the "Jewish people" in the modern era, began his relationship with this people (or "race," as he referred to Jews) with a political struggle aimed at preventing its persecuted members from taking refuge within his homeland. In the course of the 1905 parliamentary debates, Balfour maintained that Jewish immigrants married only among themselves and were neither willing nor likely to truly integrate into the British nation, and thus that Britain was morally justified in limiting their entry into its territory. To prove to the world that the decision against the Jews was not fundamentally antihumanitarian, he emphasized the Uganda option: immigrants would be offered large parcels of fertile land in colonies and should therefore refrain from complaining without good reason.[71]

This position, taken at the beginning of the twentieth century, certainly does not make Balfour an evil Judeophobe, just as the staunch efforts of early-twenty-first-century leaders to block the entry of migrant workers does not automatically make them historical Islamophobes. The term "anti-Semitism" refers to various manifestations of hostile or oppositional attitudes toward Jews along a broad spectrum. Balfour did not particularly hate Jews, although some evidence suggests he had no great love for them either. More than anything else, he did not want too many of them living in Britain itself, and as we will see, he would prove consistent on this policy in 1917 as well.

Balfour's policy in 1905 marked a turning point in the attitude of Britain, and perhaps of Western Europe as a whole, toward foreigners. While Britain was forcing its way into every possible corner of the earth without being invited to do so, it changed from being a liberal country that granted protection to refugees to being a territory that was almost completely impenetrable to others, even if they were being persecuted. During the age of imperialism, population movements were supposed to proceed in only one direction: from the center outward.

It is fair to say that the Balfourian legislation of 1905 regarding foreigners, along with a similar law enacted two decades later in the

---

71 On this subject, see Victor Kattan's informative *From Coexistence to Conquest: International Law and the Origins of the Arab-Israeli Conflict, 1891–1949,* London: Pluto Press, 2009, 18–20.

United States that further toughened the terms of immigration (the Immigration Act of 1924, also known as the Johnson-Reed Act),[72] contributed to the establishment of the State of Israel no less than the Balfour Declaration of 1917, and perhaps even more. These two anti-immigrant laws—along with Balfour's letter to Rothschild regarding the United Kingdom's willingness to view favorably "the establishment in Palestine of a national home for the Jewish people," discussed later in the present chapter—lay down the historical conditions under which Jews would be channeled to the Middle East.

How did Britain end up adopting a position that provided Zionist leaders with the diplomatic, political, and, in the eyes of the Zionists themselves, moral basis for the "national" colonization of "their homeland"? First, it is important to emphasize that in 1917, Balfour did not suddenly become a devoted activist of the Jewish cause. In January of that year, when asked by a British Jewish committee to intervene on behalf of the Jews living under terrible conditions throughout the Tsarist empire, he refrained from engaging the Russian government, with which he was then in military alliance. In a private conversation, he defended his actions as follows:

> It was also to be remembered that the persecutors had a case of their own. They were afraid of the Jews, who were an exceedingly clever people . . . [W]herever one went in Eastern Europe, one found that, by some way or other, the Jew got on, and when to this was added the fact that he belonged to a distinct race, and that he professed a religion which to the people about him was an object of inherited hatred, and that, moreover, he was . . . numbered in millions, one could perhaps understand the desire to keep him down.[73]

But Balfour was also raised by a devout Scots mother, from whom he absorbed an admiration for biblical stories and their recurrent protagonists, the ancient Hebrews. He believed that Christianity owed the Jews a great deal and criticized the Church's usual treatment of them. It is probably safe to assume that his mother also introduced him to

---

72   The 1924 act, which toughened the terms instituted by legislation enacted three years earlier, was not specifically directed at Jews but still had a significant negative impact on them.

73   Quoted in Jason Tomes, *Balfour and Foreign Policy: The International Thought of a Conservative Statesman*, Cambridge: Cambridge University Press, 1997, 202.

the idea of Jewish restoration as a necessary precursor to final Christian redemption. In contrast to Chamberlain the doer, Balfour was a man of letters who had a relatively extensive knowledge of history and dedicated time to writing. He was neither a Palmerston nor a Shaftesbury, but he possessed certain qualities of both and could certainly be considered their natural heir.

With Disraeli and other lords, Balfour shared a similar conception of race, although it is important to clarify that his attitude was far from a strict ideology of racial purity. Like many of his contemporaries, he believed in the existence of races with specific attributes and behaviors, whose blending with one another was undesirable. The Jewish race was a permanent, eternal element of history; having begun its wanderings from a specific land, it was only logical that it return there quickly. This belief provided the ideological foundation on which Balfour could turn into a sworn supporter of Zionism, which he indeed became. Although he sometimes had reservations regarding the real, somewhat "crude" Jews who lived in South London, he unswervingly admired the Zionists until the day he died. For him, they represented the historical continuity of a separate and ancient race that had categorically refused to integrate with its neighbors. He was certain that if this race were to return to its ancient homeland—a land sufficiently far from London—it would be able to demonstrate its true talents.

Such is the intellectual and psychological background of Balfour's position, but it does not shed light on the underlying logic of his concrete actions in the realms of diplomacy and international politics. Like Disraeli, Balfour was, above all, a typical British colonialist of his time, striving to promote the interests of the empire. Had the establishment of a Jewish home in Palestine conflicted with its interests, he would have been the first to oppose the idea. But toward the end of 1917, at a decisive point during the First World War, conditions grew ripe for the melding of ideology and politics. On November 2, 1917, the British Foreign Office sent the newly soldered result directly to the office of Baron Lionel Walter Rothschild. It read as follows:

Dear Lord Rothschild,
  I have much pleasure in conveying to you, on behalf of His Majesty's Government, the following declaration of sympathy with

Jewish Zionist aspirations which has been submitted to, and approved by, the Cabinet:

"His Majesty's Government view with favour the establishment in Palestine of a national home for the Jewish people, and will use their best endeavours to facilitate the achievement of this object, it being clearly understood that nothing shall be done which may prejudice the civil and religious rights of existing non-Jewish communities in Palestine, or the rights and political status enjoyed by Jews in any other country."

I should be grateful if you would bring this declaration to the knowledge of the Zionist Federation.

Yours sincerely

Arthur James Balfour

This letter made no pretense of reflecting the current demographic power relations in Palestine. At the time, the country was home to nearly 700,000 Arabs—the "non-Jewish communities in Palestine"—and 60,000 Jews (in comparison, the Jewish population of Britain itself numbered nearly 250,000).[74] But even this small minority was not Zionist, and was certainly not yet a "people." It encompassed many devoutly religious Jews who recoiled from the idea of establishing a modern state that purported to be Jewish but whose values would desecrate the Holy Land. But this data had no impact on Britain's position, which was aimed at encouraging colonization under its auspices, and perhaps also at relieving itself of some of the Jews who had managed to enter the British Isles despite the restrictions.

The notion of sanctioning the historic principle of the self-determination of nations was still very new and would not be applied to non-European populations until after the Second World War. Not only did the Balfour Declaration fail to take into consideration the collective interests of the local inhabitants—regardless of whether they were then a people or a nation—but it also went against the spirit of the assurances that Henry McMahon, the British high commissioner in Cairo, had given to Hussein bin Ali, the Sharif of Mecca. In

---

74   According to the British census of 1922, Palestine had a population of 754,549, including 79,293 Jews. See Harry Charles Luke and Edward Keith-Roach (eds.), *The Handbook of Palestine*, London: Macmillan, 1922, 33.

order to motivate the Arab leader to commit to war against the Ottomans, Britain made a vague promise of Arab political independence
in all the regions they populated, except for western Syria (the future
territory of Lebanon), which was home to a non-Muslim community.[75]
Not only did the British have no problem breaking these promises;
they also thoroughly discounted the initial signs of an Arab nationalist awakening and therefore never seriously considered keeping those
promises.

The purpose of Balfour's open letter was first and foremost to
undermine an earlier agreement that Britain had signed with France.
On May 16, 1916, when the two colonial powers decided to work
together to isolate the limping Ottoman Empire, Sir Mark Sykes
representing the British Foreign Office met with François Georges-
Picot representing the French Foreign Ministry to reach a basic
understanding regarding the division of territorial spoils. Under the
terms of their agreement, France would receive direct or indirect
control of the areas that would subsequently encompass Syria (up to
Mosul), Lebanon, southeastern Turkey, and the Upper Galilee. For
itself, Britain claimed the areas that would soon become Transjordan,
Iraq, the Persian Gulf, the Negev Desert, and the maritime enclaves of
Haifa and Acre. Furthermore, Tsarist Russia was promised control
over Istanbul, and the central portion of the Holy Land was designated an open zone under international administrative control. The
Jews were not on the agenda of the secret talks, nor were they
mentioned in the resulting historic document.[76]

In December 1916, David Lloyd George became the prime minister of Britain, and Arthur Balfour was appointed as foreign secretary
and Lloyd George's right-hand man. They were both open supporters
of Zionism. Lloyd George was a devout Welsh Baptist and, according
to his own testimony, was more familiar with the sites of the Holy
Land than with the names of the battlegrounds of the Great War. Both
men were dissatisfied with the Sykes-Picot Agreement. Their reasons
were twofold and interconnected, prosaic as well as historically majestic. On the practical level, the British aspired to expand the military

---

75   See correspondence at http://www.jewishvirtuallibrary.org/jsource/History/
hussmac1.html and in Kattan, *From Coexistence to Conquest*, 98–107.

76   For the details of the agreement, see: http://unispal.un.org/unispal.nsf/3d14c
9e5cdaa296d85256cbf005aa3eb/232358bacbeb7b55852571100078477c?OpenDocument.

security zone surrounding the Suez Canal by in fact conquering Palestine, and they were about to do so. From their perspective, it was necessary that the route connecting the Mediterranean Sea with the Persian Gulf be held by Her Majesty's representatives. They had no desire to share control of the Holy Land with unreliable French atheists. On the historical level, it was a question of the land of the Bible, from which Europe's crusading Knights had been expelled by barbarian Muslims in 1291. But now civilized Europeans could retake the land. The Holy Land was not just another colony, like Uganda or Ceylon. It was Christianity's place of origin, and Protestant lords were being offered the opportunity to direct its affairs from afar by a small and submissive band of Zionists.

On March 26, 1917, the soldiers of the British Commonwealth invaded Palestine for the first time in an attempt at conquest. Although the offensive failed, a few battalions gained control of the southern city of Beersheba, capital of the Negev; the road to Jerusalem was breached, and the fate of the Palestinians was sealed. It was during this period, between the conquest of the southern city and the surrender of Jerusalem without a battle on December 9, 1917, that Balfour sent Rothschild his famous letter, which annulled the Sykes-Picot Agreement in both theory and practice, providing the British with hegemonic perspective by means of their benevolent gift to the "Jewish people."[77]

We must remember that at the time, the world was unaware of the existence of the Sykes-Picot Agreement. Not until 1918, when the Bolsheviks perpetrated a WikiLeaks action on the archive of the Tsarist foreign ministry, would Britain's Machiavellian war game be exposed. The Sykes-Picot Agreement was a deeply cynical pact and had therefore been kept completely secret. By contrast, the Balfour Declaration had framed itself as a humanitarian gesture toward suffering Jews and was therefore made public. It was also no coincidence that the letter had been sent to Lord Rothschild, a well-known and respected political figure in the London public sphere, and not to the relatively unknown representatives of the small Zionist Organization.

---

77 For a good survey of the diverse academic literature relating to the British foreign secretary's letter, see Avi Shlaim, "The Balfour Declaration and its Consequences," in his *Israel and Palestine: Reappraisal, Revisions, Refutations*, London: Verso, 2009, 3–24. See also John Rose, *The Myths of Zionism*, London: Pluto Press, 2004, 118–29.

First and foremost, it was meant to provide cover for a sophisticated colonialist action that would affect the future of the Middle East for the remainder of the twentieth century.

Scholars point to additional factors that may have led the Lloyd George government to issue the Balfour Declaration. One was the belief within British governing circles that American Jewry could do more to persuade its government to mobilize for the Great War; after all, the ongoing massacre could not be halted until the German enemy was soundly defeated. Another was Whitehall's belief that a declaration by Great Britain in favor of a Jewish national home might motivate the Jews of Russia to favor the continuation of the desperate campaign on the eastern front, despite their support for the Bolshevik pacifists.[78]

Throughout history, both anti-Semites and philo-Semites have grossly overestimated intra-Jewish solidarity and Jewish influence. Despite their great admiration for the Jews, the Christian Zionists' overarching conceptions regarding the members of this group did not differ fundamentally from the attitudes of Judeophobes. While the views of Evangelical Protestants exhibit many nuances, they share an essentialist ethnological approach that is saturated with prejudices and suppositions regarding Jews and their ostensible ruling position in the world.[79]

A more naïve historiography attributes the British Crown's territorial generosity to the invention of an organic substance. This well-known story goes as follows: at an early stage in the war, the British were running short of acetone, a substance crucial in the production of bombs and other explosive materials. Chaim Weizmann, a leader of the Zionist movement in Britain who would later become the first president of the State of Israel, was also a talented chemist. Having discovered a method of producing acetone via the bacterial fermentation of vegetable matter, he was called on to serve

---

78 On the talks with the British government leading up to the Balfour Declaration, see Dvorah Barzilay, "On the Genesis of the Balfour Declaration," *Zion* 33:3–4 (1968), 190–202 (in Hebrew), and Meir Verete's excellent "The Balfour Declaration and Its Makers," *Middle Eastern Studies* 6:1 (1970), 48–76.

79 Tom Segev was the first to highlight this aspect of British politics, specifically with regard to Lloyd George. See his picturesque description and refreshing analysis in *One Palestine Complete: Jews and Arabs under the British Mandate*, New York: Owl Books, 2001, 36–9.

his country and succeeded in solving the wartime logistical problem. Because of Weizmann's talent and resourcefulness, the production of bombs and cannon shells could now resume at its previous pace. At the time, Lloyd George was serving as minister of munitions; Winston Churchill, whom Balfour replaced in 1915, as first lord of the admiralty. All three leaders knew Weizmann and, so the story goes, did not forget his contribution to the war effort when the time came to make a decision on the Jewish home in Palestine. In this way, the Balfour Declaration is also seen as the British leadership's fulfillment of a moral obligation to an individual and the movement he represented.

In the construction of historical narratives, almost anything can be construed as a possible factor. Unfortunately, historical scholarship is not a chemistry lab in which experiments can be repeated in order to assess the specific combination of substances that actually resulted in fermentation or explosion. Still, it seems unlikely that, at the time, the British government was unaware that the German branch of the Zionist movement was fervently supporting a German homeland. Thus we arrive at another historical irony: the fact that poison gas was invented for the German army by Fritz Haber, another chemist of Jewish descent. After the Nazis came to power, Haber, a German patriot, was forced to leave his homeland. He died in 1934, hoping to go to Palestine to join Weizmann's research institute in Rehovot.[80]

In 1917, Lord Lloyd George, Lord Arthur Balfour, Lord Alfred Milner, Lord Robert Cecil, Sir Winston Churchill, and many other British statesmen were convinced that the restoration of the Jews to Palestine would earn the British a safe imperial foothold there until the end of days and possibly even later, in the event that the Evangelicals proved to be correct.

They appear to have learned nothing from the uprising of American settlers in the late eighteenth century or the revolt of Afrikaner settlers in the late nineteenth century. Or perhaps they believed that the Jews, who possessed financial power but whose actions were

---

80   The most comprehensive study published to date on the developments leading up the British declaration in support of the Jewish national home is Jonathan Schneer, *The Balfour Declaration*, New York: Random House, 2010. Unfortunately, however, Schneer pays insufficient attention to ideological aspects and imperialist compulsions, and briefly even conveys the impression that the British had not meant to take control of Palestine.

circumscribed by politics, would achieve a different kind of relationship with the benevolent protective empire. The Jewish Zionists, too, were mistaken—in their case, in the assessment that a pro-Zionist ideology was sufficiently entrenched among the British elite to ensure its victory over other, competing imperial interests.

In any event, neither the ripeness of two thousand years of Jewish yearning for an ancient land nor the massive wave of voluntary immigration threatening to flood Britain was responsible for the diplomatic initiative that would ultimately lead to Zionist sovereignty in Palestine. Rather, during the period leading up to November 2, 1917, three distinct ideological and political axes aligned to create a decisive, and symbiotic, triad:

(1) Age-old Evangelical Christian sensitivity closely intertwined with colonial goals embraced by the British since the second half of the nineteenth century;

(2) The great hardships faced by a large proportion of Yiddish-speaking people, who found themselves caught between two dangerous and troubling processes: the rise of anti-Semitic protonationalism in East Europe, which had already begun to aggressively eject them, and the simultaneous imposition of immigration restrictions by the countries of Western Europe; and

(3) The emergence of a modern nationalist response to these events, which began to develop around the margins of the disintegration of the unformed Yiddish people, and which was aimed primarily at colonization of the land of Zion.

Without a doubt, the Balfour Declaration considerably increased the popularity of Zionism; and from this point on, we find many more Jews enthusiastically agreeing to send other Jews to "make aliyah" to the Land of Israel. Nevertheless, at least between 1917 and 1922, the declaration of British policy regarding a Jewish national home and the encouragement of British authorities still failed to convince Yiddish speakers—not to mention British Jews—to immigrate en masse to their "historic homeland."[81]

---

81 Many members of the British Jewish community were bitterly opposed to the Balfour Declaration. Figures such as the Secretary of State for India Sir Edwin Montagu; Claude Montefiore, grandnephew of the well-known philanthropist and

By the end of the five-year honeymoon between Christian and Jewish Zionism, approximately thirty thousand Zionists had arrived in British-ruled Palestine. As long as the United States permitted relatively open immigration, hundreds of thousands of Eastern European displaced persons continued to descend upon its shores. They steadfastly refused to relocate to the Middle Eastern territory that Palmerston, Shaftesbury, Balfour, and other Christian lords had been assigning them since the mid-nineteenth century.

No one should be overly surprised by this demographic situation. Although settlement in Palestine presented economic difficulties, the main reason for the lack of immigrant settlers was much more banal: during the first half of the twentieth century, most of the world's Jews and their progeny—whether ultraorthodox, liberal, or Reform, whether social democratic Bundists, socialists, or anarchists—did not regard Palestine as their land. In contrast to the mythos embedded in the State of Israel's Declaration of Independence, they did not strive "in every successive generation to reestablish themselves in their ancient homeland." They did not even regard it as an appropriate place to "return" to when that option was presented to them on a Protestant colonial golden platter.

At the end of the day, it was the cruel and horrifying blows sustained by the Jews of Europe, and the decision of "enlightened" nations to close their borders to the recipients of those blows, that resulted in the establishment of the State of Israel.

---

founder of Liberal Judaism in Britain; and even Lucien Wolf, from the Anglo-Jewish Association, publicly voiced their criticism of the Zionist idea. See Stuart Cohen, "Religious Motives and Motifs in Anglo-Jewish Opposition to Political Zionism, 1895–1920," in Shmuel Almog, Jehuda Reinharz, and Anita Shapira (eds.), *Zionism and Religion,* Hanover, NH: Brandeis University Press, 1998, 159–174.

CHAPTER FOUR

Zionism versus Judaism:
The Conquest of "Ethnic" Space

It is an eternal law: if a dividing line either passes or is made to pass between a nation state and its homeland, that artificial line is destined to vanish.

—Menachem Begin, 1948

The meaning of this victory [1967] is not only that it restored to the Jewish people its most ancient and most exalted sacred entities—those which are engraved above all others in its memory and in the depths of its history. The meaning of this victory is that it erased the difference between the State of Israel and the Land of Israel.
—Nathan Alterman, "Facing the Unprecedented Reality," 1967

British Protestants read the Bible directly seeking unmediated inter-action with the divine spirit. The Jews of the Talmud, in contrast, feared a free reading of the Book of Books, which they believed was dictated by God himself. Christian millenarian thinkers had no compunctions regarding Jewish immigration to and settlement in the Holy Land. As far as they were concerned, the ingathering of the Jews was a critical precondition of salvation. But this was not the case for Jewish rabbis, either during the medieval period, the transition to modernity, or in the course of the modern era itself. For them, the ingathering of the Jews, the living and the dead alike, would come only with redemption. In many ways, therefore, the distance between Evangelicalism and Zionism was smaller than the profound meta-physical and psychological gap between Jewish nationalism and historic Judaism.[1]

---

1 By this I do not mean to imply that Christian Zionism had a direct conceptual "influence" on the birth of Jewish nationalism in Eastern Europe. It is difficult to find unequivocal traces of such an influence in the thinking of protonationalist and Zionist intellectuals of Jewish descent. Still, it is certainly possible that Zionist Evangelicalism created a European climate that indirectly contributed to the rise of the

In 1648, one year before the Baptist mother and son Johanna and Ebenezer Cartwright called on the revolutionary government in London to put the Jews on ships and send them to their Holy Land, Sabbatai Zevi, a student from Smyrna, decided he was the Jewish Messiah. Had the Jews of Eastern Europe not been undergoing an unsettling trauma at the very same time, this young Jew might have ended up as no more than one of many anonymous lunatics consumed by messianic dreams. But the brutal massacres perpetrated by the Orthodox Christian Cossack Bohdan Khmelnytsky during his rebellion against the Polish Catholic nobility instilled terror in many communities, who were quick to devote themselves to messages of imminent redemption. To better understand this historical context, we must remember that the year 1648 was also reckoned by Kabbalistic calculations to be the year of redemption.

Sabbateanism spread like wildfire across Jewish communities in many countries and recruited a large number of followers. Only after Sabbatai Zevi's conversion to Islam in 1666 did this impassioned movement cease to thrive. The wave of messianism sent ripples through the Jewish faith for years to come. Sabbatean groups continued to be active until the eighteenth century; as a direct response, Jewish community institutions became more cautious and devised mechanisms to protect against the eruption of uncontrollable cravings for imminent salvation.

Sabbateanism was not a proto-Zionist movement and was certainly not nationalist, even if certain Zionist historiographers have tried to portray it as such. More than the uprooting of the Jews from their places of origin in order to assemble them in the Land of the Gazelle (*Eretz ha-Tzvi*), Sabbatai Zevi sought to establish spiritual rule over the world.[2] But many rabbis believed that Sabbateanism

---

idea. For more on this subject, see Amnon Raz-Krakotzkin, "The National Narration of Exile: Zionist Historiography and Medieval Jewry," Ph.D. diss., Tel Aviv University, 1996, 297–301 (in Hebrew). The emergence of Jewish nationalism resulted in close contact between Christian and Jewish Zionists, the most prominent example of which was the relationship between Theodor Herzl and the Anglican clergyman William Hechler in Vienna. For more on this, see Claude Duvernoy, *Le Prince et le prophète*, Jerusalem: Publications Department of the Jewish Agency, 1966.

2   See Avraham Elqayam's informative "Eretz ha-Zevi: Portrayal of the Land of Israel in the Thought of Nathan of Gaza," in Aviezer Ravitsky (ed.), *The Land of Israel in Modern Jewish Thought*, Jerusalem: Yad Ben-Zvi, 1998, 128–85 (in Hebrew). It is also important to note that the Frankists, the largest Sabbatean movement in

might cause Jews to look toward Jerusalem, to sin through a premature attempt to hasten redemption, and to undermine the fragile
stability of Jewish existence the world over.

The socioeconomic modernization that began in the late eighteenth century, disrupting forms of community life for centuries to
come, also contributed to the hardening of concepts of faith in rabbinical power centers. More than ever, rabbis took care to avoid being
swept up in the dangers of an eschatology that promised imminent
salvation. Despite its great spontaneity, its devotion to the Lurianic
Kabbalah, and its aversion to individual redemption, the Hasidic
movement of the eighteenth century sought, for the most part, to
exercise caution regarding the temptations of the harbingers of collective salvation and the hasteners of redemption.[3]

JUDAISM'S RESPONSE TO THE INVENTION OF THE HOMELAND

A resident of Prague prior to the emergence of Sabbateanism, Rabbi
Isaiah Halevi Horowitz, known as the saintly Sheloh, was considered
one of the great Jewish rabbis of the seventeenth century. In 1621, after
the death of his wife and in view of the quickly approaching year of
redemption (the Jewish year 5408, which coincided with 1647–48),
the rabbi relocated to Jerusalem. After living in the holy city for a
period, he moved to Safed and finally settled in Tiberias, where he
was buried with great ceremony in 1628. Many Zionist historians
regard him as a "first swallow" who, at the onset of the modern era,
decided to make aliyah, that is, to "ascend" or immigrate, to the Land
of Israel. However, the fact that he immigrated to the Holy Land while
thousands of other rabbis refused to do so teaches us more about the
major differences and epistemological detachment between traditional Judaism and the emergent Zionist idea. There can be no doubt

---

eighteenth-century Poland, also did not regard immigration to the Holy Land as a
primary messianic goal. See Jacob Frank's *Divrei ha'adon* (Words of the Lord) (in
Hebrew).

    3   One of the major elements that distinguishes Judaism from Zionism is their
differing positions on messianism, which Judaism rejects but which Zionism
remembers nostalgically. It is no coincidence that Zionist scholars such as Gershom
Scholem, Joseph Klausner, Yehuda Kaufman, and many others admired and praised
historical messianic yearnings. For more on this, see Yosef Salmon, *Do Not Provoke
Providence: Orthodoxy in the Grip of Nationalism*, Jerusalem: Shazar, 2006, 33 (in
Hebrew).

about his sense of connection to and great love for the Land. Not only did he move to a new unfamiliar place at a relatively advanced age, but he also called on others to join him, without thinking in terms of the collective immigration of all Jews.

It was in Safed that he appears to have completed writing his influential work *The Two Tablets of the Covenant*, which takes a clear position against the option of settling in the holy place in order to live a normal Jewish life. The Land was by no means intended to serve as a refuge from physical danger. To observe the commandments there would be more difficult than anywhere else in the world, and anyone desiring to settle there had to be psychologically prepared to do so. A Jew going to the "Canaanite land" did not do so in order to settle peacefully, partake in its fruits, and enjoy its pleasures. Based on biblical verses, the Sheloh concluded unequivocally that a person who settled in the Holy Land was destined to live there as a foreigner all the days of his life. Moreover, he maintained, the Land did not belong to the children of Israel, and their very existence there was precarious.

Horowitz's depiction of becoming a settler in the Holy Land was an exact description of the exilic existence of Jews in the rest of the world. He saw moving to the Land not as a first sign of redemption but as the complete opposite: the burden in the Land was greater and heavier, and therefore to bear it, in the face of fear and anxiety, was true evidence of faith. As he wrote, "The person residing in the Land of Israel must always remember the name Canaan, indicating slavery and submission . . . You shall live to be sojourners in your land, in the words of David, 'I am a sojourner on the earth' (Psalms 119:19)."[4]

A century later, Rabbi Jonathan Eybeschutz, another notable textual commentator from Prague, expressed similar opposition to the temptation of moving to the Holy Land. Although accused by his rivals of Sabbateanism, he was in fact a strict adherent to Jewish legal principles regarding redemption, and was extremely concerned by human efforts to hasten it. He contended unequivocally that Jews did not want to leave "their exile," and that doing so was, in any event, not dependent on them. "For how can I return, when it might engender in me sin?" he asked in a famous sermon in the city of Metz, which

---

4   Isaiah Halevi Horowitz, *Two Tablets of the Covenant* 2.3.11. On the views of the Sheloh, see Aviezer Ravitzky, "Awe and Fear of the Holy Land in Jewish Thought," in Ravitzky (ed.), *Land of Israel*, 7–9.

was included in his work *Ahavat Yonatan.*[5] The Land was meant to receive only Jews devoid of compulsions, who were not liable to commit a transgression or violate any of the commandments. Because such Jews were nowhere to be found, living in the Holy Land was not merely hopeless but also posed a great danger to the coming of redemption.

Perhaps most interesting is the fact that Eybeschutz's great rival, the learned Rabbi Jacob Emden, who accused Eybeschutz of Sabbateanism, was in complete agreement with him regarding the Land of Israel. His consistent critique of all tacit or explicit expressions of messianism also included the fierce rejection of all intent to hasten the redemption. If any one person made the three adjurations of the Talmud the guiding principles of his doctrine, it was undoubtedly Rabbi Emden. He viciously attacked as foolish the failed attempt by Rabbi Judah Hahasid's messianic group, which immigrated to Jerusalem in 1700 and is portrayed by Zionist historiography as the beginning of Jewish nationalist immigration to the Land of Israel.[6]

The theological fear of desecrating the Holy Land because of the major burden involved in fulfilling the commandments there was deeply rooted in Jewish religious legal thinking until the beginning of the twentieth century. Some expressed it openly, while others ignored the issue or preferred not to discuss it at all. Still others continued to glorify and extol the Land's imagined virtues without ever considering settling there. The traditional religious institutions produced neither a movement nor a stream aimed at relocation to Jerusalem so as "to build and be rebuilt" there.

However, before we consider the rabbinical streams' reactions to the rise of the new nationalist challenge, we must first consider one of the earliest voices of the Enlightenment to emerge from eighteenth-century European Jewry: Moses Mendelssohn. Mendelssohn, who knew both Eybeschutz and Emden personally, studied in a yeshivah and was well versed in rabbinical literature. However, unlike the two great traditional scholars, he began to diverge from the Jewish legal

---

5   Jonathan Eybeschutz, "Parashat Ekev," in *Ahavat Yonatan*, Hamburg: Shpiring, 1875, 72. See also the first section of *Sefer Yaarot Hadvash*, 74, and Ravitzky, "Awe and Fear," in *Land of Israel*, 23–4.

6   On the Hasidic immigration, see Jacob Barnai's praiseworthy *Historiography and Nationalism: Trends in the Research of Palestine and its Jewish Yishuv, 634–1881*, Jerusalem: Magnes, 1996, 40–159 (in Hebrew).

frameworks and to develop an independent system of thought. For this reason, Mendelssohn is considered the first Jewish philosopher of the modern era.

To a great extent, he was also one of the first Germans. When most subjects of the kings and princes still did not know the literary German language, Mendelssohn, like other great intellectuals, had already started writing it with remarkable virtuosity. That is not to say he stopped being a Jew. He was a faithful observer of the commandments; he expressed a deep connection to the Holy Land and objected to the integration of the Jews into Christian culture, even within the framework of an egalitarian religious coexistence. At the same time, however, he worked to improve the socioeconomic condition of Jews and to facilitate their cultural departure from the ghettos, which, though providing their residents with a sense of protection from the onslaught of modernization, had been forced on them. He therefore retranslated the Bible into literary German (in Hebrew characters) and added his own philosophical comments. His struggle for equal rights for Jews also led him to engage in one of the last intellectual discussions of his life.

In 1781, ten years before Mendelssohn's death, Christian theologian Johann David Michaelis launched an attack against the provision of equal rights to Jews. It was one of the first of many bitter debates on the subject that would continue into the first half of the nineteenth century. In Michaelis's approach, we can already detect a Judeophobic, protonationalist tone. One of his major claims against the Jews was that they already had another homeland in the East. Indeed, haters of Jews within the German territories were the first to invent a faraway Jewish national territory, long before the birth of Zionism. Mendelssohn responded immediately, fearlessly presenting his position. His view was based on principle and resonated with most devout Jews during the nineteenth century. "The hoped-for return to Palestine, which troubles Herr. M.[ichaelis] so much," he wrote,

> has no influence on our conduct as citizens. This is confirmed by experience wherever Jews are tolerated. In part, human nature accounts for it—only the enthusiast would not love the soil on which he thrives. And he who holds contradictory religious opinions reserves them for church and prayer. In part, also, the precaution of our sages accounts for it—the Talmud forbids us *even to think* of a

return [to Palestine] by force [i.e., to attempt to effect Redemption through human effort]. Without the miracles and signs mentioned in the Scripture, we must not take the smallest step in the direction of forcing a return and a restoration of our nation. The Song of Songs expresses this prohibition in a somewhat mystical and yet captivating verse (Song of Songs 2:7 and 3:5): I charge you, O daughters of Jerusalem,

By the gazelles, and by the hinds of the field, That you stir not up, nor awake my love, Till it please.[7]

In this passage, on the eve of the birth of national territories in Europe, Mendelssohn felt the need to clarify why the Holy Land was not his homeland. He relied on two main arguments: one that could have been taken straight from Hellenistic Judaism, which maintained that the Jews were normal human beings and therefore loved the land in which they lived; and another that drew explicitly on the Talmud, which cited the theological excuse of the three adjurations and which from then on would be articulated by the Jewish Haskalah, which regarded itself as part of the emerging of the German nation. From this perspective, we can understand Mendelssohn as a milestone of sorts, bridging the gap between Philo of Alexandria, the first Hellenistic Jewish philosopher, and Franz Rosenzweig, possibly the last great German Jewish philosopher, who also categorically rejected every attempt to link Judaism to land.[8] At the same time, Mendelssohn can be viewed as the harbinger of the large Reform Judaism movement, which also objected to proto-Zionist and Zionist ideas.

---

7   Moses Mendelssohn, "Remarks Concerning Michaelis' Response to Dohm (1783)," in Paul Mendes-Flohr and Jehuda Reinharz (eds.), *The Jew in the Modern World: A Documentary History*, Oxford: Oxford University Press, 1995, 48–9. For the original German text, see Moses Mendelssohn, *Gesammelte Schriften* 3, Hildesheim: Gerstenberg, 1972, 366.

8   Like Martin Buber, Rosenzweig conceived of Jews as a blood community. However, unlike Buber, he refused to link blood to land and rejected the view of the Holy Land as a homeland: "We alone have put our trust in blood and have parted with the land . . . For this reason, the tribal legend of the eternal people begins otherwise than with indigenousness. Only the father of humanity . . . is sprouted from the earth . . . Israel's ancestors, however, immigrated." Franz Rosenzweig, *The Star of Redemption*, trans. Barbara E. Galli, Madison: University of Wisconsin Press, 2005, 319. On Buber's position regarding the organic connection between land and nation, see Martin Buber, *Between a People and Its Land*, Jerusalem: Schocken, 1984 (in Hebrew).

Mendelssohn believed that the idea of a Jewish state in the Holy Land was negative and destructive, and in this he was no different from the traditional rabbinate. The ascent of nationalism in Europe during the nineteenth century would not change this fundamental point of faith in any meaningful way. Aside from a few atypical rabbis such as Zvi Hirsch Kalischer and Judah Alkalai who tried to combine religious messianism with national territorial realism, earning them the praise of Zionist historiography, mainstream Jewish institutions demonstrated no openness to early expressions of proto-Zionism. On the contrary, they responded with a barrage of hostility toward the very idea of turning the Holy Land into a national homeland.

We must remember that the efforts by historical, traditional Judaism to contend with the changes of the period were not initially geared toward Zionism, that is to say, the project of collective assimilation into modernity. Rather, the initial struggles of the nineteenth century were aimed at semicollective integration (Reform Judaism) and individual, primarily secular assimilation. Through these two latter processes, Jews sought to join the still evolving national cultures in the countries they inhabited. Legislative progress regarding equal rights for Jews in the countries of Western Europe, and subsequently those of Central Europe, accelerated the disintegration of the superstructures that had long constrained Jewish existence. The penetration of enlightened ideas of skepticism into Eastern Europe, and the sway of these ideas over the educated strata and the younger generations, began to disrupt Jewish community institutions, which sought to respond to the challenge in any way possible.

Reform Judaism began to flourish everywhere that political liberalism was well established, and at times even helped bring it about. In the Netherlands, Britain, France, and especially Germany, newly established religious communities tried to adapt Jewish practices and tactics to the spirit of enlightenment that had been spread by the French Revolution. Everything in the tradition that was perceived as counterintuitive was modified and imbued with new substance and new expression. Synagogue and prayer observances were changed, and new houses of worship developed invigoratingly original rituals.

Aside from the efforts to modernize community activities, what most characterized the Reform enterprise was the attempt to adapt it to the consolidation of nations and national cultures that was then under way. Reform Jews, seeking their place in this process, saw themselves first and foremost as an immanent component of the new collective identities. Hebrew prayers were translated into the increasingly dominant standardized national languages. In addition, Reform Judaism removed from the liturgy all references to redemption that suggested a return to Zion at the end of days. According to the Reform ethos, each Jew had only one homeland: the country where he or she lived. Jews, before being anything else, were German, Dutch, British, French, and American believers in the faith of Moses.

Reform Jews voiced strong opposition to the proto-Zionist ideas that emerged during the second half of the nineteenth century, fearing that insistence on highlighting difference that was cultural rather than religious would intensify Judeophobia and impede the cause of civil equality. Yet this opposition did not prevent the rise of modern anti-Semitism in Central and Eastern Europe. Nationalisms typically needed Jews, in addition to other minority groups, in order to delineate the still insufficiently clear-cut borders of their nations. In the end, proto-Zionism and Zionism emerged as immediate and direct responses to ethnocentric nationalism, which began to exclude Jews on religious and mythologically historical grounds, and, within a short time, on biological grounds as well. But the development of political Zionism was of even greater concern to liberal Reform Jews, who expressed their fears in hundreds of publications. In their eyes, Zionism was beginning to look more and more like the flip side of Judeophobic nationalism: both streams of thought refused to see Jews as patriots of their resident homeland and both suspected them of dual loyalty.

In Germany, Reform Judaism emerged as the most populous Jewish stream, producing numerous religious intellectuals, from Mendelssohn's student David Friedländer to the learned rabbi Abraham Geiger and figures such as Sigmund Maybaum and Heinemann Vogelstein. Judaic Studies (*Wissenschaft des Judentums*), which contributed more to the study of Jewish history than did any other cultural movement during the first half of the nineteenth century, developed within its orbit. Without taking into account the impact of Reform Judaism, it is impossible to understand, for example, the anti-Zionist Jewish thinking of Hermann Cohen, the great neo-Kantian philosopher.⁹ Particularly after the Revolutions of 1848, the movement empowered groups in the United States as well, where it spread and strengthened.¹⁰

Despite their great rivalry, Reform Judaism and traditional Judaism were in agreement on one fundamental point: the steadfast refusal to regard Palestine as national property, a destination for Jewish immigration, or a national homeland. As we have seen, Jews in Western and Eastern Europe were as nationalized as other citizens, not in the sense of embracing a unique Jewish political identity but rather in the sense of being integrated into their respective individual nations. In the closing years of the nineteenth century, an important Jewish newspaper explained the phenomenon in the following terms: "On this question of love for the Kaiser and the Reich, for the state and the homeland, all the parties of Jewry are of one opinion—the orthodox and the Reform, the ultraorthodox and the well-educated [*die Aufgeklärtesten*]."¹¹

One prominent example of this dynamic was Rabbi Samson Raphael Hirsch, the major nineteenth-century German leader of Orthodox Judaism. At the time, he could already read and write fluently in German and is still renowned as a brilliant commentator whose talented students and followers outnumbered those of all other rabbis of his day. With the first reverberations of proto-Zionism resulting from the ideas of Rabbi Kalischer and former Communist Moses Hess, Hirsch immediately undertook to stop this deviation, which he believed was a falsification of historic Judaism and a likely cause of serious injury to it. He was concerned that those who regarded

---

9   On this philosopher's anti-Zionist positions, see Hermann Cohen, *Selected Essays from* Jüdische Schriften, Jerusalem: Bialik, 1977, 87–104 (in Hebrew), and *Religion und Zionismus*, Crefeld: Blätter, 1916.

10   It was only in 1937, after the rise of Nazism and within the liberal climate of American nationalism, that progressive Judaism began to come to terms with the Jewish nationalist idea. After the Israeli victory in the 1967 war, its identification with the State of Israel became complete, and in 1975 it even joined the World Zionist Organization. For more on this, see Michael A. Meyer, *Response to Modernity: A History of the Reform Movement in Judaism*, New York: Oxford University Press, 1988. Unfortunately, the author of this study dedicates very little attention to the struggle between liberal Judaism and Zionism (326–7).

11   *Der Israelit* 79/80, October 11, 1898, 1460, quoted in Yaakov Zur, "Zionism and Orthodoxy in Germany," in Haim Avni and Gideon Shimoni (eds.), *Zionism and Its Jewish Opponents*, Jerusalem: Hassifriya Hazionit, 1990, 75 (in Hebrew).

the Holy Land as a Jewish homeland and were demanding sovereignty over it would repeat Bar Kokhba's mistake from the time of Hadrian and bring about a new Jewish tragedy. He therefore reminded all Jews, lest they forget:

> Yisrael was given the Torah in the wilderness, and there—without a country and land of its own—it became a nation, a body whose soul was Torah . . . Torah, the fulfillment of the Divine Will, constitutes the foundation, basis and goal of this people . . . Therefore, a land, prosperity and the institutions of statehood were to be put at Yisrael's disposal not as goals in themselves but as means for the fulfillment of the Torah.[12]

The notion that the holy scriptures had completely replaced the Land sparked developments among other traditional scholars, and when Herzl attempted to invite the Union of German Rabbis to the opening of the First Zionist Congress in 1897, he was met with resounding rejection. The situation was so serious that the Jewish community in Munich, where the congress was to have convened, flatly refused to allow the meeting to take place on German soil. As a result, Herzl was forced to move it to Basel, Switzerland. Of ninety representatives of the German rabbis, all but two signed a harsh letter of protest against the convening of the Zionist Congress.

Naftali Hermann Adler, chief rabbi of the United Kingdom, who initially supported the Jewish community in Palestine and even expressed support for the Lovers of Zion movement, immediately opposed the political Zionist colonization project and refused public contact with Herzl. The same was true of Zadoc Kahn, chief rabbi of France. Although he was supportive of the philanthropic enterprise of Edmond James de Rothschild and was initially intrigued by Zionism, French Jewry's allegiance to the French homeland was far more important to him than the new Jewish national "adventurism."

But the most intriguing attitude of a European rabbi toward Zionism was that of Moritz Güdemann, chief rabbi of Vienna and a prominent scholar of Jewish history. In 1895, even before writing *The Jewish State*, Herzl approached the influential rabbi with the aim of

---

12   Samson Raphael Hirsch, "The Eighth Letter: The Founding of the Jewish People," in *The Nineteen Letters*, New York: Feldheim, 1995, 115–16.

securing his assistance in making contact with the Viennese branch of the Rothschild family. His curiosity piqued, the rabbi was certain Herzl was inclined to join the struggle against anti-Semitism and perhaps also inclined to enlist the *Neue Freie Presse*, the widely circulated Viennese newspaper for which Herzl wrote, in defense of the persecuted Jews. However, Güdemann grew concerned after his visit to Herzl's home, where he was surprised to learn that the journalist had a Christmas tree.[13] Herzl was known not to be an especially observant Jew and not even to have had his son circumcised (most likely because he regarded circumcision as detrimental to masculinity). But Rabbi Güdemann overcame his hesitations regarding the strange young *goy* and continued a correspondence with the intriguing journalist.

In his theatrically rich imagination, Herzl saw Güdemann as the chief rabbi of the capital city of the future Jewish state.[14] In this context, the significant "misunderstanding" that erupted between the two was quite telling. Although Güdemann was a traditional, not a Reform, rabbi, he steered clear of all forms of nationalism. His cosmopolitanism accurately reflected the antinationalist political and cultural aspects of the Austro-Hungarian Empire. In 1897, the year of the First Zionist Congress, the rabbi of Vienna published a booklet bearing the title *National Judaism*.[15] This short work is one of the most enlightening theological and political critiques of the Zionist vision ever written.

As a rabbi and a devout Jew, Güdemann did not question the biblical narrative. However, his commentary on the Torah and the books of the prophets display a craving for universalism and human solidarity. His deep anxieties regarding modern anti-Semitism made him a consistent and methodical antinationalist thinker. From his viewpoint, even if the Jews had been a people in antiquity, since the destruction of the Temple they had been nothing more than an important religious community with the aim of disseminating the message of monotheism throughout the world and turning humanity into one great people. The Jews always adapted

---

13   Journal I, December 24, 1895, in Theodor Herzl, *Writings*, Tel Aviv: Neuman, 1960, 212 (in Hebrew).

14   June 7, 1895, in ibid., 35.

15   Moritz M. Güdemann, *National Judaism*, Jerusalem: Dinur, 1995 (in Hebrew).

well to diverse cultures (Greek, Persian, and Arab, for example) while preserving their faith and their Torah. Both the traditional Rabbi Güdemann and the rabbis of Reform Judaism, including Rabbi Adolf Jellinek, leader of the Liberal community in Vienna, agreed in principle that the Jews of Germany were German, the Jews of Britain were British, and the Jews of France were French—and that this was a good thing:

> The most important chapters in the history of the Diaspora were reflected in names such as Philo, the Rambam, and Mendelssohn. These men were not only the flag-bearers of Judaism but also shone brilliantly in the general culture of their times.[16]

The nationalist egoism spreading throughout the world, argued Güdemann, fundamentally contradicted the spirit of the Jewish religion, and devout followers of the Bible and Jewish religious law should avoid falling under the enticing and dangerous influence of chauvinism. It was precisely this path along which the Jews should not follow the gentiles: in other words, assimilation into modern secular culture—yes, but assimilation into modern politics—no. Every educated Jew knew that the basic political concepts that derived from Greco-Roman culture did not exist within Judaic culture. The charismatic rabbi did not hide his fear that one day a "Judaism with cannons and bayonets would reverse the roles of David and Goliath to constitute a ridiculous contradiction of itself."[17] However, because of the threat of anti-Semitism, Güdemann was not opposed to the immigration and settlement of Jews in other countries, and therein lies the basis for Herzl's fundamental misunderstanding of the scholarly rabbi:

> Giving those Jews, for whom the struggle for survival in their current homeland has become too difficult, an opportunity to settle elsewhere is a praiseworthy deed. We can only ask and hope that the Jewish colonies that already exist and those that will be established in the future, in the Holy Land or elsewhere, will continue to exist and to prosper. However, it would be a grave error running

16   Ibid., 27.
17   Ibid., 28.

contrary to the spirit and history of Judaism if these settlement activities, which are worthy of great appreciation, are linked to nationalist aspirations and regarded as the fulfillment of the divine promise.[18]

According to Güdemann, Judaism had never been dependent on time or place and had never had a homeland. Many Jews, he maintained, intentionally forgot Jewish history and knowingly falsified it, interpreting the yearning and love for the Holy Land and the desire to be buried there as a nationalist mentality, which it was not. The reason was simple:

> In order to prevent the misunderstanding that Israel's existence is dependent on the ownership of land or tied to the land of its heritage, the Bible explains: "But the Lord's portion is his people, Jacob his allotted heritage" (Deuteronomy 32:9). This perspective, which regards the people of Israel more as God's heritage than as the owners of this heritage, cannot serve as the basis of a nativism linked by an unbreakable bond to the land in question. Israel never relied on the autochthony or aboriginality that served the other peoples of the ancient period.[19]

It is no surprise that after the publication of this stinging pamphlet, Herzl lost all hope in both the Reform and traditional rabbis of Western and Central Europe. He also knew that he had no hope of finding support among the Jews of the United States. After all, Rabbi Isaac Mayer Wise, founder of the Central Conference of American Rabbis, had publicly and unequivocally classified Zionism as false messianism and had proclaimed the United States—not Palestine—to be the Jews' true place of refuge. By doing so, he dashed all hopes of support or assistance from America's new and increasingly strong Jewish community.[20]

---

18   Ibid. Although Güdemann uses the terms "Holy Land" and "Palestine," the Hebrew translation replaces these terms with the standard term "Land of Israel."

19   Ibid., 20. For Herzl's response, see "The National Judaism of Dr. Güdemann," at the Ben-Yehuda Internet Project, http://benyehuda.org/herzl/herzl_009.html (in Hebrew).

20   See Melvin Weinman, "The Attitude of Isaac Mayer Wise Toward Zionism and Palestine," *American Jewish Archives* 3 (1951), 3–23.

From then on, Herzl pinned his hopes solely on the rabbis of Eastern Europe, the spiritual guides of the large Yiddish-speaking population of the region. Indeed, the few traditional Jews of the Mizrachi movement who attended the historic assembly of the young nationalist movement in 1897 came mostly from the Russian empire. Unlike the rabbis of Britain, France, Germany, and the United States, who already spoke and wrote in their respective national languages, the rabbis of Eastern Europe still had their own language—Yiddish, in which most of them wrote—as well as their sacred language, Hebrew. The use of Russian or Polish met with the bitter opposition of the Eastern rabbinical establishment.

As we know, the state of Eastern Europe's Jews was completely different from that of Western Europe's. Millions of Jews still lived in neighborhoods or small towns that were segregated from those of their neighbors; moreover, by contrast to the Jews of the West, this population exhibited clear signs of a unique and lively popular culture. In such places, therefore—but not necessarily elsewhere—secularization and politicization played a role in shaping a specific culture. Political parties, newspapers, and literature were organized, managed, and published in Yiddish. Like all other inhabitants of Tsarist Russia, these Jews were not citizens of the empire but only its subjects; as a result, no significant non-Jewish local nationalism developed. And when we take into consideration the bitter Judeophobia that crystallized in these areas, we understand why it was there, of all places, that Zionism acquired its first foothold and achieved its first successes.

The pioneering, albeit marginal, efforts from the 1880s onward to settle in Palestine—while espousing no national aspirations and taking care to observe the Jewish commandments—had received a degree of encouragement from the traditional rabbinical establishment. The rabbis were most concerned with the secular socialist radicalism that had been spreading among Yiddish youth. Although the rabbinate was not overly enthusiastic about the immigration to the Holy Land initiated by the Lovers of Zion, which did include some traditional Jews, the phenomenon initially appeared to pose no significant threat to Jewish religious frameworks. Nor did the early reports of Zionist political organization arouse immediate concern. It was hoped that nurturing the longing for holy Zion would help safeguard the core of Jewish belief from the influence of the secularizing force of modernization.

Soon the rabbis came to understand that Zionism's gracious gestures in their direction were purely instrumental.[21] For a moment, the proponents of religion had hoped to use nationalism to their own benefit. However, they quickly discovered that even though they shared a lot with Zionism, the goal of the two movements was exactly opposite. Herzl and his colleagues in the new movement courted the traditional leadership because they were aware of its hegemonic power for Jewry. They sought to turn religious Jews into nationalists as well, and had no intention of preserving religion that was antimodern and therefore antinationalist.

Between the first Zionist Congress in 1897 and the fourth in 1900, the leading rabbis of Eastern Europe spoke out in opposition to the transformative vision of turning the Holy Land into a homeland where all Jews would gather to establish a Judaic state. After years of bitter struggles between *Mitnagdim* and Hasidic rabbis, the broad-based hostility toward Zionism succeeded in unifying them into one fighting Eastern front, which included Yisrael Meir Kagan of Raduń (known as the Chofetz Chaim); Yehudah Aryeh Leib Alter (the Gerrer Rebbe, author of and also known as Sfas Emes); Chaim Halevi Soloveitchik of Brisk; Yitzchak Yaakov Rabinovich (the Rabbi Itzele Ponevezher); Eliezer Gordon of Telz, Lithuania; Eliyahu Chaim Meisel of Lodz; David Friedman of Karlin-Pinsk; Chaim Ozer Grodzinski of Vilna; Yosef Rosen of Dvinsk, Latvia (known as the Rogatchover Gaon); Sholom Dovber Schneersohn, the Rebbe of Lubavitch; and a long list of others. Each of these figures spoke out in defense of the Torah against what they regarded as the harbinger of their destruction.[22]

---

21 The first Jewish anti-Zionist book was Dob-Baer Tursz's *Herzl's Dream*, Warsaw: Tursz, 1899. On this book and the writings of rabbis who opposed Zionism, see Yosef Salmon's thorough "Zionism and the Ultraorthodox in Russia and Poland 1898–1900," in Salmon, *Religion and Zionism: First Encounters*, Jerusalem: Hassifriya Hazionit, 1990, 252–313 (in Hebrew).

22 Although I have not listed the names of rabbis from outside the Russian empire, outspoken opponents of Zionism also included most rabbis of Hungary, traditional and Reform (Neologs) alike. From Rabbi Chaim Elazar Spira (the Munkaczer Rebbe) to Rabbi Isaac Breuer to Rabbi Dr. Lipót Kecskeméti, all streams of Judaism were united in their staunch opposition to Zionism. For more on Spira, see Aviezer Ravitzky, "Munkács and Jerusalem: Ultra-Orthodox Opposition to Zionism and Agudaism," in Shmuel Almog, Jehuda Reinharz, and Anita Shapira (eds.), *Zionism and Religion*, Hanover, NH: Brandeis University Press, 1998, 67–92. On Kecskeméti, see Yehuda Friedlander, "The Thoughts and Deeds of Zionist and Anti-Zionist Rabbis in Hungary," Ph.D. diss., Bar-Ilan University, 2007, 123–43 (in Hebrew).

This was the elite of Eastern European Jewry, major leaders of Judaism who led large communities throughout the Russian empire. They were the brilliant Torah commentators of their age and, in this capacity, they, more than anyone else, were responsible for shaping the spirit and sensibilities of hundreds and thousands of believers. This Jewish elite broke the momentum of Zionism much more effectively than the combined influence of the Bund, the socialists, and the liberals, preventing it from emerging as a leading force among the Jews of Eastern Europe. The great rabbis did not allow Zionist activists into their synagogues or places of Torah study; they also prohibited the reading of the Zionists' writings and strictly forbade all political cooperation with them.

The writings of these rabbis reveal a skillful and sober diagnosis of nationalism. Although their conceptual tools may at times have been naïve and inadequate, few secular scholars of their day articulated such sharp insights. This stemmed not from the rabbis' brilliance but rather from the fact that they were the only intellectuals of the late nineteenth century who were capable of analyzing nationalism from the outside. As foreigners to the modern era and strangers in a foreign land, they intuitively identified the prominent attributes of the new collective identity.

In 1900 a group of major influential rabbis jointly compiled and published a volume titled *The Book of Light for the Righteous, Against the Zionist Method*. Already in the introduction, the editors make their position clear:

> We are the people of the book, and in the books of the Bible, the Mishnah and the Talmud, the Midrash, and the legends of our holy teachers of blessed memory, we find no mention of the word "nationalism," neither in its Hebrew derivation from the word "nation" nor in the intimations or the language of our teachers of blessed memory.[23]

Considering the volume's many ultraorthodox collaborators, it was evident that the Jewish world was facing an unprecedented historical phenomenon. Certainly, the rabbis explained, the Jews are a people

---

23   S. Z. Landa and Y. Rabinovich (eds.), *The Book of Light for the Righteous, Against the Zionist Method*, Warsaw: Haltar, 1900 (in Hebrew), 18.

because God chose to establish them as such; this people, however, was defined only by the Bible, and not by any authority from outside the faith. For tactical reasons, the enticing Zionists were arguing that the nation could accommodate believers and nonbelievers alike, and that the Torah was of secondary importance. This was an innovation, as the claim that Judaism was a national political grouping and not a religious one had never before been asserted in the Jewish tradition. The Zionists had also intentionally chosen the Holy Land as the territory on which a state should be established because they understood how precious it was to the Jews. They had even appropriated the name Zion with the intent of luring naïve believers into becoming supporters of nationalism. For all types of Zionists, Jewry was a fossilized people that needed to be rehabilitated. However, for the authors of the volume in question, the statement meant modern Hellenization and a new species of false messianism.

Rabbi Meisel of Lodz held that the "Zionists are not in search of Zion" and had merely donned this verbal cloak in order to deceive naïve Jews.[24] Rabbi Chaim Soloveitchik and the Rogatchover Gaon regarded them as a "cult," and could not seem to find enough words to denounce them as a whole. The Rebbe of Lubavitch warned that "their entire desire and aim is to throw off the burden of the Torah and the commandments and to maintain only nationalism, and that is what would constitute their Judaism."[25] The popular Hasidic leader lashed out with particular venom against the Zionists' selective use of the Bible, skipping over elements that they found inconvenient and creating a new faith in practice and in theory, a nationalized Torah that was completely different from that which had been given to Moses at Mount Sinai.

In conjunction with other books and articles, this joint publication unmistakably reflected the contention of the traditional rabbinate that Zionism represented a reproduction of individual secular assimilation on the collective, national level. In Zionism, the Land replaced the Torah, and the sweeping worship of the future State replaced the strong adherence to God. From this perspective, Jewish nationalism

---

24   Ibid., 53.
25   Ibid., 58. See also "Statement by the Lubbavitcher Rebbe Shulem ben Schneersohn, on Zionism (1903)," in Michael Selzer (ed.), *Zionism Reconsidered*, London: Macmillan, 1970, 11–18.

posed a much greater danger to Judaism than did individual assimilation, greater even than contemptible religious reform. In the case of
these two latter phenomena, there was the chance that Jews would
return to their original faith after being disappointed. In the case of
Zionism, however, there was no chance of return.

Traditional Judaism's fear of the power of nationalism ultimately
proved justified. With the terrifying assistance of history, Zionism
defeated Judaism, and after the Second World War, large segments of
world Jewry that had survived extermination accepted the decisive
verdict: the principle of a state designated as Jewish and located in the
Holy Land, which would be a Jewish national homeland. With the
exception of a tiny community based in Jerusalem and the great
Hasidic courts in New York, most faithful Jews became followers of
the new nationalism to one degree or another. Some even came to
support an extremely aggressive nationalism. When the master of the
universe began to show signs of weakness and possibly even death,
they too, like the secular radical right, came to see human beings—
that is to say, nationalism—as the all-powerful master of the earth.

Vayoel Moshe, an influential book by the Satmar Rebbe Yoel
Teitelbaum, can be regarded as the culmination and impressive theoretical conclusion of Judaism's opposition to proto-Zionism and
Zionism.[26] Although the text—the first part of which was written in
the 1950s—contains very little that is new, it does breathe life into the
three languishing Talmudic adjurations by prohibiting collective
immigration to the Holy Land prior to the redemption; by stressing
that the land of the Bible was never a national territory and forbidding
settlement without meticulous observance of the clear commandments that apply to it; and by maintaining that Hebrew is a sacred
language meant strictly for prayer and legal discussion, and should
not be used as a secular language for business, for curses, for blas-
phemy, or, according to the rabbi, for military commands.

Until the birth of Zionism at the end of the nineteenth century,
few Jews imagined that the Holy Land was or could become a national
territory for the world's Jewry. Zionism disregarded tradition, the
commandments, and the opinions of the rabbis, and spoke in the
name of those who completely rejected these things and publicly

---

26   Yoel Teitelbaum, *Vayoel Moshe*, Brooklyn: Jerusalem Publications, 1961 (in
Hebrew).

expressed contempt for them. This was certainly not the first such surrogate act in history: just as the Jacobins spoke with absolute confidence in the name of the French people, which did not yet really exist, and as the Bolsheviks presented themselves as a historic replacement for the proletariat, which was just coming into being in the Russian empire, so too did the Zionists locate their imagined homeland within Judaism and understand themselves to be its successors and its mandated, authentic representatives.[27]

At the end of the day, the Zionist revolution succeeded in nationalizing the main elements of Jewish religious discourse. From then on, the Holy Land became a more or less defined space that should be owned by the eternal people. In short, during the twentieth century, the Holy Land became the "Land of Israel."

HISTORICAL RIGHT AND THE OWNERSHIP OF TERRITORY

Herzl's diagnosis of the state of Eastern and Central European Jewry was more accurate than that of all his rivals, thus explaining why his ideas have been so powerful over the long haul. The traditionalists, reformists, autonomists, socialists, and liberals all failed to understand the brittle, aggressive nature of nationalism in those regions of Europe and therefore failed to identify, as Herzl did, the grave threat posed to Jewish existence. Today, in retrospect, we also know that the choice of the poverty-stricken, homeless immigrants who left old Eastern Europe en masse for the shores of the Americas was ultimately a better choice than that of those who chose to stay where they were. But it is still too early to know for certain whether they were right in their stubborn refusal to immigrate to Palestine. In any event, the great westward migration saved millions of lives. Unfortunately, the same was not true of the Zionist project.[28]

---

27   For the best and most comprehensive study on Jewish opposition to nationalism published to date, see Yakov Rabkin, *A Threat from Within: A Century of Jewish Opposition to Zionism*, London: Zed Books, 2006.

28   The Zionist movement did not and could not have truly saved Jews from the hands of the Nazis. However, its overall approach to the genocide was fairly problematic. On this subject, see Shabtai Beit-Zvi's courageous and pioneering book *Post-Ugandan Zionism on Trial: A Study of the Factors that Caused the Mistakes Made by the Zionist Movement During the Holocaust*, S.B. Beit-Zvi, 1991. On the Zionist movement's attitude toward the victims of Nazi persecution and anti-Semitism prior to the outbreak of the Second World War, see Herzl Schubert, "The Evian Question in Context," M.A. thesis, Tel Aviv University, 1990 (in Hebrew).

However, although the diagnosis of the founders of Zionism was accurate, the medicine they prescribed was problematic because of its striking resemblance to the ideological core of modern anti-Jewish sentiment. The Zionist mythoi regarding the delineation of the imagined Jewish nation and the territory designated for this "nation" were meant to "ethnically" isolate it from other nations, thereby appropriating land on which and from which others were living.

Herzl himself may have been less ethnocentric and, in truth, less "Zionist" than the other important leaders of the young movement. In contrast to most, he did not really believe that the Jews were a unique race-based nation; moreover, for him, unlike most members of the movement, Palestine was of less importance as a country of destination. Most decisive in his vision was the urgent need to find collective national refuge for helpless, persecuted Jews. In his 1896 book *Der Judenstaat* (The State of the Jews), he clarifies his position on the issue of refuge as follows: "Shall we choose Palestine or Argentina? We shall take what is given us, and what is selected by Jewish public opinion."[29] And during the debate on Uganda that took place at the sixth Zionist Congress, he successfully forced his colleagues to accept the British proposal for colonization in East Africa.

But as a realistic statesman, Herzl also knew that the only way to penetrate the Eastern European Jewish public was by means of an unbreakable bond between tradition and vision. For a mythos to be credible and sturdy, its foundation had to have a layer of "ancient" images. Not only could this imagery be completely re-fabricated, it was essential that it be so. Nonetheless, it was irreplaceable as a starting point. Such endeavors have been common in the construction of national memory in the modern era.

However, by what right was it permissible to establish a Jewish nation-state in a territory where the decisive majority was not Jewish? In all the debates with the traditionalists, on both sides of the

---

29 Theodor Herzl, *The Jewish State*, Mineola, NY: Dover Publications, 1988, 95. In this context, it is important to remember that Leon Pinsker, the proto-Zionist who preceded Herzl, still did not regard Palestine as the Jews' exclusive country of destination. In his 1882 essay "Auto-Emancipation," Pinsker wrote: "The goal of our present endeavors must be not the 'Holy Land,' but a land of our own. We need nothing but a large tract of land for our poor brothers, which shall remain our property and from which no foreign power can expel us." (http://www.jewishvirtuallibrary.org/jsource/Zionism/pinsker.html).

campaign, the presence of Arabs in Palestine was almost never raised. There were, of course, a few individuals who understood the importance of this issue, but they were necessarily located far from both nationalism and the Torah on the Jewish political spectrum. For example, as early as 1886, Ilya Rubanovich, a Narodnaya Volya (People's Will) member of Jewish descent who went on to be a leader of the Russian Socialist Revolutionary Party, posed the following penetrating question. Even if wealthy Jews succeeded in purchasing the "historic homeland" from the Turks,

> What is to be done with the Arabs? Would the Jews expect to be strangers among the Arabs or would they want to make the Arabs strangers among themselves? . . . The Arabs have exactly the same historical right and it will be unfortunate for you if—taking your stand under the protection of international plunderers, using the underhand dealings and intrigue of a corrupt diplomacy—you make the peaceful Arabs defend *their* right.[30]

To use such logic in argument, one had to be a revolutionary who espoused a universal morality—meaning neither a religious Jew nor a Zionist. It was the height of the age of colonialism, when nonwhite inhabitants of the planet were still not considered the equals of Europeans, and were certainly not entitled to the same civil and national rights. Although most Zionists well knew that Palestine had many local inhabitants, and periodically mentioned them in their writings, they did not construe their presence as meaning that the Land was not open for free colonization. Their fundamental consciousness on this point was consistent with the general climate of the late nineteenth and early twentieth centuries: as far as the white man was concerned, the non-European world had for all intents and purposes become a space devoid of people, just as America had been desolate two hundred years earlier, prior to the arrival of the white man.

---

30   Ilya Rubanovich, "*Chto delat evreiam v Rosii?*" *Vestnik narodnoi voli* 5 (1886), 107, quoted in Jonathan Frankel, *Prophecy and Politics: Socialism, Nationalism, and the Russian Jews, 1862–1917*, Cambridge: Cambridge University Press, 1981, 129. Later, similar arguments would be advanced by members of the Bund movement. See, for example, Victor Alter's Yiddish essay *Der Emet Wagen Palestina*, Warsaw: Die Welt, 1925.

Among the Zionists, however, there were a few exceptions. One was Ahad Ha'am (Asher Hirsch Ginsberg), the leader of spiritual Zionism, who, after a visit to Palestine in 1891, wrote passionately about Palestine's local population with great misgivings:

> From abroad, we are accustomed to believe that Eretz Israel is presently almost totally desolate, an uncultivated desert, and that anyone wishing to buy land there can come and buy all he wants. But in truth it is not so . . . From abroad we are accustomed to believing that the Arabs are all desert savages, like donkeys, who neither see nor understand what goes on around them. But this is a big mistake. The Arab, like all children of Shem, has a sharp intellect and is very cunning . . . if the time comes when the life of our people in Eretz Israel develops to the point of encroaching upon the native population, they will not easily yield their place . . . how careful we must be not to arouse the anger of other people against ourselves by reprehensible conduct. How much more, then, should we be careful, in our conduct toward a foreign people among whom we live once again, to walk together in love and respect, and needless to say in justice and righteousness. And what do our brethren in Eretz Israel do? Quite the opposite! They were slaves in their land of exile, and they suddenly find themselves with unlimited freedom . . . This sudden change has engendered in them an impulse to despotism, as always happens when "a slave becomes a king," and behold they walk with the Arabs in hostility and cruelty, unjustly encroaching on them.[31]

By the end of the nineteenth century, the basic mold of Jewish-Arab relations resulting from the colonization of the country had already been cast, and this moral thinker, who supported the existence of a nonpolitical Jewish spiritual center in the Land of Israel, was shocked by what he saw. Ahad Ha'am was by no means a marginal figure within the Zionist camp. Rather, he was a highly respected author of lucid and penetrating essays, with a wide readership across the Jewish public. Despite his status, his pained protest aroused no serious discussion within the emerging nationalist camp. This might have

---

31   For an English translation of Ahad Ha'am's article, see Alan Dowty, "Much Ado about Little: Ahad Ha'am's 'Truth from Eretz Yisrael,' Zionism, and the Arabs," *Israel Studies* 5:2 (2000), 154–81. This quotation in ibid., 161–75.

been expected, even if Ahad Ha'am himself was unable to understand why: after all, such a discussion would have neutralized the drive of the movement and damaged the moral foundation for much of its claim.

The above excerpt suggests that the first settlers typically ignored the locals and had not been educated to see them as equals. One exception may have been Yitzhak Epstein, a linguist who immigrated in 1895 to Palestine, where he worked as a Hebrew teacher. In 1907, Epstein published an article in the Berlin-based Zionist journal *Ha-Shiloah*, which, not coincidentally, had been founded by Ahad Ha'am. Titled "A Hidden Question," Epstein's article opened with the following assessment:

> Among the difficult questions linked to the idea of the rebirth of our people on its land, there is one question that outweighs all the others: the question of our attitude toward the Arabs. This question, upon whose correct solution hangs the revival of our national hope, has not been forgotten, but has been completely hidden from the Zionists and in its true form is scarcely mentioned in the literature of our movement.[32]

Epstein was also concerned that the purchase of land from wealthy effendis, which resulted in the systematic dispossession of peasant farmers, was an immoral act that would produce hostility and conflict in the future.

Like Ahad Ha'am's protest, Epstein's article fell on deaf ears. The sense of ownership, of having a right to the Land, was too strong in Zionist consciousness for its adherents to take the time to consider those whom they regarded as uninvited guests in their promised land. But how could a movement that was fundamentally secular in nature, despite the tallith of tradition in which it wrapped itself, base its right to land on religious texts written in the distant twilight of ancient history?

One religious minority faction that participated in early Zionist Congresses exercised caution in its attitude toward the land of the

---

32   For an English translation of Epstein's article, see Alan Dowty, "'A Question That Outweighs All Others,' Yitzhak Epstein and Zionist Recognition of the Arab Issue," *Israel Studies* 6:1 (Spring 2001), 34–54. Above quotation in ibid., 39. See also Epstein's pamphlet *The Question of Questions in Settling the Land*, Jaffa: Hever Emunei Hayishuv, 1919 (in Hebrew).

Bible, and established itself as a movement in 1902. This group, Mizrachi, did adopt the new national idea of *shivat Tziyon* (the return to Zion) as a viable human action paving the way for the coming of redemption. However, in contrast to the secular Zionists, who lacked faith in divine power, the members of Mizrachi asserted, based on biblical knowledge, that although God had promised the Land to the children of Israel, it did not come with a deed of ownership. Because of its sacredness, it had been granted only conditionally and would never become the full property of human beings, whether or not they belonged to the chosen people.

The first religious Zionists regarded a Jewish state as a solution to a concrete problem, not necessarily as the realization of a divinely granted right. For this reason, during the fiery Uganda debate, in contrast to the passionate secular "Palestinocentrics," who were unwilling to give up the Holy Land under any circumstances, Mizrachi supported Herzl's proposal and voted in favor of accepting the offer of a temporary land of refuge. Only later did the movement's spokespersons hesitantly, and in internal contradiction, begin to articulate the religious right to the Land of Israel. Many forget that during the seven decades that elapsed between the First Zionist Congress in 1897 and the power-driven "miracle" of the 1967 war—aside from clear exceptions such as Abraham Isaac HaCohen Kook—the majority of religious Zionists were among the least dogmatic where authority over the land was concerned.[33]

In the modern world, it is virtually impossible to justify political practices without invoking some sort of universal moral dimension. Power is necessary to the execution of collective projects, but if lacking in ethical legitimacy, such projects must remain impermanent and unsound. Zionism understood this as it took its first steps, seeking to mobilize the principle of right in order to fulfill its nationalist aims. From Moses Leib Lilienblum in 1882 to the Israeli Declaration of Independence in May 1948, Jewish nationalism mobilized a system of ethical and legal justifications based on a common denominator of historical right, or the right of precedent, or, in plain language, "we were there first, and now we're back."

---

33   Professor Yeshayahu Leibowitz, who regarded himself as a Zionist until his dying day, can be thought of as the authentic spiritual heir of the initial members of the Mizrachi movement.

Just as the French Revolution produced the idea of "natural rights" to a national territory, it was the Franco-Prussian War that crystallized the concept of "historic rights." Between 1793 and 1871, the concept of homeland gained currency throughout Europe, at times giving birth to new conceptions of rights. When Alsace-Lorraine was annexed to Germany, the major argument of the German historians was that the regions in question had belonged to the German Reich in the distant past; the French, by contrast, championed the inhabitants' right to determine their own country of affiliation, based on their right to self-determination.

Ever since the controversy surrounding this territory, the nationalist right and at times the liberal right have tended to invoke "historic rights," while the liberal and socialist left has typically adopted the idea of self-determination for people living on their land. From the Italian fascists, who claimed the Croatian coast because it had earlier belonged to the Venetian empire (and before that, to the Roman Empire), to the Serbs, who claim sovereignty over Kosovo based on the battle of 1389 against the Ottoman Muslims and the existence in the region of a Christian majority that spoke Serbian dialects until the end of the nineteenth century, reliance on the principle of historic rights has fueled some of the ugliest territorial struggles in modern history.[34]

Even before the appearance of Herzl, Lilienblum, a leader of the Lovers of Zion, advised the Jews to leave hostile Europe and

> to settle in the nearby land of our fathers, to which we have a historical right that was neither extinguished nor lost with our loss of rule, just as the rights of the Balkan people were not extinguished with their loss of rule.[35]

---

34   Although the Nazis justified their annexation of Alsace-Lorraine with claims of historical rights, they based their demand to annex the Sudetenland on the right of self-determination. It was the Czechs who, in 1919, convinced the victorious Allies to punish the vanquished Germans by incorporating the German-speaking region into the new Czechoslovakia based on "historical rights" reaching back to the days of the Bohemian monarchy. Hitler made effective use of this act in his nationalist propaganda before he rose to power, and subsequently in the international realm. "Historic rights" also played a role in the bitter conflict between Poland and Lithuania during the first half of the twentieth century.

35   Moses Leib Lilienblum, *On the Revival of Israel on the Land of Our Fathers*, Jerusalem: Zionist Organization, 1953, 70 (in Hebrew).

Lilienblum grew up in a traditional Jewish home and became a secular scholar for whom the religious conception of the Holy Land was supplanted by an overwhelmingly political conception. As one of the first Jews to read the Bible not as a theological work but as a secular text, he asserted: "We have no need for the walls of Jerusalem, for the Temple, or for Jerusalem itself."[36] In his view, therefore, it was not a right of religious connection to a holy city, but rather a right to national territory.

As the first Zionists began to learn of the Arabs in Palestine, Menachem Ussishkin, a major Zionist leader, decided to extend Lilienblum's position with the demand "that those Arabs live in peace and solidarity with the Jews and acknowledge the children of Israel's historic right to the Land."[37] This rhetorical hypocrisy elicited an immediate and decisive response from Micah Joseph Berdichevsky, an early Modern Hebrew author who, unlike Ussishkin, was a man of exceptional integrity. Berdichevsky responded to these rationalizations with simple logic:

> For the most part, our fathers were not natives of the Land but its conquerors, and the right they acquired was also acquired by the conquerors who subsequently conquered it from us . . . They do not acknowledge our rights but rather deny them. The Land of Israel is not virgin land before us; it is populated by a people cultivating its land, with rights to its land.[38]

Like many others of his generation, Berdichevsky truly and naïvely regarded the Bible as an accurate historical text. But he read it without relying on the various Zionist premises that justified the logic of conquest only when the conquerors, whether present or past, were "children of Israel."

From this point on, the Bible as secular text would serve as a primary component of Jewish moral arguments for the eternal rights of the Jewish people. It was also necessary to cite the ostensibly indisputable fact that the Jews were forcibly exiled from the Land in

---

36   Ibid., 71.

37   Shmuel Almog, *Zionism and History*, Jerusalem: Magnes, 1982, 184 (in Hebrew).

38   Micah Joseph Berdichevsky, "From the Land of Israel to Just a Land . . . ," in *The Writings of Micah Joseph Berdichevsky*, vol. 8, Tel Aviv: Hakibbutz Hameuchad, 2008, 270 (in Hebrew).

the year 70 CE (or a bit later) and to believe that most modern Jews were "racially" or "ethnically" descended from the ancient Hebrews. Only the acceptance of these three premises made it possible to establish and maintain belief in the Jews' historical right. To undermine any one of them would disrupt their integrated functioning as a mythos capable of arousing and mobilizing the Jewish public.

On this basis, as we have noted in previous chapters, the Bible came to serve as the first history book to be studied by all schoolchildren within the Zionist community in Palestine as well as, under the auspices of the Israeli education system, within the modern State of Israel. The story of the exile of the Jewish people after the destruction of the Temple now emerged as a historical axiom, neither to be researched nor questioned, but rather to be used in political declarations and official national displays. The kingdoms that had been converted to Judaism, whose populations came to constitute some of the world's most important Jewish communities—from the Adiabene kingdom of Mesopotamia to the Khazar empire of southern Russia—now became a taboo subject, simply not to be discussed. It was these ideological conditions that enabled "historical right" to serve as a sturdy ethical platform for Zionist consciousness.

Herzl himself had too colonialist a mind-set to be concerned about the issue of right or to be troubled by complicated historical questions. Living in the era of imperialism, he did not consider the acquisition of a homeland outside Europe that would serve as a territorial branch of the bourgeois "civilized" world to be a goal requiring justification. Herzl was also a wise politician, however, and for pragmatic reasons, he too came to believe the national narratives that began to be woven around him.

The first protests articulated by Arabs against the implications of the Balfour Declaration forced Jewish nationalism to make increasing use of variations on its moral superweapon, "historical right." Proponents of that ideology skillfully translated long-term religious ties to the Holy Land into the right of ownership to a national land. Among those invited to take part in talks on the future of Ottoman territories were representatives of the Zionist Organization, who proposed the following resolution:

> The High Contracting Parties recognize the historic title of the Jewish people to Palestine and the right of the Jews to reconstitute in

Palestine their National Home . . . The land is the historic home of
the Jews; there they achieved their greatest development . . . By
violence they were driven from Palestine, and through the ages they
have never ceased to cherish the longing and the hope of a return.[39]

In 1922 the League of Nations adopted the text of the Mandate for
Palestine, which named Britain as the Mandatory. Although it did not
confirm the Jews' right to Palestine, the international body had already
recognized their "historical connection" to the territory. After that
point, in conjunction with the new "right under international law,"
the conception of historical right emerged as the rhetorical cornerstone of Zionist propaganda. As a result of the increasing pressure on
the Jews of Europe, and the absence of countries willing to grant them
entry and refuge, more and more Jews and non-Jews alike came to be
convinced of the importance of this new consciousness of right, transforming it into an indisputable "natural right." The fact that for
thirteen hundred years the inhabitants of the region had been overwhelmingly Muslim was countered by maintaining that this local
population did not possess the unique attributes of a nation and had
never claimed self-determination. By contrast, according to Zionist
discourse, the Jewish nation had always existed and, in every generation, had aspired to return to its country and realize its right, although
to its great misfortune it had always been prevented from doing so by
political circumstance.

There were of course some Zionists, especially from the political
left, who felt uncomfortable with justifications based on the conception of historical right, which negated the rights of the living and gave
priority to the rights of the dead from an ancient past. Hesitation and
opposition were voiced by members of Brit Shalom, a small pacifist
group that existed on the margins of the Zionist movement for a short
period during the 1920s, and even by some Zionist socialists, notably
those affiliated with the HaShomer HaTzair movement. These individuals well knew that according to the liberal and socialist heritage
of the nineteenth century, land always belonged to its cultivator.
Efforts were therefore made to link multiple rights, and at times even
to equate the indigenous population's right to continue living on their

39 Quoted in Gideon Shimoni, *The Zionist Ideology*, Hanover: Brandeis
University Press, 1995, 352–3.

land with the historic right of the new settlers. Nevertheless, local resistance to the settlers intensified and increasing pressure was brought to bear on the British to curb immigration. This resulted in the writing of considerable numbers of articles, stories, and legal essays that attempted to base the historical mythos in any way possible on the wandering race-based people who, though exiled by force, had begun to return to their homeland at the earliest opportunity.

April 1936 marked the start of the Arab Revolt in Palestine. The leaders of the Zionist community portrayed it not as an authentic protonationalist uprising against external rule and foreign invasion, but rather as the product of anti-Semitic incitement on the part of hostile Arab leaders. However, in light of the mass awakening and the increasing apprehensions of the British, the distressed Jewish Agency for Palestine quickly prepared a lengthy memorandum titled "The Historical Connection of the Jewish People with Palestine."[40] It was submitted to the Palestine Royal Commission, also known as the Peel Commission, after its appointed head, Lord William Peel. This text, composed with great effort and meticulous care, is a fascinating document reflecting the Zionist conception of right as of the 1930s.

In order to understand why the country belonged to the people of Israel, the text explained, it was necessary to begin at the beginning, with the book of Genesis. The Land had been promised to Abraham by a divine power that is known and accepted by all. Jacob's son Joseph was the first scion of the race to be exiled from the Land,[41] and Moses was the first Zionist who intended to return to it. The first exile uprooted the nation to Babylonia, from which it quickly returned to its land by dint of national mental fortitude. This mental determination was also responsible for the revolt of the Maccabees, which again established a large Jewish kingdom. During the Roman period, the Land was home to four million inhabitants, and two national revolts resulted in the displacement of some of the Jews from their native land, causing their dispersion among the nations. But not all the Jews were exiled: many remained on their land, and Palestine remained the territorial center of the Jewish people throughout its entire existence. The Arab conquest resulted in additional exiles, and the foreign regime bitterly oppressed the Jews of the country. Still, the

---

40   Jerusalem: Jewish Agency for Palestine, 1936.
41   Ibid., 4.

memorandum informs us, the Jews who remained held steadfastly to their homeland, and the "mourners of Zion" returned to Jerusalem and remained there. For the Jews, the Wailing Wall had always been the most sacred place in the world. In this sense, all the messianic movements had been Zionist in essence, even if they were not explicitly classified as such.

The historical survey dedicated significant space to sympathetic British figures such as Disraeli, Lord Palmerston, and other supporters of the people of Israel, transforming them into active Zionists. In fact, the memorandum dedicated more time to Shaftesbury than to Abraham and Moses combined, and of course made no mention of the British lord's secret aspiration to convert all Jews to Christianity.[42] Only Herzl and the birth of the Zionist movement were allocated more pages than Christian Zionism. According to this document, Jewish history in its entirety had been directed toward the appearance of the Zionist idea, the Zionist movement, and the Zionist enterprise. No mention was made of the rights of the non-Jewish majority of Palestine which, for the time being, was also living within the same small territory.

This critical theoretical document was unsigned. We do not know who its authors were, but it is fairly safe to assume that it was composed by the new historians of the Hebrew University of Jerusalem, headed by Ben-Zion Dinur, patriarch of the study of the past within the young Zionist community. This important political historian left his mark on numerous aspects of the memorandum, including its emphasis on the Land's centrality throughout Jewish history, on the fact that the two revolts of the ancient period were not followed by true exiles and that the Arab conquest resulted in more exiles, and on the fact that there had always been a Jewish presence in the territory.

Those who established the foundations for the conception of historical right were not legal experts. Primarily they were historians, biblical scholars, and geographers.[43] From the 1930s onward, most

42   Ibid., 23–5.

43   One "legal" study, however, was written by a religious author. See Reuven Gafni, *Our Legal-Historical Right to Eretz-Israel*, Jerusalem: Tora Ve'avoda Library, 1943 (in Hebrew). This study holds that whereas the Jews always maintained a historical, legal, and moral connection with the Land, "there is no nationalist spiritual connection between this land and the Arabs. They settled here as individual citizens out of economic interest . . . and therefore the Land of Israel has no national Arab history" (58). Years

Zionist historians were hard at work establishing and preserving the "Land of Israel" as the focus of Jewish experience. It was during this period that we see the beginning of efficient and consistent production of a new kind of collective identity that reshaped the Jewish past, making it more territorial. Because Jewish historiography—from Isaak Markus Jost, the modern period's first Jewish scholar of the past, to Simon Dubnow, the most important Jewish historian of his time—had been neither Palestinocentric nor Zionist, the historians from the Hebrew University had to expend great effort to wipe away its dangerously non-nationalist writings. At the same time, they also had not only to craft a narrative demonstrating that there had always been one Jewish people, which had originated in the Land of Israel, but also to counterbalance and expunge the long Jewish heritage that stood in opposition to the "return to Zion" as the national secular goal of world Jewry.

Early in this process, in order to entrench the conception of the Jewish right to the Land, major Zionist activists such as Israel Belkind, David Ben-Gurion, Yitzhak Ben-Zvi, and others attempted to prove that the Arabs of the country were ancient descendants of the Jews. However, the revolt of 1929 put a quick end to the "ethnoracial unification of these two components of the people." As a result, Ben-Zion Dinur and his colleagues took it upon themselves to convince the Jewish readership that between the destruction of the Temple and the modern period, there had been a more authentic Jewish presence in the Land of Israel. They argued that there had always been strong Jewish communities in the Land, which had been strengthened and expanded by waves of Jewish immigration over the generations. It was no simple matter to prove these questionable theses, but with a great deal of persuasiveness, a strong desire to believe in the righteousness of the approach, and the consistent support and funding of the Zionist establishment, the construction of this new past got under way and ultimately achieved full pedagogical success.

---

later, an Israeli historian reiterated this logic with the following words: "The uniqueness of this land throughout the generations was based only on the spirit of the People of Israel, and it is only because of this reality and this consciousness rooted in the People of Israel that we can speak of a history of the Land of Israel." In contrast to its original inhabitants who did not regard it as unique, "for the People of Israel . . . the land was made singular as a result of the Children of Israel's entry into it." Yaacov Shavit, "The Land of Israel as a Geographical-Historic Unit," in Israel Efal (ed.), *The History of Eretz Israel*, vol. 1, Jerusalem: Keter, 1982, 17 (in Hebrew).

The source that best reflects this blind drive to document a consistent Jewish presence in the supposed homeland as the basis for the Jewish right to the Land was the multivolume anthology *Sefer ha-Yishuv*, whose publication began in 1939.[44] The project was edited by Samuel Klein, the first important geographer at the Hebrew University of Jerusalem, and contained every shred of evidence of a Jewish presence in Palestine between 70 CE and 1882. In his introduction to the collection, Ben-Zion Dinur acknowledged that "ironically, the Land whose changes in destiny merge with the dispersed nation to form a single historical unit has not yet been paid the attention it deserves by the Jewish historiography."[45] This marked the beginning of the writing of a new history of both the people and the Land, the nature of which has changed little until today.

Dinur was not only a talented writer but also a multitrack agent of memory. He edited dozens of volumes and collections of documents, he published journals, and eventually he became a member of the Israeli Knesset and from 1951 to 1955 served as the young country's minister of education. An interview with Dinur provides a good overview of his ideological legacy. Published under the title "Our Right to the Land," the interview was subtitled "Arabs in the Land of Israel have all rights, but over the land of Israel they have no right," clarifying his theoretical doctrine and empirical claim.[46] Dinur's historical narrative was always lucid, and he returned to it at every opportunity. The Arabs had conquered the land in 634 CE and had remained in it as foreign occupiers ever since. The Jews, in contrast, had always held on to their homeland and never abandoned it, even if at times they were pushed into a corner within it. With historical and legal logic that might sound ironic to us today, this leader of the Zionist left and pioneer of Israeli historiography maintained:

Occupation does not create historical possession. An occupier's possession of the land he conquers is valid only if the owner of that

44   Samuel Klein (ed.), *Sefer ha-Yishuv*, vol 1: *From the Second Temple Period to the Arab Conquest of the Land of Israel*, Tel Aviv: Dvir, 1939 (in Hebrew).

45   Ibid., 9.

46   Ben-Zion Dinur, "Our Right to the Land," in Mordechai Cohen (ed.), *Chapters in the History of Eretz-Israel*, vol. 1, Tel Aviv: Ministry of Defense, 1981, 410–14 (in Hebrew). It is interesting to consider how Palestinians today might make use of the same sentence by replacing the word "Arabs" with "Jews."

land is absent and does not object to the theft for a long period of time. But if the owner was present on his land . . . pushed into a corner for hundreds of years, [this] does not detract from their rights [but] rather enhances them.[47]

The creators of a mythos are usually the first to believe in it. Indeed, the historians who worked alongside Dinur, all of whom were European immigrants and not "cornered" natives of Palestine, did not think otherwise. Yitzhak Baer, Gershom Scholem, Israel Heilprin, Joshua Prawer, Nahum Slouschz, and others employed their considerable talents in their respective fields of study to prove that Jewish history was never theological-religious but always teleological-nationalist. That is to say, it was never the long-term tale of a community of believers who adhered to unique rituals of worship, but rather the history of a nation that always strove to reach its supreme goal: return to the Land of Israel. Yitzhak Baer, the most prominent historian working alongside Dinur, articulated the essence of the Zionist narrative at the beginning of his professional career while interpreting the writings of the sixteenth-century Maharal of Prague with enthusiastic patriotism:

> God designated an inheritance of land for every people, and the People of Israel's inheritance is the Land of Israel. It is its natural place, and everything uprooted from its natural place loses its natural grasp until it returns to its place.[48]

This is not to say that there is no value in the many studies produced by these scholars over the course of many years. However, most of the conceptual mechanisms underlying "Land of Israel" studies have resulted in empirically defective achievements, calling into question their historiographical conclusions.

After a decade-long ideological campaign to incorporate a rights-oriented consciousness into the Zionist ethos, it is no wonder that the authors of Israel's Declaration of Independence in 1948 regarded it as self-evident that the establishment of the State of Israel in the Land of Israel was justified by their dual "natural and historical" right to the

---

47   Ibid., 410-411.
48   Yitzhak Baer, *Galut*, New York: Schocken Books, 1947, 118-19.

Land.[49] However, after the establishment and stabilization of the state, historians, archaeologists, philosophers, biblical scholars, and geographers continued to work to reinforce the historical right and its by-products, seeking to transform them into axioms—immune to all analytical efforts to disprove them.

From Ze'ev Jabotinsky through his heirs in the early twenty-first century, the intellectuals and politicians of the Zionist right wing have regarded their right to the land as self-evident and have made little effort to clarify it. However, it is important to emphasize that even they did not limit themselves to the philosophy of "right" in order to justify conquest of the land. The Revisionist stream of Zionism has always sincerely believed that history is a chronological framework in which nothing fundamental ever changes. Accordingly, the right to the land is conceptualized as an eternal right, which holds identical weight in the past, the present, and the future. For this reason, the territorial right remains intact from generation to generation, and will cease to exist only with the destruction of the planet. On this basis, Menachem Begin, Israel's prime minister in the late 1970s and early 1980s, was able to sum up this heritage with great simplicity: "We returned to the Land of Israel not by virtue of power but by virtue of right, and thank God we have the power to realize the right."[50]

In contrast to this unequivocal position, a more nuanced group of scholars affiliated with the Zionist left has for many years regarded the Jewish historical right to the Land as a problematic issue that is yet to be completely resolved. In every generation, self-persuasion has required repeated justification through complex moral rhetoric; it is not always an easy undertaking. For example, the historian Shmuel Ettinger has argued that a right may not have existed, but that the Jewish people's long-term affinity with the land—that is to say, the fact that over the course of thousands of years the Jews never forgot their land, saw the exile as an unnatural situation, and always sought to return to their place of origin—justified the revival and endowed it with validity. Despite his knowledge of the history of the Jewish faith,

---

49   The word "right" (*zekhut*) appears in the Israeli Declaration of Independence eight times. The right is natural, apparently because a portion of the Jewish people always "remained" in their land, and historical, because it belonged to them before they were "exiled" by force nineteen hundred years earlier.

50   Menachem Begin, "The Right That Created the Power," in Joseph Nedava (ed.), *Our Struggle for the Land of Israel*, Tel Aviv: Betar, 1986, 27 (in Hebrew).

Ettinger could proclaim, with scientific certainty: "In their religious creation and national thinking, the Land of Israel remained the important center, the heart of the Jewish nation."[51]

In contrast, Yehoshua Arieli, a historian commanding no less respect than Ettinger, established the premise that just as rights create affinity, affinity may also become rights. "On this basis, the historical affinity became a right by virtue of public international recognition [the Balfour Declaration and the Palestine Mandate] of the Zionist claim for the solution of the Jewish question."[52] The fact that "public international recognition" actually amounted to British and Western colonialism's recognition of its own actions, without regard for the indigenous population, was set aside when it was necessary to present a moral justification for Zionist colonization at any cost.

Political scientist Shlomo Avineri also typically preferred to highlight affinity rather than right:

> There is no doubt that we have a historical affinity to all parts of the historical Land of Israel, and this Land of Israel . . . includes not only Judea and Samaria and Gaza, but also areas that are not under our control today (is our affinity to Mount Nebo and Amman weaker than our affinity to Nablus?). However, not all places with which we have a connection must be under our political rule.[53]

To this, a shrewd settler from "Judea and Samaria" would most certainly have answered, "There is indeed no obligation to bring it under our political rule, but it is nonetheless desirable."

For this purpose, Saul Friedländer, an important Israeli historian, mobilized a more subjective rationale. In his opinion, the Jewish right to the land is sui generis,

---

51   Shmuel Ettinger, "Historic Uniqueness and Connection to the Land of Israel," in *Modern Anti-Semitism*, 260.

52   Yehoshua Arieli, *History and Politics*, Tel Aviv: Am Oved, 1992, 401 (in Hebrew). David Ben-Gurion already understood that this claim was not a strongly moral one when he wrote: "I am here by right. We are not here by virtue of the Balfour Declaration or the Palestine Mandate. We were here long before that . . . Only the Mandate power is here by virtue of the Mandate." From Ben-Gurion, "Israel's Declaration in Its Land" (testimony before the Anglo-American Committee of Inquiry), Jerusalem: The Jewish Agency, 1946, 4–5 (in Hebrew).

53   Shlomo Avineri, *Essays on Zionism and Politics*, Jerusalem: Keter, 1977, 66 (in Hebrew).

because the Jewish people define themselves as a people only by their ties to this land . . . During their entire existence in Diaspora for almost two thousand years, the Jews have felt driven out, dispersed, exiled from this ancestral land, which they longed to return to. This is unique in history. I think that such a strong bond, such a fundamental bond, gives this people a right to this land. Only the Jews have placed such a high value on it and considered it irreplaceable, even if for a time—and that time lasted centuries—they lived in other places.[54]

In addition to his problematic depiction of the temporary and the permanent in this partly historiographic, partly mythological assertion, Friedländer fails to notice that even if this was not his intention, his words served to bolster the ideology of the Jewish Israeli settlers in the occupied territories. He wrote these words just as the settlers were starting a national campaign to actualize their "strong bond" to the heart of their historic land by asking why they had a right to Tel Aviv, Jaffa and Haifa, the non-Jewish cities of the coastal plain, but not to ancient Jerusalem, Hebron, or Bethlehem.

Chaim Gans, a senior legal scholar, has pondered the question of historical right at length and, in a statement much more consistent with the Zionist narrative than with distributional justice, ultimately reduces the Jewish right to a "right to formative territories."[55] Fortunately for Zionism, its "formative territory" did not lie in the heart of England or central France, but rather in a colonial region populated only by powerless Arabs.

Contrary to the consensus that has taken form and deepened within Israeli society, particularly after the conquests of 1967, these scholars have all maintained that the Jews have connections to "the Land" in its entirety and have national rights in "the Land," but do not possess rights to all "the Land." This distinction may be important, as it stems from a moral sense of discomfort vis-à-vis ongoing control over a population that enjoys no rights, and yet it has never proved capable of translating itself into meaningful and effective politics. The

---

54   Mahmoud Hussein and Saul Friedländer, *Arabs and Israelis: A Dialogue*, New York: Holmes, 1975, 175–6.

55   Chaim Gans, *The Limits of Nationalism*, Cambridge: Cambridge University Press, 2003, 118.

primary reason for this was that most intellectuals of the later Zionist left failed to understand that, although religious connections did not necessarily have to be translated into rights, ties of ownership in patriotic garb did, as such rights are always included within the paradigms of ownership over homeland territories, and these paradigms are deeply embedded in all national pedagogies. That is to say, in the case of Israeli political culture, the area considered to constitute the Land of Israel is ultimately regarded as the property of the Jewish people, and abandoning parts of this imagined land is considered the equivalent of an owner of private property willingly giving up some of his assets. While such a scenario is of course possible, most people would agree that it is nonetheless rare and problematic.

Despite the rationalizing discourse that has accompanied it since its inception, Zionist colonization never spent much time on ethical nuances that had the potential to limit or even to entirely prevent its hold on the land. As with all other colonizations, the only boundaries that have restrained the Zionist enterprise have been those dictated by the limits of its own power, not those resulting from concessions or from the quest for pacific compromise with the local inhabitants.

We still know very little about the meaning of the "concession" of property in Zionist thought, which now brings us to two additional questions: (1) According to the Zionist imagination, what tracts of land have, without question, always belonged to the Jewish people? 2) What land did the nationalist vision deem sacred, and did this land ever have concrete borders?

ZIONIST GEOPOLITICS AND THE REDEMPTION OF THE LAND

Settlement Zionism, which borrowed the term "Land of Israel" from the Talmud, was not overly pleased with the borders it had been assigned by Jewish law. As already noted, the lines that cordoned off sacred land were short, extending only from Acre to Ashkelon. Furthermore, the land contained by these boundaries was not sufficiently contiguous to serve as a national homeland. For the *Olei Bavel* (traditionally, the "exiles" who "returned" from Babylonia), the Land of Israel did not include Gaza, Beit-She'an, Tzemah, Caesarea, and other places. The borders of the divinely promised land were much more enticing than those of the religious legal entity and possessed immense potential to evolve into a large Jewish country, a territory

worthy of its name, consistent with the vast areas of European colonization that existed at the beginning of the twentieth century.

In the book of Genesis, it is written: "On that day the Lord made
a covenant with Abram, saying, 'To your offspring I give this land,
from the river of Egypt to the great river, the river Euphrates" (15:18).
In this way, the authors of the first books of the Bible, who had most
likely come from Babylonia, incorporated part of their land of origin
into the theological Promised Land. It is interesting to note that these
lines of delineation were based on natural borders, in this case rivers.
And because different biblical texts were written by different authors
with different territorial imaginations, there are other borders delineated as well. In the book of Numbers, God promises Moses slightly
less impressive borders: from the Egypt River (Wadi El-Arish) via the
modern day Negev Desert to the Dead Sea, to modern-day Amman,
and from there, in a curved line, to the Druze Mountain in the Damascus basin, and then north to what is now the Lebanese city of Tyre (it
is not always easy to identify the sites; see, for example, Num. 34:3–12).
In the book of Joshua, we again read of a more generous version:
"Every place that the sole of your foot will tread upon I have given to
you, just as I promised to Moses. From the wilderness and this Lebanon as far as the great river, the river Euphrates, all the land of the
Hittites to the Great Sea toward the going down of the sun shall be
your territory" (1:3–4). The imagined kingdom of David and Solomon
also almost corresponds with the Promised Land, extending as far as
Mesopotamia (Psalms 60:2).[56]

When Heinrich Graetz wrote the first protonationalist history
book in the mid-nineteenth century, he invented a Jewish people in
the modern sense of the word and located the birth of this people in an
exotic and mysterious Middle Eastern land: "This strip of land was
Canaan (now known as Palestine), bordering Phoenicia to the south
and sitting on the coast of the Mediterranean."[57] The borders to which
this pioneering scholar refers are blurry and undefined, and so they
would remain for some time among the Zionists attending their annual
congresses at the turn of the twentieth century. The Lovers of Zion, the
first settlers, were also uncertain of the extent of their sacred land.

---

56   On this subject, see Moshe Brawer, *Israel's Boundaries: Past, Present and
Future*, Tel Aviv: Yavneh, 1988, 41–51 (in Hebrew).

57   *History of the Jews*, vol. 1 (1855), Tel Aviv: Jezreel, 1955, 5 (in Hebrew).

At the same time, in his *Book of the Land of Israel*, published in Jerusalem in 1883, Eliezer Ben-Yehuda, one of the inventors of the new Hebrew language, imagined his new land according to the "borders of the Torah of Moses," from Wadi El-Arish to Sidon, from Sidon to Mount Hermon, and from 52 degrees to 55 degrees in the east, for a total area of approximately 33.6 square kilometers.[58] In 1897 Israel Belkind, the first practical Zionist, drew a map of the Land of Israel that reached as far as Acre in the north, the Syrian Desert in the east, and the River of Egypt in the south: "The Jordan splits the Land of Israel into two different sections," asserted Belkind, whose assessment was subsequently adopted by most settlers of the period.[59] A geography syllabus compiled by the early Zionist teachers association offers an experimental model for homeland studies based on the same generous borders. The land depicted is large and wide, with a full Jordan River flowing powerfully down its middle.[60] In 1918 Zionist activists went one step further in demarcating the borders of the Land of Israel, this time in a somewhat more scientific manner, when David Ben-Gurion and Yitzhak Ben-Zvi decided to "reasonably and rationally" map the borders of their country, which, as might have been expected, were not consistent with the borders of small Palestine.

As far as the future founder of the State of Israel and his classmate were concerned, the borders of the biblical promise were too expansive and untenable, while the borders of the Talmudic commandment were too narrow and did not suit the natural state of the Land and the needs of a large nation. According to the two authors, the desired borders of the Land of Israel must be drawn objectively in accordance with physical, cultural, economic, and ethnographic considerations, as follows:

> In the west—the Mediterranean Sea . . . In the north—the Litani River, between Tyre and Sidon . . . In the south—the latitude line that passes diagonally from Rafiah to Aqaba—In the east—the Syrian Desert. The eastern border of the Land of Israel should not be precisely demarcated . . . As the destructive impact of the desert

---

58   Eliezer Ben-Yehuda, *The Book of the Land of Israel*, Jerusalem: Yoel Moshe Salomon, 1883, 1–2 (in Hebrew).

59   Quoted in Yoram Bar-Gal, *Moledet and Geography in One Hundred Years of Zionist Education*, Tel Aviv: Am Oved, 1993, 126 (in Hebrew).

60   Ibid., 34.

decreases . . . the Land's eastern borders will be diverted eastward, and the area of the Land of Israel will expand.[61]

In other words, it went without saying that the Land of Israel included the East Bank of the Jordan River up to Damascus and what would later be demarcated as Iraq, as well as the region of El-Arish (despite the fact that, according to the authors, this area was located outside of "Turkish Palestine"). What is important to note here is the fact that both banks of the Jordan River constitute one indivisible natural entity. These borders are neither ideological nor maximalist, claimed the authors, but are more realistic and more likely to accommodate the ingathering of the Jewish people.

Ben-Gurion and Ben-Zvi were both socialist revolutionaries at the time, and at this early stage in their political careers they paid little attention to diplomacy. On the other hand, the leaders of the Zionist movement were much more apprehensive and tended to be extremely cautious when expressing their views on the demarcation of the Jewish state they sought to establish. Nonetheless, the borders sketched by the two "left-wingers" were actually located well within the crystallizing national consensus. The same year that Ben-Gurion and Ben-Zvi wrote their book, Chaim Weizmann wrote a personal letter to his wife in which he expressed his support for the establishment of a Jewish state on both sides of the Jordan River. This state, which would cover sixty thousand square kilometers and would contain and control the sources of the river, was the only one he believed capable of maintaining the economic existence of the Jewish community in Palestine.[62]

In the Zionist memorandum submitted to the League of Nations in 1919, the movement's territorial claims were already largely consistent with the borders proposed by Ben-Gurion and Ben-Zvi one year

---

61   David Ben-Gurion and Yitzhak Ben-Zvi, *The Land of Israel in the Past and in the Future*, Jerusalem: Yad Ben-Zvi, 1980, 46 (in Hebrew). In *Memoirs*, which Ben-Gurion wrote years later, he explains that "during all periods, the northern region of Transjordan, which the Sykes-Picot Agreement allocated to France, was an integral part of the Land of Israel . . . The growth of the Jewish population in the Land of Israel will increase its inhabitants' connection to the crops brought from Transjordan." *Memoirs*, vol. 1, Tel Aviv: Am Oved, 1977, 164–5 (in Hebrew).

62   The letter, dated June 17, 1918, is quoted in Eliezer Pney Gil, "Conceptions of Borders of Eretz Israel," M.A. thesis, Tel Aviv University, 1983, 7 (in Hebrew).

earlier. Here, too, the Jewish land is envisioned as containing Trans-jordan, but only up to the Hejaz Railway, that is to say, up to the line extending from Damascus to Amman.[63] When, during a closed session of the Zionist Action Committee, Weizmann was criticized for his willingness to accept these "narrow" borders, the leader, who the following year would become president of the Zionist Organization, responded thus:

> The borders we proposed provide us with enough space. Let us first fill the space within our borders. It will take a generation of Jewish settlement for us to reach the Hejaz Railway. Once we reach it, we will be able to cross it.[64]

In 1937, when Samuel Klein, the father of Israeli geography, wrote his influential book *The History of the Study of the Land of Israel in the Jewish and General Literature*, the cartographer in him was struck by the fact that the Bible reflected "scientific precision in demarcating the borders of the Land as well." For him, as for his readers, it was clear that the land of Canaan was only the "western Land of Israel,"[65] and almost all future geographers of the State of Israel would follow suit in this assessment. Indeed, in the year 2000, a senior expert on borders from Tel Aviv University would still feel comfortable using this "scientific" term, which he perceived as a fully professional geographic term, not as a needless expression of linguistic politics.[66]

Israeli readers today will certainly find it strange to learn that from the end of the nineteenth century until at least the 1967 Six-Day

---

63   Itzhak Galnoor, *The Partition of Palestine: Decision Crossroads in the Zionist Movement*, Albany: SUNY Press, 1995, 37–9. In a 1921 tourist book ordered by the Land of Israel Express Company, the Hejaz railway already appears as the natural border of the land of the Jews. See Yeshayahu Peres, *The Land of Israel and Its Southern Secret*, Jerusalem, Berlin, Vienna: Hertz, 1921, 19 (in Hebrew).

64   Quoted in Yigal Eilam, "Political History, 1918–1922," in Moshe Lissak (ed.), *The History of the Jewish Yishuv in Eretz Israel since the First Aliyah*, vol. 1, Jerusalem: Bialik, 1993, 161 (in Hebrew).

65   Samuel Klein, *The History of the Study of the Land of Israel in the Jewish and General Literature*, Jerusalem: Bialik, 1937, 3 (in Hebrew). See also A. J. Brawer, *The Land: A Book to Study the Land of Israel*, Tel Aviv: Dvir, 1927, 4 (in Hebrew).

66   Gideon Biger, *Land of Many Boundaries: The First Hundred Years of the Delimitation of the New Boundaries of Palestine–Eretz Israel, 1840–1947*, Sede Boqer: Ben-Gurion University, 2001, 15 (in Hebrew).

War, the term "Land of Israel" as used in the Zionist tradition always included the East Bank of the Jordan River and the Golan Heights. The logic behind this understanding was simple, and Ben-Gurion explained it with great clarity:

> The view voiced at times even among Zionists that Transjordan is not the Land of Israel is based on a complete lack of knowledge of the history of the nature of the country. It is known that the Hebrews' hold over the east side of the Jordan preceded their conquest of the west side of the Jordan.[67]

According to the biblical mythos, two and a half tribes of Israel settled east of the Jordan, and David and Solomon ruled there as well. Therefore, from the perspective of Jewish history, this region was no less important than the west bank of the river, not to mention the coastal lowlands of Palestine-Canaan, which, as we know, were of no special interest to the ancient children of Israel. Economic interests also suggested the desirability of controlling the water sources on both banks of the Jordan.

In the early stages of Jewish national territorial imagination, the Jordan River served not as a dividing border but as a water course linking two parts of one united land. For this reason, the common terminology used in all Zionist academic and political literature spoke of a "western Land of Israel" and an "eastern Land of Israel," while the "Whole Land of Israel" constituted a single geographical entity that encompassed both. In this context, withdrawal from any part of this Land was regarded as a painful national concession.

Indeed, even if the primary colonization efforts were carried out in the relatively greener and more fertile western Land of Israel, some took place to the east of the Jordan, primarily in the north. From Laurence Oliphant, the first Christian Zionist (mentioned in the previous chapter), to Charles Warren, another active Christian Zionist, and the Baron Edmond de Rothschild, some even assigned a degree of priority to colonization across the Jordan. One fifth of the

---

67   David Ben-Gurion, "The Borders of Our Land" (1918), in *We and Our Neighbors*, 41. Even after 1967, Benjamin Akzin, a legal scholar from the Hebrew University in Jerusalem, continued to assert that "we conceded the eastern part of the Land of Israel, despite our rights to it." *Tfutzot Hagolah* (1975), 27 (in Hebrew).

lands purchased by the baron himself were located east of the river, where land was cheaper and more readily available, the population was less dense, and foreign settlement attracted less attention. By 1888, a temporary settlement had been established east of the Sea of Galilee by a settlement group known as Bnei Yehuda, and in 1891 an attempt was made to settle on land east of the Druze Mountain. Various associations began to purchase land, primarily in the southern Golan Heights and the region northeast of the Jordan; only the exclusion of the Golan Heights in 1920 from the area under British rule halted attempts to settle there. The severing of Transjordan from the British Mandate for Palestine in 1922 caused great disappointment in the Zionist camp. The fact that the Jewish national home now did not include the areas east of the river caused major grievances but did not counteract the Zionists' territorial appetite for a large country. The Zionists' prevailing assumption was that the partition was only temporary and would eventually be annulled. In 1927 a large electricity production plant was built at Naharayim, where the Yarmuk River flows into the Jordan, and a Jewish settlement established right next door. In the 1920s, hopes for Jewish colonization in the Whole Land of Israel had still not disappeared.[68]

The dream of a large biblical homeland sustained a powerful blow from the violent clashes of 1929 and was further traumatized by the outbreak of the Arab Revolt in 1936. As a result of the massive uprising of the native population of Palestine, the British government appointed the Peel Commission to investigate the cause of the violence and to propose countermeasures. In 1937, despite the great Zionist lobbying effort to the contrary, the commission reached the conclusion that Palestine had to be partitioned.[69]

After the "concession" of the "eastern Land of Israel" in 1922, the loss of large portions of the "western Land of Israel" was considered intolerable within the Zionist movement. Prominent intellectuals from the Jewish community in Palestine immediately voiced their

---

68   For a comprehensive account of all the settlement efforts undertaken east of the Jordan River and the territorial dreams that accompanied them, see Zvi Ilan, *Attempts at Jewish Settlement in TransJordan, 1871–1947*, Jerusalem: Yad Ben-Zvi, 1984 (in Hebrew).

69   The proposal to establish a Jewish state and an Arab state required, according to the full Report of the Palestine Royal Commission, a population exchange that would have seen 225,000 Arabs and only 1,250 Jews displaced from their homes.

opposition. Major political figures and factions who joined forces to oppose the partition included Menachem Ussishkin, Ze'ev Jabotinsky, Berl Katznelson, Yitzhak Tabenkin, the Zionist left, and the religious Zionists. More pragmatic leaders such as David Ben-Gurion and Chaim Weizmann not only called for accepting the Peel proposal but even succeeded in convincing the twentieth Zionist Congress to half-heartedly approve the plan, primarily because of the difficult conditions facing European Jewry at the time.[70]

Their logic was similar to Herzl's rationale during the Uganda debate. They held that it was better to get a small Jewish state then and there than to risk what had already been achieved through colonization. Furthermore, the Zionist movement had little choice. At this stage of the national enterprise, only close military and diplomatic cooperation with the British rulers could repel and suppress the rebellion of the local population, which lasted for three years and was aimed simultaneously at both the foreign colonial power and the steadily expanding community of Zionist colonizers.

This did not mean, however, that the supporters of partition had given up their dream of gaining control over the Whole Land of Israel. When asked about the parts of the country that had not been included in the Jewish area of control, Chaim Weizmann pointed out, with his unique brand of humor, that they were not going anywhere. Soon after the twentieth congress, Ben-Gurion, who by this point was serving as chair of the Jewish Agency executive, told the British press: "The debate has not been for or against the indivisibility of Eretz Israel. No Zionist can forego the smallest portion of Eretz Israel. The debate was over which of two routes would lead quicker to the common goal."[71]

In the overall balance of considerations in 1937, as would be true of the UN partition plan a decade later, the possibility of achieving a

---

70 On the arguments for and against the proposal, see Shmuel Dothan's comprehensive book *The Partition of Eretz-Israel in the Mandatory Period: The Jewish Controversy*, Jerusalem: Yad Ben-Zvi, 1979 (in Hebrew).

71 Quoted in Christopher Sykes, *Crossroads to Israel: Palestine from Balfour to Bevin*, London: New English Library, 1967, 212. At a June 7, 1938, meeting of the Jewish Agency executive, Ben-Gurion explicitly stated that he ultimately intended to annul the partition and to expand into the entire Land of Israel, based, of course, on "Arab-Jewish agreement." See excerpt from the meeting minutes in Efraim Karsh, *Fabricating Israeli History: The New Historians*, London: Frank Cass, 1997, 44.

sovereign Jewish majority was more enticing than the long-term actu-alization of the mythos of the Whole Land. In the late 1930s, Zionist leaders from the movement's central stream began to exercise extreme caution and reached the conclusion that it was now better "to refrain from talking about maps." The mythos of the land continued to guide Zionist politics and yet by 1967 had still not replaced it. Another equally decisive and mobilizing ethos limited the historical aim: the construction of an "ethnic" nation, living in its own sovereign state, that did not risk assimilation or integration within the great mass of local inhabitants. Jewish immigration to Palestine had initially been quite modest compared with the mass immigration to the West. Faced with the subsequent extermination of European Jewry, Zionism's territorial fervor temporarily cooled, and its leaders learned to conduct more balanced politics.

Their willingness to accept narrowed borders was therefore, in essence, a product of pragmatic and flexible tactics and a function of fundamental "ethnocentric" policy. In the long run it proved to be the more effective strategy. Thus, diplomacy can be seen as merely a sophisticated political translation of the colonizing principle of "another *dunam*, another goat" (one *dunam* = one thousand square meters) that had directed Zionist conquest of the land from the outset. Creating facts on the ground has been a guiding principle of Zionist policy from the outset, and it remains so today.

Colonization itself got off to a slow start in the late nineteenth century.[72] Carried out in the shadow of the sweeping and mobiliz-ing image known as redemption of the land, it was, in practice, a cautious, calculated, multiphase enterprise. Like other key guiding concepts within the Zionist ethos—such as the "Land of Israel," to which a Jew could only "ascend" (*oleh*) and never "immigrate"—the purchase and initial cultivation of land was referred to by a mythicized term, "redemption of the land." In the Jewish tradition, the word "redemption" signified salvation and rebirth, cleanliness and purity, and the liberation of prisoners from enemy hands. This

---

72   In the mid-1890s, the number of Jewish settlers in Palestine stood at 2,000. This can be compared to the 1,400 Templar settlers living in the area at the time. Ran Aaronsohn, "The Scope and Character of the First Wave of New Jewish Settlement in Eretz-Israel (1882–1890)," in Yehoshua Ben-Arieh, Yossi Ben-Artzi, and Haim Goren (eds.), *Historical-Geographical Studies in the Settlement of Eretz Israel*, Jerusalem: Yad Ben-Zvi, 1987, 9–10 (in Hebrew).

triple meaning injected power into the psychological needs of the new immigrants, who became more than simply tillers of the soil. After all, the petty bourgeoisie, even those who are poverty stricken, never seek to turn themselves into farmers. No: they had come to redeem land that had become desolate and abandoned following the exile of their ancestors some nineteen hundred years earlier.

The few immigrant-settlers who arrived in Palestine beginning in the 1880s were a mixture of traditional Jews and young men and women saturated with the radical populism prevalent in Russia at the time. Both groups commonly invoked the term "redemption," along with its enveloping aura. By the late 1880s a small association known as the Redeemers of Zion had been established, and the 1887 program of the Lovers of Zion asserted "that the essence of redeeming the country is the purchase of land [karka`] and its redemption from gentiles."[73]

The term grew increasingly entrenched during subsequent waves of immigration, particularly among the young idealists. In Zionism, the redemption of the enslaved farmer that was characteristic of Russian populist romance was replaced by the redemption of the land itself. For the "pioneers," land became a focus of mystical and even sexual desire.[74] The land was therefore conceived as having been metaphorically empty until the long-awaited arrival of the pioneers coming to redeem it. The overarching image of a desolate land was integral to the redemption process. Desolation signified a special, boundless, virginal environment enthusiastically awaiting the *yishuv* (the organized Zionist community in Palestine) to penetrate and fertilize it. According to this conception, the abandoned land was a dismal combination of desert and swamp until the historic moment of being entered by the pioneers.[75] Even if "foreign" peasant farmers

73 Quoted in Shmuel Almog, "Redemption in Zionist Rhetoric," in Ruth Kark (ed.), *Redemption of the Land of Eretz Israel: Ideology and Practice*, Jerusalem: Yad Ben-Zvi, 1990, 16 (in Hebrew).

74 See Ruth Kark, "Land and the Idea of Land Redemption in Traditional Culture and in The Land of Israel," *Karka* 31 (1989), 22-35 (in Hebrew). See also Boaz Neumann, *Land and Desire in Early Zionism*, Tel Aviv: Am Oved, 2009 (in Hebrew).

75 On the role of wilderness in the Zionist conception and its association with the desert, see Yael Zerubavel, "The Desert As a Mythical Space and Site of Memory in Hebrew Culture," in M. Idel and I. Grunwald (eds.), *Myths in Jewish Culture*, Jerusalem: Zalman Shazar, 2004, 227-32 (in Hebrew).

were living in the Jewish region, they were not likely to make the wasteland bloom, for they were, in essence, limited and backward. They also did not truly love the Land, as only the Zionists were capable of doing.

For all Zionist leaders and most Zionist intellectuals, it was more convenient to imagine themselves not as conquerors of foreign lands but as saviors of the Land of Israel, which had always been theirs. Aaron David Gordon, a major thinker of the Zionist labor movement, effectively defined this still-evolving mythos in 1912:

> What are we coming to do in the Land of Israel? To redeem (for our purposes, it makes no difference whether in the broad or the narrow sense of the word) and to revive the People. These, however, are not two separate aims, but two aspects of the same thing. The Land cannot be redeemed without reviving the People, and the People cannot be revived without redeeming the Land. The monetary purchase of land cannot be redemption in the national sense as long as it is not cultivated by Jews.[76]

From 1905 onward, the new emphasis on the value of redemption inherent in labor itself was reflective of a new generation of socialist immigrants. It also expressed indirect criticism of the tendency of inhabitants of the colonies supported by Edmond de Rothschild, as well as other Jewish settlers, to employ primarily seasonal non-Jewish workers. Zionist criticism of this sort now became part of the consensus within the settlement enterprise, and perhaps therein lies the secret of its success: redemption could not be achieved through the use of Arab labor.

The colonizations of the modern era have accommodated many different types of territorial control. Long ago, scholars divided European settlement into a number of categories: occupation colonies of a conquering army (for example, India and large parts of Africa), mixed colonies of settlers and locals (Latin America), plantation colonies (the southern United States, South Africa, Algeria, and Kenya), and pure "ethnic" settlement colonies (the Puritans in the northeastern United States, the British in Australia and New Zealand). Clearly,

---

76 A.D. Gordon, *Letters and Writings*, Jerusalem: Hassifriya Hazionit, 1954, 51 (in Hebrew).

these are only archetypes. In reality, the models were not absolute and there were many intermediate cases.[77]

The Jewish colonization of the 1880s began as a mixture of the plantation model and the pure model. The first *moshavot* (Hebrew for "colonies," and the name of the first settlements established in Palestine) initially refrained from integrating with the local population but were quickly forced to rely on them to an increasing extent. In some ways the Zionist settlement process resembled various phases of the European colonization of Algeria, which was already under way during this period. For this reason, Baron de Rothschild could fit into its plans with relative ease, and although the financial assistance he provided had initially saved the very existence of the Jewish settlements, he would later condition funding on streamlining and productivity, thus forcing them to become profitable. These measures made certain sectors of agricultural cultivation dependent on inexpensive labor, which the "natives" could supply and with which the "pioneers" could not compete. As a result, significant numbers of settlers were forced to leave Palestine and immigrate to the countries of the West.

Ultimately, the solution was the new wave of radical young immigrants, who were in fact particles of radical circles shed through the centrifugal force of the 1905 Russian Revolution. During this wave of immigration, it was understood that redemption of the land had to be combined with the conquest of labor. This led to the emergence of a pure colony model that, on the one hand, was based on an ethnocentric mythos and, on the other hand, expressed the basic economic need for the promotion of colonization.

Gershon Shafir, an Israeli-born sociologist who lives and works in the United States, was the first to effectively analyze and to discuss clearly and in great detail the attributes of this new and original form of settlement.[78] In addition to the communal-collectivist ethos that the immigrants brought with them from the revolutionary storm in Russia, the Prussian model implemented in Germany during the second half of the nineteenth century played a major role. The

---

77 For more on this, see David Kenneth Fieldhouse, *The Colonial Empires: A Comparative Survey from the Eighteenth Century*, London: Macmillan Press, 1982.

78 Gershon Shafir, *Land, Labor and the Origins of the Israeli-Palestinian Conflict, 1882-1914*, Cambridge: Cambridge University Press, 1989.

government of the Second Reich, balking at the immigration of German-speaking farmers to the cities and to the United States and their gradual replacement by Polish farmers, began to finance the settlement of "more German" tillers of the soil in ethnically "threatened" regions.

German Jewish sociologist Franz Oppenheimer learned from this historical experience. After visiting Palestine in 1910, he was infected with enthusiasm regarding "the new race of Jewish masters" that was emerging in Palestine and was capable of behaving aggressively toward the Arabs.[79] And because the Zionist Organization lacked the means enjoyed by the German rulers, he recommended that his Zionist colleagues adopt the ethnocommunal settlement model, which he regarded as a general solution to the contradictions of unchecked capitalism throughout the world.

Against the background of the Zionist movement's treading of water during the period in question, Oppenheimer's pioneering national-cooperative project was warmly received. Zionist institutions quickly adopted the idea of having communal groups of settlers. Despite initial failures, this practice began its slow evolution into the settlement framework that would later come to be known as the kibbutz movement. The kibbutz—crowning achievement of redemption of the land—was not only a product of the egalitarian idealism that young settlers brought with them from Russia and that provided psychological fuel for sacrifice and effort. It was also a historical product engendered by two local economic needs: (1) the need to create a production sector that was closed to the competitive labor market (that is, to less expensive Arab laborers); and (2) the need for collective settlement of the land, in a context where settlements based on nuclear families were particularly difficult to sustain (because of the relatively dense and often hostile local population).

Oppenheimer's model worked. From the outset, kibbutz land was not private but rather belonged to the World Zionist Organization's Jewish National Fund (*Keren Kayemeth le-Israel*), and was thus the property of the "nation." It could not be sold, and could be leased only to Jews. In 1908 a Jaffa-based bureau known as the Palestine Office, agent of the Zionist Organization, began to serve as the body responsible for purchasing most of the land. Arthur Ruppin, a talented and

---

79   Almog, "Redemption in Zionist Rhetoric," 29.

accomplished man who, more than any other Zionist leader, was responsible for the growth of the landed assets of the "nation," was appointed as head of the new institution.[80]

After the First World War, and especially after the 1920 establishment of the General Federation of Hebrew Workers in the Land of Israel, or Histadrut, the kibbutz movement, which had always consisted of a select minority of the Jewish population, became the spearhead of the young settler society. The role of the kibbutz as the most dynamic redeemer of land earned it a hegemonic status that it maintained for decades to come, even after the establishment of the State of Israel, and its security role as a military stronghold in frontier regions added to its elite status. Until the 1967 war, the cream of the country's Jewish political, cultural, and military elite came from the kibbutzim and skillfully defended the movement's achievements. However, after fulfilling its historical role, this form of settlement ended up in the waste bin of history. The new settlements established after 1967 would be based on a different kind of ideology and on government financial assistance.

It is important to remember not only that land, once purchased for the Jewish nation, could not revert to non-Jewish ownership, but that the kibbutz, with its egalitarian lifestyle, did not accept members of the local population into its ranks. That is to say, under no circumstances could an Arab join a kibbutz. And later, when the occasional female kibbutz member wished to live with a Palestino-Israeli, she was usually forced to leave the pioneering collective.[81] In this way, Zionist communal socialism served as one of the most effective mechanisms for maintaining a pure settler society, not only by means of its exclusive practices but also as a moral model for the society as a whole.

The struggle to exclude Arab labor from the Zionist labor market did not end with the creation of cooperative producer collectives. All

---

80   See Ruppin's description of the idea of kibbutz in his 1924 article "The Group" (*Ha-Kvutsa*) in *Thirty Years of Building Eretz Israel*, Jerusalem: Schoken, 1937, 121-9. For an English version of this book, see Arthur Ruppin, *Three Decades of Palestine: Speeches and Papers on the Upbuilding of the Jewish National Home*, Westport, Connecticut: Greenwood Press, 1936.

81   The kibbutzim of Hashomer Hatzair, the Marxist-Zionist movement that supported a binational state with a Jewish majority, were also unwilling to accept Arabs as members.

other settlements that were established—agricultural and urban alike—were also exclusively for Jews. In addition to this intentional politics of segregation, an intensive political/ideological campaign, carried out under the slogan of "Hebrew labor" (*avoda ivrit*), was initiated in all production sectors of the Zionist community. Employers in all sectors of the economy felt heavy pressure to refrain from hiring Arabs, regardless of the circumstances. During the very same years that propaganda in Germany was calling for the dismissal of Jews from their positions and the closure of Jewish stores (*Juden raus!*), Mandatory Palestine was the site of a comprehensive and public Zionist campaign against all economic interaction with the local population. In both instances, the campaigns were more effective than expected. As a result, many new Jewish immigrants arrived in Palestine in the 1930s, by which point two almost completely separate market economies had emerged: one Jewish, and the other Arab.[82]

The bulk of the struggle was conducted by the Histadrut, an organization meant exclusively for Jews (that opened its doors to Palestino-Israelis only in 1966). The Histadrut was not merely a labor union; it was an all-encompassing framework that established and maintained a broad assortment of enterprises, directed public works, provided medical and banking services, and served other functions as well. Known also as the Society of Workers (Hevrat ha-Ovdim), the Histadrut functioned as the power base of the Zionist left wing until the late 1970s and evolved over time into a kind of state within a state.

It is important to remember that this left wing—both the labor federation and the political left—did not come into existence through the same process that produced the European left: that is, through a conflict between capital and labor. Rather, it was born out of the needs of the "conquest of the land" and the construction of pure national

---

82 The comparison implied by the above sentences applies only to the ethnocentric politics of segregation of the 1930s and should by no means be understood as suggesting an analogy between the Nazi extermination campaign of the 1940s and the Zionist settlement enterprise, which was and always remained devoid of any trace of the idea of exterminating the other. On the idea and the practices of "Hebrew labor" that were already being implemented in the 1920s, see Anita Shapira, *The Futile Struggle: The Jewish Labor Controversy, 1929–1939*, Tel Aviv: Hakibbutz Hameuchad, 1977 (in Hebrew). Originally Shapira's doctoral dissertation, it is interesting despite its pervasive apologetic tone.

colonies. For this reason, a social democratic movement with a broad working-class base never emerged within the Zionist community or, subsequently, in Israel. The morality of the Zionist left has always been purely in-group, and could therefore always adhere openly and uninhibitedly to biblical morality. In truth, the Zionist left never had a deeply rooted tradition of universalism, and it is this, among other things, that helps explain its rapid divestment from all values of social equality with the demise of its hegemony toward the end of the twentieth century.

Zionist colonization was a unique process of colonization, in that it was carried out by a national movement that was not at first politically and economically dependent on an imperialist mother country.[83] Until 1918 it achieved its foothold in the Land without assistance from local authorities and, at times, despite their opposition. Although the British Mandate created a political and military umbrella that facilitated and sheltered the expansion of the Zionist community in Palestine, it had significant limitations. The main drive behind Zionist colonization also differed from other colonizing projects in that economic gain was not a primary motivation. Palestinian land was expensive, and the more the Zionist movement purchased, the higher its price rose. Land purchase, too, was uniquely problematic in comparison to other settlement enterprises. Some land, known in Arabic as *mushā*, was not truly private property; it was cooperatively cultivated by a village collective. The land available for purchase was for the most part large estates held by wealthy effendis who lived elsewhere, and purchasing land from them required the expulsion of tenants who until then had cultivated and lived on it. Indeed, this is what happened in practice, as vividly described in Yitzhak Epstein's 1907 essay that warned the Zionist movement of the dangers involved in dispossession.

The creeping agrarian reform that took place in Palestine between 1882 and 1947 had the same overall effect as similar reforms in other parts of the world: the transfer of land ownership from the few to the many. However, in Palestine this flow of landed property went from the indigenous population to the settler community. On this basis, 291

---

83   For an interesting comparison between Zionist colonization and other colonizing processes, see Ilan Pappé, "Zionism as Colonialism: A Comparative View of Diluted Colonialism in Asia and Africa," *South Atlantic Quarterly* 107:4 (2008), 611–33.

thriving Jewish agricultural settlements were established by 1947. Still, we must also remember that by 1937, Zionist institutions had purchased only 5 percent of all the cultivable private land in Mandatory Palestine, which was concentrated for the most part on the coastal plain and in the internal valleys. By the time partition was officially endorsed by the United Nations in November 1947, only 11 percent of all land in the country, and 7 percent of all the cultivated land, had been brought under Jewish ownership.

On the eve of the passage of the UN partition resolution, David Ben-Gurion wrote the following lines in his personal journal:

> The Arab world, the Arabs of the Land of Israel with the help of one, some, or possibly all the Arab countries . . . are likely to attack the *yishuv* . . . We must . . . defend the *yishuv* and the settlements and conquer all or a large portion of the Land, and maintain the occupation until the achievement of an authorized political settlement.[84]

Although the pragmatic statesman's foresight in this case was much more applicable to the post-1967 reality than that of post-1948, the war of the late 1940s and the Israeli land policy implemented in its wake brought about the complete transformation of land tenure relations in the country.

FROM INTERNAL SETTLEMENT TO EXTERNAL COLONIZATION

The Zionist community was overjoyed by the 1947 resolution regarding the partition of Palestine and the establishment of a Jewish state. A mere two years had elapsed since the end of the epic massacre of European Jewry, and tens of thousands of refugees who were refused permission to immigrate were still living in temporary camps, mostly in Germany (the author of this book was born and spent the first few years of his life in one such camp). The Western countries found it convenient to get rid of the Jewish refugees by channeling them to the Middle East. This was the hour of opportunity for stagnant Zionism. Despite the brutal anti-Jewish persecution that characterized the period, only half a million immigrants had arrived in Palestine

---

84   Quoted in Michael Bar-Zohar, *Ben-Gurion: A Political Biography*, vol. 2, Tel Aviv: Am Oved, 1978, 663 (in Hebrew).

between 1924, when the United States all but closed its gates to immigration, and 1947, when the number of Jews in Mandatory Palestine reached approximately 630,000. At the same time, the country's Arab population totaled more than one and a quarter million.

Although in retrospect it did not turn out to be in their best interest, the Arabs' refusal to support the partition of their country and to recognize the Jewish state was logical and understandable. Very few populations around the world would have agreed to be colonized by land-hungry foreigners who were slowly acquiring pieces of their territory, who were unwilling to live together with them, and who aspired to establish their own nation-state. Moreover, the UN partition plan granted only 45 percent of the land area of British Mandate Palestine to its 1.25 million "native" inhabitants, while the settler population was allocated 55 percent of the land. Even though some of the Jewish area consisted of desert, it would seem clear, based on the demographic relationship between Arabs and Jews at the time, that the partition was unlikely to be considered just by those against whom it discriminated.

Equally absurd from the perspective of the venerable inhabitants of Palestine was the fact that, under the original UN plan, the large landholdings of some 400,000 Arabs, or approximately one third of Palestine's Arab population, would have ended up within the borders of the proposed Jewish state. It is an irony of history that, had it not been for the 1948 war, which truly was initiated by Arab leaders, the newly established State of Israel would have to have included a large Arab minority that would have gained strength with the passage of time, ultimately counteracting the state's Jewish isolationist nature and possibly even its very existence. It seems unlikely that the new state would have initiated sweeping mass expulsions without military conflict. It also seems unlikely that hundreds of thousands of Arab inhabitants would have fled had it not been for the fierce battles.

For years, Zionist rhetoric attempted to convince the world in general and the supporters of Zionism in particular that the Arabs of Palestine had fled in response to their leaders' propaganda. Since the publication of studies by Simha Flapan, Benny Morris, Ilan Pappé, and others,[85] however, we know this was not the case—the

---

85   Simha Flapan, *The Birth of Israel: Myths and Realities*, New York: Pantheon Books, 1987; Benny Morris, *The Birth of the Palestinian Refugee Problem Revisited*,

leaders of the local population did not recommend its departure, and the Nakba was certainly not carried out on the advice of Arab leaders. Many Palestinians fled out of fear, and the Jewish forces used a variety of methods to encourage them to do so (for a better understanding of this process, see the afterword of the present book). Many were loaded directly onto trucks and taken as far away as possible. All in all, more than four hundred villages were destroyed and close to seven hundred thousand inhabitants—more than the entire Jewish population of the country at the time—became homeless refugees.

The debate that has played out in recent years, which has focused on determining whether the majority of Palestinians chose to leave "willingly" or were in fact expelled, is important but, in my view, not of decisive significance. The debate over whether the "ethnic cleansing" was systematic or only spontaneous and partial is also important from the perspective of history and propaganda, but is less relevant than the fundamental ethical premise that families of refugees fleeing whizzing bullets and falling bombs are entitled to the basic human right to return to their homes once hostilities end. Yet it is widely known (and on this point, there is no academic debate) that, since 1949, Israel has adamantly refused to allow the refugees to return, even though most did not take part in the fighting.[86] In addition to this categorical refusal, the young State of Israel quickly enacted the 1950 Law of Return—a law that enables all who can prove they are Jewish to immigrate to Israel and receive immediate and full citizenship, even if they are full citizens of their own countries and have not been persecuted because of their religion or ethnic origin. Moreover, even if they subsequently choose to return to their country of origin, these Jewish immigrants to the State of Israel do not forfeit their rights in their "historic homeland."

Cambridge: Cambridge University Press, 2004; Ilan Pappé, *The Ethnic Cleansing of Palestine*, London: Oneworld, 2006. See also Uri Ben-Eliezer, *The Emergence of Israeli Militarism, 1936–1956*, Tel Aviv: Dvir, 1995, 232–79 (in Hebrew). It should be noted that these scholars were preceded by Palestinian scholars, who repeatedly stressed these facts over the years.

86   On Israel's refusal to allow the return of refugees, see Morris, *The Birth of the Palestinian Refugee Problem Revisited*, 309–40. On Israel's hesitant and evasive agreement, under heavy American pressure, to allow the return of 100,000 of the 700,000 refugees see pp. 570–80 of the same source.

During the 1948 war, the young state was also able to significantly modify the borders it had been assigned by the UN resolution. The newly occupied territories were not returned with the signing of the armistice agreement but instead were immediately annexed. In this context, it is important to remember that although the Zionist institutions accepted the idea of partition and the establishment of the State of Israel, it is no coincidence that its borders are not mentioned in the Israeli Declaration of Independence. By the end of the 1948 war, Israel controlled 78 percent of Mandatory Palestine, or the "western Land of Israel."[87] More important than the expansion of its borders, however, was the "disappearance" of the Arabs—the true miracle for which the new country had been waiting, even if it had not truly been planned.

Despite the flight and expulsion of seven hundred thousand Palestinians, a hundred thousand miraculously managed to remain in place throughout the entire war, and some forty thousand others either returned to their homes during the implementation of the armistice agreements or succeeded in crossing back over the border soon after. These "fortunate" Arabs, who had become a minority in their country overnight, received Israeli citizenship as explicitly required by the UN partition resolution, but most were forced to live under a strict system of military government until the end of 1966. Cut off from the Jewish immigrant population, which continued to expand, they were left isolated in a pale of settlement that they were permitted to leave only after receiving the military's authorization. Their movements were restricted, and their chances of finding employment far from home became infinitesimal. This state of affairs, in addition to Israeli legislation that specifically bars civil marriages between people classified as Jews and non-Jews, enabled the Zionist state to continue its successful implementation of its policy of pure "ethnic" colonization.[88]

---

87   The partition recommended by the Peel Commission allocated the Jewish state an area of approximately 5,000 square kilometers, and the UN partition plan of 1947 envisioned the establishment of a Jewish state on 14,000 square kilometers of Mandatory Palestine. In contrast, the 1949 armistice lines contained 21,000 square kilometers; today, at the time of writing, Israel controls 28,000 square kilometers, an area larger than British Mandate Palestine but still a far cry from the 1918 vision of Ben-Gurion and his associates.

88   The military government operated on the basis of the Defence (Emergency) Regulations, which Israel inherited from the pre-1948 colonial British regime. For more on the situation of Palestino-Israelis during this period, consult Sabri Jiryis's

As the hostilities of the 1948 war continued, kibbutzim spontaneously seized the abandoned fields of their former Arab neighbors who had fled or were expelled from their homes and villages, and their abundant crops were harvested by new cultivators. Israel established settlements outside the borders of the partition plan even before the end of the war, and by August 1949, 133 such settlements were already in existence. A bit later came the beginnings of the massive nationalization of "absentee" property—a legal classification applied not only to external refugees but to many Palestinian Arabs who remained in Israel as citizens, and who therefore came to be referred to by the oxymoronic term "present absentees." By means of the Absentee Property Law of 1950, the state expropriated some two million *dunams*, representing approximately 40 percent of all privately-held Arab land. At the same time, the Israeli legislature took measures to ensure the legal transfer of all state land of British Mandate Palestine (amounting to 10 percent) to the state of Israel. Overall, these actions resulted in the expropriation of two-thirds of the land that had belonged to Palestino-Israelis. At the end of the twentieth century, at a time when they constituted 20 percent of the Israeli population, Palestino-Israelis held only 3.5 percent of the land within Israel's pre-1967 borders.[89]

After 1948, "redemption of the land," "draining the swamps," and "making the desert bloom" were infused with new incentive and momentum, and were now administered by sovereign state authorities. Some of the land was transferred at token prices to the Jewish Agency and the Jewish National Fund, both of which were extraterritorial bodies whose bylaws prohibited them from transferring land to non-Jews. In this way, a considerable portion of the expropriated land became property that did not belong to the citizens of the new state but rather to world Jewry. Even today, 80 percent of Israel's land area can still not be purchased by non-Jews.[90]

groundbreaking *The Arabs in Israel*, New York: Monthly Review Press, 1976. The original Hebrew-language version of this translated book was completed just before the lifting of military rule in 1966.

89   On the Judaization of the land immediately following the establishment of the State of Israel, see Baruch Kimmerling's thorough study *Zionism and Territory: The Socio-Territorial Dimensions of Zionist Politics*, Berkeley: University of California Press, 1983, 134–46.

90   Oren Yiftachel, "Ethnocracy, Geography, and Democracy: Comments on the Politics of the Judaization of Israel," *Alpayim* 19 (2000), 78–105.

"Judaization of the country" became the new slogan, gradually replacing "redemption of the land" and embedding itself in the consensus of the Zionist left and right wings alike. Later, the term "Judaization of the Galilee" gained currency because of the steadfast Arab majority that continued to populate this region. Because the population of Israel tripled from 1949 through 1952 as a result of the mass immigration that followed the establishment of the state, the authorities were able to populate the appropriated lands with tens of thousands of new Jewish citizens. Kibbutzim, moshavim, and, to a lesser degree, development towns were granted large amounts of land free of charge. By 1964, 432 new settlements had been established, including 108 kibbutzim.[91] Most kibbutzim were established in "frontier areas" along the borders, in order to prevent the cross-border movement of Arab refugees (whom Israeli jargon of the period called infiltrators) trying to return to their villages or to recover some of their lost property. A significant number also crossed the border to take revenge on their dispossessors. In 1952 alone, 394 "infiltrators" were killed, and a large number of new settlers were wounded. The Palestinian refugees found it hard to accept the border that separated them from their homes and fields. For many Israelis, too, the border was not self-evident.

During the two decades prior to 1967, Israel appeared to have accepted the armistice lines that had been demarcated in 1949 as its final borders. The Zionist movement's great desire to achieve Jewish sovereignty had been fulfilled both in theory and in practice. The State of Israel had been recognized by most countries, albeit not by its Arab neighbors, and massive Jewish immigration to the new country had continued undisturbed since the 1950s. During the same period, the state succeeded in bringing to Israel survivors of the Holocaust who had not been permitted to immigrate to the United States, as well as a large proportion of the Arab Jews who were quickly pushed out of the Arab countries as a result of the conflict with Israel and the rise of nationalism. In the meantime, the immense energies invested in the economic and cultural organization of the new society, along with the

---

91   On internal Jewish discrimination between "Ashkenazim" and "Mizrahim" in the allocation of this land, see Oren Yiftachel, "Nation-Building and the Division of Space in the Israeli 'Ethnocracy': Settlement, Land, and Ethnic Disparities," *Iyunei Mishpat* 21:3 (1998), 637–64 (in Hebrew).

need to finish populating the 78 percent of British Mandate Palestine under Israeli control, curbed the emergence of an irredentism bent on pursuing the appropriation of the ancestral Land of Israel in its entirety. With the exception of the young members of the right-wing Zionist youth movement Betar, who continued their fervent singing of Ze'ev Jabotinsky's refrain "the Jordan has two banks, this is ours, and the other is too," the national pedagogy did not employ explicit rhetoric suggesting an aspiration to breach and expand the borders of the State of Israel. The first nineteen years of statehood appeared to have facilitated the consolidation of a new Israeli culture with a patriotism focused much more on language, culture, and the territory already populated by Jews.

But at the same time, it must not be forgotten that in all state schools, Bible studies played a major role in shaping the national territorial imagination of all Israeli children other than those in the Arab and the ultraorthodox Jewish sectors. Every student knew that Jerusalem, the city of David, was conquered by Arabs; every graduate of the Israeli education system was aware of the fact that the Cave of Machpela, where their putative forefathers were buried, was now an Islamic mosque. A prevalent practice in geography textbooks was the tendency to obscure the armistice lines and instead emphasize the "broad physical" borders of the historical homeland.[92] Even though it was not translated into daily political propaganda, the mythic Land of Israel continued to inhabit the interstices of Zionist consciousness.

The general Israeli population did not perceive the armistice lines as constituting the final borders of the Israeli state. In addition to the Zionist right wing, which never stopped dreaming of a large-scale Israel, and the Zionist left-wing Ahdut Ha'avodah party, whose appetite for land never diminished,[93] there was also a generational division that has been astutely pointed out by Israeli sociologist Adriana Kemp.[94] The generation of native-born Israelis who grew up in Manda-

---

92   For more on this, see Bar-Gal, Moledet *and Geography*, 133–6.

93   On this political movement's views on the Land of Israel, see the following small collection published in memory of Yitzhak Tabenkin, the movement's leader: Aryeh Fialkov (ed.), *Settlement and the Borders of the State of Israel*, Efal: Yad Tabenkin, 1975 (in Hebrew). Specifically, see the short testimony of former IDF general Rehavam Ze'evi delivered during the conference in question (25–31).

94   Adriana Kemp, "From Territorial Conquest to Frontier Nationalism: The

tory Palestine in the 1920s and 1930s, in an atmosphere formed in part by the ongoing settlement experiment, had a psychological dynamic of refusal to recognize territorial limitations and obstacles. Young Israelis, perhaps most prominently represented by Moshe Dayan and Yigal Alon, adopted what we might call an ethnospatial nationalism. During the 1948 war, these Israelis were the best fighters and proved to be excellent commanders, but were also conspicuously unrestrained and determined in their sweeping evacuation of Arab villages.

That generation of fighters was displeased with the 1949 armistice agreements and felt that, had it only been permitted to do so, the young Israel Defense Forces could have continued to advance into the Sinai Peninsula and easily conquered the West Bank.[95] Indeed, during the 1950s, former combat soldiers would cross the border in acts of adventurism that challenged the country's "narrow and artificial" borders. Making nighttime treks to the Nabataean city of Petra became fashionable for many young Israelis, and the occasional casualties among them emerged as cultural heroes overnight.[96] But in response to border crossings by Palestinian "infiltrators," the IDF established Unit 101 under the command of Ariel Sharon, a unit that crossed borders without hesitation and attacked villages and camps suspected of serving as the Palestinians' bases. Many new Israelis regarded the borders more as flexible frontier areas than as unequivocal permanent boundaries.[97]

However, it was the Sinai War of 1956 that exposed startling layers

---

Israel Case," Tel Aviv University: The David Horowitz Institute, Paper 4, 1995, 12–21.

95   On March 24, 1949, Yigal Alon sent a letter to David Ben-Gurion in which he expressed his opposition to the armistice lines and proposed an alternative border, based on the assertion that "one cannot imagine a line more sturdy than the line of the Jordan, which runs the entire length of the country." He confirmed this position in a 1979 interview, in which he recalled nostalgically, "Toward the end of the War of Liberation, a one-time chance emerged in which it was possible to fearlessly take the entire western Land of Israel." Ze'ev Tzur, *From the Partition Debate to the Alon Plan*, Efal: Yad Tabenkin, 1982, 74 (in Hebrew).

96   See Nessia Shafran, "The Red Rock in Retrospect," in Aharon Amir (ed.), *Keshet Te'uda: The Old Land of Israel*, Ramat Gan: Masada, 1979, 169–89 (in Hebrew).

97   On Israel's unwillingness to recognize the 1949 armistice lines as final borders, see Adriana Kemp's important work "Talking Boundaries: The Making of Political Territory in Israel, 1949–1957," Ph.D. diss., Tel Aviv University, 1997 (in Hebrew). See also Adriana Kemp, "From Politics of Location to Politics of Signification: The Construction of Political Territory in Israel's First Years," *Journal of Area Studies* 12 (1998), 74–101.

of territorial imagination that had not risen to the surface of Israeli politics during peacetime. Egyptian leader Gamal Abdel Nasser's nationalization of the Suez Canal led to a war coalition consisting of Britain, France, and Israel, aimed at invading Egypt and toppling its regime. It was a standard colonial reflex, which Israel saw fit to use on the pretext that its participation would prevent infiltrators from penetrating its territory.

A preparatory meeting took place in 1956 in the Parisian suburb of Sèvres, attended by Israeli prime minister David Ben-Gurion, French prime minister Guy Mollet, and British foreign secretary John Selwyn Lloyd. Ben-Gurion presented a daring plan to reorganize the Middle East: upon military victory, the Hashemite Kingdom of Jordan should be split into two, with Iraq, which was then still pro-British, receiving the East Bank in exchange for its promise to resettle the Palestinian refugees there, and Israel receiving the West Bank as a semiautonomous region. In addition, Ben-Gurion asserted, Israel should be permitted to shift its northern border northward to the Litani River and to annex the Straits of Tiran and the Bay of Eilat in their entirety.[98]

The founder of the Israeli state did not return to his territorial conceptions of 1918. Now Ben-Gurion was sincerely ready to concede eastern Transjordan. However, his new vision also reflected a change with regard to the southern Sinai Peninsula: in his younger years, this Zionist socialist activist had not regarded the area south of Wadi El-Arish as part of the Land of Israel. It is no coincidence that during his flight to Paris in 1956, he spent some time reading up on historical references, made by the Byzantine geographer Procopius, to a Jewish kingdom on the island of Tiran, known as Yotvat.

The coalition's quick military victory in the Sinai Peninsula breathed new life and strength into the seventy-year-old Israeli leader, who publicly demonstrated that his craving for territory had not dissipated with old age. In a letter to the IDF brigade that conquered Sharm el-Sheikh, he wrote: "Eilat will once again be the primary/first Jewish harbor in the south . . . And Yotvat, [now] called Tiran . . . will once again become part of the Third Israeli [i.e., Jewish] Kingdom/

98   Avi Shlaim, *The Iron Wall: Israel and the Arab World*, London: Penguin, 2001, 171–2.

Commonwealth."[99] Just as he had regarded the annexation of conquered territory lying outside the borders of the partition plan as a "natural" national act in 1948, the passionate Israeli prime minister now portrayed the conquest of the Sinai Peninsula as the liberation of authentic regions of the homeland. Each time there arose an international context in which the territorial dream could be linked to power, the "Land of Israel" returned to center stage and once again became the focus of pragmatic work.

On December 14, 1956, just over two months after the end of the fighting, the first Israeli settlement was established at Sharm el-Sheikh. It was named Ofira, meaning "toward Ofir," a region mentioned in the Hebrew Bible.[100] The IDF had already started to withdraw from parts of the Sinai Peninsula, but its chief of general staff, Moshe Dayan, who initiated the project, remained convinced that it was possible to settle along the banks of the Red Sea. The prime minister came to visit the new fishing village, where he delivered a speech on Jewish settlement, sparking hope for the establishment of additional settlements along the coast.

A second settlement was set up during the same period in Rafiah, in the southern Gaza Strip. Soldiers of the IDF's Nahal (Fighting Pioneer Youth) brigade settled in an abandoned army camp and began plowing a thousand *dunams*. The goal was to establish a chain of settlements as quickly as possible to cut off the strip from the peninsula and transform it into Israeli territory. There was also a plan to have a group from the Hashomer Hatzair movement establish a fishing village on the region's sandy white beaches. Dayan was responsible for executing the practical measures of the settlement operation, and in this he received the full political backing of his eternal political rival, Yigal Alon. In December 1956, Alon, the promising young leader of the Zionist left, declared confidently:

> If we are truly determined to defend Gaza ... I am certain that the city of Samson will remain an Israeli city, part of the State of Israel. This policy is consistent with our historical right to the Strip, our

99   Quoted in Benny Morris, *Israel's Border Wars, 1949–1956*, Oxford: Oxford University Press, 1993, 444. On the same day the letter was sent, Ben-Gurion made reference to Procopius in a speech to the Knesset.

100   See Meron Rapoport, "The Settlement Enterprise Was Already Dreamed Up by Moshe Dayan in 1956," *Haaretz*, July 10, 2010 (in Hebrew).

interest in our existence, and the principle that guides us—the principle of the wholeness of the Land.[101]

But the first settlement enterprise outside the 1949 armistice lines quickly sustained a mortal blow. A UN resolution calling for withdrawal from the entire Sinai Peninsula, coupled with US and Soviet pressure, put an end to the hopes of Ben-Gurion and his young colleagues to establish the "third Israeli kingdom." Moreover, the swift compulsory withdrawal cooled Israel's annexationist enthusiasm, and its leaders, seeming to have learned a lesson, began to restrain the colonization urges that had thus far been characteristic of state action. Although Israel's borders may not have been completely peaceful during the years 1957–67, this relatively golden decade ended with Israel's termination of military rule over its Arab citizens, and a sense of normalization pervaded its presence in the Middle East. The fact that, during this period, Israel joined the ranks of countries in possession of nuclear weapons may have also contributed to a greater sense of security and calm among Israel's political and military elite.

"Of all the Arab-Israeli wars, the June 1967 war was the only one that neither side wanted. The war resulted from a crisis slide that neither Israel nor her enemies were able to control."[102] This concise characterization was written by Avi Shlaim, a scholar of the Arab-Israeli conflict. We might add only that despite the now-prevalent view that Nasser was not in favor of war and that the generals of the IDF played an indirect role in causing its outbreak, it is difficult to refute the conclusion that the Egyptian leader was primarily responsible for the crisis. Although it is true that at the end of the 1956 war, Egypt, while innocent of any crime, was punished by being forced to demilitarize the Sinai Peninsula and accept the deployment there of an emergency international force, this punishment cannot serve as historical justification for the warlike (even if hollow) discourse conducted in the Egyptian media. Nasser fell into a trap that he himself had set, and that the IDF proved adept at exploiting.[103]

---

101   Yigal Alon, "Release the Strip," *LaMerhav*, December 12, 1956 (in Hebrew).

102   Shlaim, *The Iron Wall*, 236.

103   A few days before the war, Colonel Eli Zeira, who would later serve as the director of Israeli military intelligence, informed his subordinates, officers of the elite Sayeret Matkal unit: "There will be war within a week. Two or three Arab armies will take part, and we will defeat them all within a week . . . And the Zionist enterprise will

In 1967, at the age of nineteen, Israel may have achieved an amazing military victory, but as a result, it fell into an even bigger trap. Israel did not start the war nor did it plan to conquer the parts of the Land of Israel it had "lost" in 1948 (even if there had always been contingency plans for such a possibility), but it was nonetheless not shocking that it succeeded in that conquest.

The Israelis' joy of victory intoxicated many, imbuing them with a deep feeling that now anything was possible. The siege mentality that had stemmed from the armistice lines—or "the Auschwitz borders," as Israeli foreign minister Abba Eban is said to have called them—was replaced with dreams of space, a return to ancient landscapes, spiritual uplift, and the image of a Jewish empire reminiscent of the kingdom of David and Solomon. A large segment of the Israeli population felt it had finally attained the parts of the homeland to which the Zionist vision, almost from the outset, had directed the national imagination. Indeed, as early as 1967, the Israeli government issued an order to the Survey of Israel to stop marking the 1949 armistice lines— "the green line"—on maps of the country. From then on, Israeli schoolchildren ceased to learn about the country's previous, "temporary" borders.

Immediately following the conquest of East Jerusalem, and before the war had even ended, Moshe Dayan declared: "We have returned to our holiest places. We have returned in order to never part with them again. Especially at this time, we extend a hand in peace to our Arab neighbors."[104] It should therefore come as no surprise that on June 28, given the hypnotic and euphoric atmosphere, the Israeli Knesset voted to annex East Jerusalem and the surrounding area, and at the same time announced its intention to strive for peace and direct negotiations with all its enemies in exchange for withdrawal from the territories in the Sinai Peninsula and the Golan Heights. Today it is difficult to imagine how level-headed Israeli figures could think that Arab leaders, humiliated by defeat, would agree to begin sincere peace talks with Israel in light of the immediate official annexation of Arab and Muslim Al-Quds by the "Jewish state." Nonetheless, this was the

---

take one more step forward toward its fulfillment." Quoted in Ran Edelist, *Where Did We Go Wrong*, Jerusalem: November Books, 2011, 25–6 (in Hebrew).

104   Dayan's words were broadcast by the Voice of Israel on June 7, 1967, and are quoted in Arye Naor's broad study, *Greater Israel: Theology and Policy*, Haifa: Haifa University Press, 2001, 34 (in Hebrew).

Zionist Israeli logic that prevailed in the summer of 1967. To a large degree, this logic appears still to be at work today.[105]

In September 1967, just a few months after the war, the "Manifesto for the Whole Land of Israel" was published. Its signers consisted primarily of figures associated with the Israeli labor movement but also included figures from the Zionist right. In this document, some of the greatest Israeli intellectuals of the time formally declared: "The Land of Israel is now held by the Jewish people . . . we are loyally obligated to the integrity of our Land, and no government of Israel has the right to concede this integrity."[106] Poets such as Nathan Alterman, Haim Gouri, Yaakov Orland, and Uri Zvi Grinberg joined together to promote the territorial integrity of the homeland. Prominent authors such as Shai Agnon (S. Y. Agnon), Haim Hazaz, Yehuda Borla, and Moshe Shamir joined security and military figures such as former Mossad chief Isser Harel and General Avraham Yoffe in an effort to prevent Israeli politicians from withdrawal. Even highly praised, award-winning professors such as Dov Sadan and Harold Fisch forged an alliance with former fighters of the Warsaw Ghetto Uprising, such as Yitzhak Zuckerman and Zivia Lubetkin, to encourage settlement in all parts of the Land of Israel. Many other individuals held similar opinions but preferred not to make declarations that to them seemed self-evident and superfluous. The age-old tradition of not "talking about maps" in public now spread to most of the political, economic, and cultural elite.

In the course of its victory, Israel seized control of the Sinai Peninsula, the Golan Heights, and the West Bank, including East Jerusalem. Israel managed to be "liberated" of the Sinai Peninsula within a decade, primarily as a result of the bloody war of 1973 and the effective intervention of US president Jimmy Carter, but an external redeemer capable of releasing Israel from the Golan Heights, the West Bank,

---

105   One of the moving patriotic songs that expressed this paradoxical, deceptive spirit after the 1967 war was "Sharm el-Sheikh" (lyrics by Amos Ettinger, music by Rafi Gabay). Its lyrics include the following lines: "Sharm el-Sheikh, we've returned to you once again. You are in our hearts, always in our hearts . . . The evening sets, bringing another dream, brings on the water a hope for peace."

106   The manifesto was published on the same day (September 22, 1967) in Israel's most widely-read newspapers: *Yedioth Aharonot, Maariv, Haaretz,* and *Davar.* For an informative analysis, see Dan Miron, "*Te'uda b'Israel*" *Politics,* August 1987, 37–45 (in Hebrew).

and Arab Jerusalem has yet to emerge. Moreover, pro-Zionist Jewish institutions that had maintained relatively cool relations with small, weak Israel prior to the lightning victory of 1967 now suddenly became sworn supporters of the new, large, strong Israel.[107] Thus, with the financial and political support of "the Jews of the Diaspora," who were looking out for their expanded assets across the sea without any real desire to live there in person, the State of Israel began to sink into the quagmire of ongoing occupation and oppression. In this context, the ever-expanding settlement enterprise and the military regime, which implemented a local, "apologetic" version of apartheid with an almost indecipherable historical logic, became integral to the fabric of Israeli experience.

In 1967, Israel was not as lucky as it had been in 1948. Large-scale population transfers had still been possible within the postwar reality of the late 1940s and early 1950s but were much less acceptable in the postcolonial world of the late 1960s. Aside from the numerous local inhabitants of the Golan Heights who fled and were expelled during and immediately following the fighting, as well as the inhabitants of three leveled Palestinian villages in the Latrun area near Jerusalem and a refugee camp near Jericho, the majority of the conquered population—the Palestinians of the West Bank and the Gaza Strip—remained in their homes. Although a few voices called for the immediate expulsion of the local population,[108] Israel clearly understood the impossibility of doing so. It is therefore no coincidence that the first settlement to be established, approximately one month after the conclusion of the fighting, was located in the recently "evacuated" Golan Heights and that thirty-two additional settlements have been established in the region since then. The absence of a large local population encouraged Israel to officially annex the territory in 1981,

---

107   This stemmed not only from their admiration of Israeli power but also from the decline of the traditional nationalisms, which demanded unequivocal loyalty to a single homeland, and the simultaneous strengthening of transnational community identities across the Western world.

108   See, for example, the public statement of author Haim Hazaz, recipient of the Israel Prize for Literature and a major figure in the Israeli intellectual world: "There is the question of Judea and Efraim, which contain large populations that will need to be evacuated and sent to neighboring Arab countries . . . Each people to its own – Israel to the Land of Israel, and the Arabs to Arabia . . ." Haim Hazaz, "Things of Substance," in Aharon Ben-Ami (ed.), *The Book of the Whole Land of Israel*, Tel Aviv: Friedman, 1977, 20.

indicating disregard for the possibility of a future peace deal with Syria. Underlying this measure was the assumption that, just as the world was forced to accept the conquests of 1948, so too would it come to accept Israeli control over the conquests of 1967.

The first Nahal settlement was set up in the Sinai Peninsula relatively early as well: Neot Sinai, built northeast of El-Arish in December 1967. This pioneering effort was followed by another twenty permanent settlements in the region. Under the terms of Israel's eventual peace treaty with Egypt in 1979, all of these were subject to forced evacuation along with the withdrawal of Israeli military forces. The first Israeli settlement in the Gaza Strip was established only in 1970 and was followed by seventeen other thriving settlements, all of which were evacuated by Israel in 2005.

But at the very heart of the "historical homeland," matters were handled from the outset through the use of different strategies and under the influence of very different emotional baggage. During the first decade following the war, the old Zionist left remained in power in Israel. As we have seen, this Zionist left had no less territorial drive than did the Zionist right. Unlike the Zionist right, however, the Zionist left had a sense of pragmatism that resulted in self-restraint at decisive points in history—1937, 1947, 1957—and that in 1967 caused it to hesitate and deliberate before acting.

One important factor was Israeli concern that the two large superpowers of the day would again engage in joint diplomatic action, forcing Israel to withdraw from all the territories it had occupied. But 1967 was not 1957, and this time around, to Israel's great misfortune, it was not subject to any serious international pressure. The second, and more troubling, factor was that, at the time of conquest, the West Bank had a population of 670,000 Palestinians, with the potential for sharp demographic growth. To establish Jewish settlements in the midst of this population would have placed into question the principle of the pure colony that had been guiding the Zionist movement since its first steps in Palestine. Because of the high birth rate of the Arab population incorporated into the state in 1948, Israel never considered granting them citizenship. Maintaining the West Bank as an autonomous region, ruled by Israel but without the introduction of settlements, as some intelligence officials proposed, was more consistent with the interests of the state. Nevertheless, the long-term nature of the Zionist enterprise ultimately proved decisive.

Establishment of the first settlement in the West Bank was supported by several factors: veneration of the dead, the mythos of stolen land, and eradication of national insult. In September 1967, just a few months after the war, Kfar Etzion was established on the ruins of a Jewish settlement that had been evacuated and destroyed during the 1948 war (the same was true of Kfar Darom in the Gaza Strip). Similar logic guided the group that invaded a hotel in Hebron and declared its intention to renew the city's former Jewish community, which had sustained painful injury in 1929 and was forced to evacuate the city altogether in 1936.[109] But if in the first instance the settlement was established in an area adjacent to the 1949 armistice line and therefore received immediate, sweeping government support, the second settlement was established in the very heart of the Palestinian population. In this way, the Jewish settlement in Hebron must be seen as a decisive turning point in the history of the Israeli-Palestinian conflict.

In retrospect, we can identify three significant moments in the long history of the occupation and the settlements in the occupied territories—moments that most likely were decisive in shaping the future of both Israel and its neighbors. The first was Israel's unilateral annexation of East Jerusalem and the surrounding area without taking into consideration the wishes of the local inhabitants and without granting them full citizenship. Israel never truly united the city, unless we understand the term "unification" as being applicable not to people but to stones, dirt, houses, and graves. This particular act of annexation, which at the time was even supported by sworn peace-seekers such as Uri Avnery, represented the complete victory of mythos over historical logic and of holy ground over the principle of democracy.

The other two decisive moments were linked to the city of Hebron, where the graves of the Jewish patriarchs and matriarchs are found. The first occurred when the new Israeli pioneers invaded the city during Passover of 1968, and Prime Minister Levi Eshkol, a moderate, requested that they be removed at once. But the combined force of a powerful mythos and mounting public pressure, which Yigal Alon and Moshe Dayan effectively and cynically translated into personal political capital, led him to relent and agree to a compromise: the

---

109   On the importance of the Jewish settlement in Hebron, see Michael Feige, *One Space, Two Places: Gush Emunim, Peace Now, and the Construction of Israeli Space*, Jerusalem: Magnes, 2002, 101–25 (in Hebrew).

establishment of the Jewish settlement of Kiryat Arba adjacent to the Arab city of Hebron. The dam breached, Israel began slowly but surely to seep into the West Bank.

The third moment came in 1994, immediately following Israeli American physician Baruch Goldstein's massacre of twenty-nine Muslim worshippers in the city of Hebron. In light of the profound public shock it caused, the event provided Prime Minister Yitzhak Rabin with a rare opportunity to evacuate the settlers not merely from Hebron but also perhaps from Kiryat Arba. Such a decision would have solidified the coalescing intentions to extricate Israel from its occupation of all or part of the West Bank and significantly strengthened the forces of conciliation among the Palestinians. But the mythos of ancestral land and the fear of public protest again tamed the response of Prime Minister Rabin, a political figure who was growing more moderate. Although a recipient of the Nobel Peace Prize, Rabin supported "security" settlement in the occupied territories. In fact, during his second term as prime minister (1992–5), settlement construction continued at nearly its previous level. He was murdered in November 1995, even though he had not dared evacuate even one Jewish settlement.[110]

The various incarnations of the Labor Party—which lost its control over the government for the first time in 1977, returned to power in 1992, and again formed the government in 1999—behaved toward the settlement enterprise in the West Bank like a cow wanting to be milked. Far from rebuffing those who came to do the milking and who often employed illegal means to do so, Labor ultimately gave them its milk with much grief, conciliation, and love. According to the principles espoused by this moderate-left government, the "positive" settlements (those established in accordance with the 1967 Alon Plan) were ostensibly "security settlements," located primarily in areas that did not have a dense Palestinian population, such as the expanded Jordan Valley, as distinct from the new Jewish neighborhoods that would surround Arab Jerusalem for eternity.

---

110   It should be noted that in the Oslo Accords, in exchange for the Palestinian delegation's agreement to disavow terrorism and violence, Israel did not agree to stop settlement. In a speech to the Knesset on October 6, 1995, Rabin laid out the principles guiding him in the process: the unity of Jerusalem (including Ma'ale Adumim); a Palestinian entity that would be less than a state; no return to the pre-1967 borders; and a security border that would run through the Jordan Valley.

But a dynamic and active minority found common cause with the colonization drive and swept the hesitant regime forward. At the beginning of the present chapter, we discussed the small nationalist-religious stream that joined the Zionist movement in 1897, imbued with strong faith in the power of God and in the fundamental weakness of the individual believer. However, each step in the appropriation of the Land increased the sanctity of the Land and made it more important in the eyes of the religious nationalists. God's replacement by the Land as the central focus of religious Zionism, and the move from a passive awaiting of the Messiah to an active engagement in national action to hasten his arrival, occurred long before 1967 but was relegated to the political margins of religious nationalism. After the stunning Israeli military victory, this change from passivity to activity came to entice the national religious political lobby that was part of the ruling coalition.

In Kfar Etzion as early as 1967, and even more so in Hebron in 1968, we see the emergence of a new type of avant-garde that began to set the pace of settlement. Graduates of religious high schools and students of nationalist yeshivas, who until then had occupied the margins of Israeli culture, suddenly became the heroes of the day. And whereas Zionist settlers from the beginning of the twentieth century had been primarily secular socialist Zionists, henceforth the most dynamic segment of the conquerors of the Land came wrapped in talliths and wore nationalistically symbolic knitted yarmulkes. They also despised the "humanistic pacifists" who questioned the authenticity of God's promise of the Land, just as earlier generations of religious Jews had despised the modern nationalism that had turned the Land into the focus of ritual worship. Thus was born the pioneering movement known as Gush Emunim—the "Block of the Faithful"—which facilitated the expansion of Israeli settlement in the occupied territories and enabled it to attain much greater proportions than it would have otherwise.

Although Gush Emunim represents a minority in Israeli society, no other political stream, faction, or coalition has been able to successfully oppose its rhetoric, which is based on the concept of the People of Israel's undeniable right to its Land. In light of the ideological and territorial antecedents of Jewish nationalism, the entire Zionist camp has consistently felt compelled to submit to the demands of this minority, even when it confounds the political, diplomatic, economic, and logical balance sheet of the existing sovereign state.[111] As we have seen, even the most moderate forces have been unable to sustain long-term resistance to the triumphant patriotic discourse in defense of national territorial property.

The Zionist right's rise to power in 1977 significantly accelerated the pace of settlement. Menachem Begin, who "conceded" the entire Sinai Peninsula in exchange for a peace treaty with Egypt in 1979, simultaneously did all he could to promote Jewish settlement in the West Bank. Since the establishment of Kfar Etzion in 1967, this region has witnessed the establishment of more than 150 settlements, cities, and villages, and many more outposts.[112] At the time of writing, the number of Israelis living in the settlements exceeds half a million. Not all are ideological settlers seeking to liberate the Land of Israel from foreign occupiers. Some are economic settlers, who live in the West Bank because it allows them to have a house with some land and a mountain view at a token price. In addition, with the help of generous government funding, the quality of the pedagogical, medical, and welfare services provided in the pioneering settlements is vastly higher than within Green Line Israel. Whereas the welfare state in the latter crumbled fairly quickly, in the occupied territories it has expanded and flourished. Some people even purchased homes in the territories as an investment, based on the expectation that they would be well compensated if Israel were to implement a forced withdrawal.

The majority of settlements were built by local Palestinian laborers living under military occupation. They worked in the settlements by day, sometimes even building the security fences, and returned to their villages in the evening. By the outbreak of the First Intifada in late 1987, the Palestinian labor force had also penetrated the business sectors in cities, kibbutzim, and moshavim located in sovereign Israeli territory. Unintentionally, and out of purely economic interests, Israel found itself turning into a typical plantation colony, with a peaceful and submissive population that lacked both citizenship

111   This holds true except with regard to the politics of water in the West Bank. The way water is managed in the occupied territories is profitable for both the Jewish settlements and the State of Israel.

112   On the world of the settlers, the pace of settlement, and their relationships with different Israeli governments, see Akiva Eldar and Idith Zertal, *Lords of the Land: The Settlers and the State of Israel 1967–2004*, Or Yehuda: Kinneret, Zmora-Bitan, 2004 (in Hebrew).

and sovereignty, working for masters who possessed not only citizenship and sovereignty but also a protective sense of paternalism. It was Moshe Dayan's paternalistic fantasy that shaped the "enlightened" occupation, which stood the test of time for twenty years only to completely collapse in 1987. This "soft" occupation policy delayed a Palestinian uprising for a decade, allowed the world to remain indifferent, and facilitated an ongoing, creeping colonization. Ultimately, however, it indirectly contributed to the eruption of a major rebellion.

The popular Intifada and the brutal terrorism that accompanied it undermined the calm relations of control and by so doing again saved the principle of the "ethno-democratic" state. Israel drove the Palestinian "invaders" back into their places of residence in the West Bank, halted the economic symbiosis that had been under way until then, and began to import cheap labor from the markets of East Asia. The massive wave of immigrants that arrived from the crumbling Soviet Union during this same period provided Israel with additional working hands;[113] in this case (to the consternation of the nationalist ultraorthodox), Israel was not deeply concerned whether these hands were Jewish, just as long as they were "white."

Between 1967 and 1987, the Palestinians' standard of living rose significantly, and their birth rate spiked accordingly. In 2005 the population of the West Bank stood at 2.5 million, while the combined population of the West Bank and Gaza Strip was 4 million. Since then these figures have continued to rise. Those who were born under the occupation in the late 1960s became the leaders of the uprising in the late 1980s and early 1990s and filled the rank and file of the armed popular resistance. Despite having never known another regime, these young Palestinians quickly learned that very few people on earth at the end of the twentieth century shared the unusual situation of officially possessing no citizenship, no self-sovereignty, and no homeland, in a world where such a status had become almost entirely infeasible and, in the view of most, wholly intolerable.

Most Israelis were surprised at the new unrest and found it hard to understand. "They have better lives than all the other Arabs in the region" was one prevalent justification within the Israeli ruling discourse. The intellectuals of the Zionist left, who felt uncomfortable

---

113   On this, see Juval Portugali, *Implicate Relations: Society and Space in the Israeli Palestinian Conflict*, Tel Aviv: Hakibbutz Hameuchad, 1996, 204-6 (in Hebrew).

living permanently alongside a veiled apartheid regime, communi-
cated with one another through a sophisticated terminology of protest
regarding the "administered territories" (*ha-shtakhim ha-mukhza-
kim*) as opposed to the "occupied territories" (*ha-shtakhim
ha-kvushim*). More than anything, they feared that the ongoing occupation would damage the state's "Jewish" character and took
consolation in the basic assumption that it was only temporary, even
after it had existed for twice as long as the "narrow-hipped" pre-1967
Israel. This resulted in the entrenchment of moral indifference toward
colonial control, an indifference reminiscent of the attitude of numerous Western intellectuals toward colonialism during the period
preceding the Second World War.[114]

The intifadas that erupted in 1987 and 2000 brought about minimal changes in the spatial reality. The First Intifada resulted in the
Oslo Accords and the establishment of the Palestinian Authority,
which received European and American support and therefore helped
decrease the Israeli cost of the occupation but did nothing to slow
colonization. Indeed, since the signing of the accords in 1993, the
settler population has increased almost threefold. The Second Intifada, by contrast, resulted in the uprooting of the Israeli settlements
from the Gaza Strip. However, it is no secret that Prime Minister Ariel
Sharon's initiative, which created a hostile "Indian reservation" that
was denied the right of direct communication with the outside
world,[115] was aimed primarily at evading an overall compromise with
the Palestinian leadership. In actuality, both of Israel's unilateral with-
drawals—from Lebanon in 2000 and from the Gaza Strip in
2005—were designed and executed, without negotiations, with the
goal of permitting Israel to retain other territories (specifically, the
Golan Heights and the West Bank). Even the security fence with
which Israel surrounded itself in order to reduce the number of deadly
suicide bombings perpetrated within its borders was not erected
along the 1967 border, but rather cut through Palestinian territory so

---

114   For the most comprehensive study published to date on the system of
military control over the Palestinian people and the capacity of Israeli culture and
politics to contend with it, see Ariella Azoulay and Adi Ophir, *Occupation and
Democracy Between the Sea and the River (1967–)*, Tel Aviv: Resling, 2008 (in Hebrew).

115   I use the term "reservation" to refer to the Gaza Strip because a decisive
majority of its inhabitants are descendants of Palestinian refugees from the 1948 war.
Ariel Sharon is known as one of the architects of Israeli settlement in the West Bank.

as to encircle a large number of the settlements. At the same time, settlements located outside the fence continued to grow stronger, and additional outposts were established.

From Menachem Begin in the late 1970s, through Yitzhak Rabin and Ehud Barak in the 1990s, to the Israeli prime ministers of the early twenty-first century, Israeli leaders have been willing, under pressure, to grant Palestinians a limited and divided autonomy surrounded and splintered by land, air, and sea zones under Israeli control. The most they have been willing to accept is two or three bantustans that submissively accept the dictates of the Jewish state.[116] As expected, security has always provided the justifications for this position, as the discourse of defensive war continues to shape the major contours of Judeo-Israeli identity and consciousness. But the deep historical reality concealed by this discourse is quite different: even today, the political elite in Israel—left wing and right wing alike—have found it extremely difficult to acknowledge the Palestinians' legitimate right to full national self-sovereignty within areas located inside the territory that the elite regard as the Land of Israel. In their view, this territory is precisely what its name declares it to be: an ancestral inheritance that has always belonged to the "People of Israel."

In its fifth decade, the occupation appears to be paving a territorial path for the evolution of a binational state, as the increasing penetration of Israeli settlers into densely populated Palestinian areas seems to hinder every attempt at future political separation. On a psychological level, however, the oppressive nature of Israeli control, the international criticism, and most important, the violent and desperate Palestinian resistance all contribute to the increasingly extreme consciousness among many Israelis of "a people dwelling alone" (Num. 23:9). The posture maintained by the fictional Israeli *ethnos* reflects a mixture of contempt and fear toward its neighbors, spawned by its own fictitiousness and its own lack of confidence in its national-cultural identity (especially vis-à-vis the Middle East). Israelis continue to refuse to live together, and certainly to live together in equality, with the Others who dwell in their midst.

---

116   Israel had done everything in its power to divide the West Bank in half through massive construction in the territorial space between Jerusalem and Jericho.

Under extreme circumstances, this fundamental contradiction could lead Israel to the aggressive displacement of the Arabs living under its control—whether they live as citizens within the segregated Israeli state or, having been trapped within the unique apartheid system, possess no citizenship whatsoever. We are all undoubtedly capable of imagining the ways in which this dangerous, dead-end, ethnoterritorial policy could degenerate in the event of a mass civil uprising of all non-Jews within the "Whole Land of Israel."

In any event, at the time of writing, a major compromise—involving an Israeli withdrawal to 1967 borders, the establishment of a Palestinian state alongside Israel (with Jerusalem as its joint capital), and the formation of a confederation between two sovereign democratic republics, each of which belongs to all their respective citizens—appears to be a fading dream, growing increasingly faint as each day passes and seeming fated to disappear into the abyss of time.[117]

After two difficult intifadas, large segments of Israeli society have tired of the mythologies of the Land. But this ideological weakening and weariness, and the underlying hedonism and individualism, are still far from generating a stable and meaningful electoral outcome. We have thus far witnessed no decisive change in public opinion in the direction of a massive removal of settlements and a fair compromise regarding Jerusalem. Although with each confrontation Israelis grow increasingly sensitive regarding Israeli soldiers' loss of life, a serious mass peace movement has yet to emerge. Zionist in-group morality still enjoys absolute hegemony. And not only has the political balance of power within Israel not changed directions thus far, but in actuality the ethnoreligious and secular-racist streams have grown stronger. Surveys conducted at the time of writing reflect that 70 percent of all Judeo-Israelis naïvely yet sincerely believe they are members of the chosen people.[118]

---

117 The Palestinian and Palestino-Israeli population living between the Mediterranean Sea and the Jordan River stood at 5.6 million people as of 2011, and the number of Judeo-Israelis living in the same space was 5.9 million. In a very short time, there will be demographic equality between the two populations. See Barak Ravid, "The Demographic Demon Lives On, but the Right Is Trying to Bury It," *Haaretz*, January 3, 2012 (in Hebrew).

118 See Nir Hasson, "80% of the Jews in the Country Believe in God," *Haaretz*, January 27, 2012.

Israel's increasing diplomatic isolation in the region and the world does not appear to trouble the Israeli political and military elite, whose power is contingent on the ongoing sense of siege. As long as the United States—under pressure from the Jewish and Evangelical pro-Zionist lobbies as well as from representatives of the arms industry[119]—continues to support the status quo and give Israel the feeling that its policies are legitimate and its power unlimited, chances of progress toward a meaningful compromise remain slim at best.

Under these historical conditions, the prospect of combining rational interests with a vision based on universal morality appears purely utopian. And as we know, at the beginning of the twenty-first century, the power of utopias has all but disappeared.

---

119   A large portion of America's generous aid to Israel remains in the hands of weapons and munitions manufacturers in the United States. For more on the pro-Zionist coalition, see John J. Mearsheimer and Stephen M. Walt, *The Israel Lobby and U.S. Foreign Policy*, New York: Farrar, Straus and Giroux, 2007.

The Sad Tale of the Frog and the Scorpion

Only direct cooperation with the Arabs can create a dignified and safe life . . . What saddens me is less the fact that the Jews are not smart enough to understand this, but rather, that they are not just enough to want it.

—Albert Einstein, letter to Hugo Bergman, June 19, 1930

One day, a scorpion wanted to cross the river, and asked a frog to carry him across on his back. "But you sting anything that moves!" the frog remarked in astonishment. "Yes," responded the scorpion, "but I will not sting you, because then I would die as well." The frog accepted the logic of this response. Midway across the river, the scorpion stung the swimmer. "Why did you do that?" wailed the frog. "Now we both will die!" "It's my nature," moaned the scorpion, moments before he sank into the watery depths.

—By an anonymous author, at an unknown time

The tale of the frog and the scorpion is a well-known story with a familiar moral: that not everyone determines their actions based on common sense, and that nature and essence are often what determine how we act. Historical processes and movements do not exactly possess a nature, and certainly do not possess an essence. However, they do possess, or at least are accompanied by, inert mythoi that are not always suited to the changing logic that results from changing circumstances. As the British saying goes, "common sense is not always common." The features of the current phase of the Zionist enterprise reinforce this observation.

The construction of the mythos of a wandering Jewish people that was uprooted from its homeland two thousand years ago and that aspired to return to it at the first possible opportunity is imbued with a practical logic, even if it is based entirely on historical fabrications. The Bible is not a patriotic text, just as the *Iliad* and the *Odyssey* are not works of monotheistic theology. The agricultural inhabitants of Canaan had no political homeland because no such homelands existed in the ancient Middle East. The local population that began to espouse a belief in a singular God was never uprooted from its home but simply changed the nature of its faith. It was not a question of a unique people being scattered around the world but a dynamic new religion spreading and acquiring new believers. The masses of converts and their descendants longed passionately and with great mental fortitude for the holy place from which redemption was supposed to come, but they never seriously considered moving there and never did so. Zionism was not at all the continuation of Judaism but rather its negation. Indeed, it is for this reason that the latter rejected the former at an earlier period of history. Despite all this, the mythos has permeated a certain historical logic, which has in turn contributed to its partial fulfillment.

The outbreak of nationalism, with its inherent Judeophobia, that swept across Central and Eastern Europe in the second half of the nineteenth century instilled its principles within a small portion of the persecuted Jewish population. This select avant-garde sensed the danger that hovered over the Jews and therefore began to sculpt a self-portrait of a modern nation. At the same time, it grasped hold of its sacred center and worked it into an image of an ancient site from which the "ethnic" tribe had ostensibly sprouted and expanded. This national territorialization of hitherto religious ties was one of Zionism's most important, even if not completely original, achievements. It is hard to assess the role played by Christianity in general and Puritanism in particular in bringing about the new patriotic paradigm, but these forces were undoubtedly present behind the scenes during the historic encounter between the conception of the children of Israel as a nation on the one hand, and the project of colonization on the other.

Under the political conditions that prevailed in the late nineteenth and early twentieth centuries, the notion of settlement in "desolate" areas was still credited with considerable logic. It was the high point of the age of imperialism, and the project was enabled by the fact that its land of destination was populated by an anonymous local population, devoid of national identity. Had the vision and the movement appeared earlier, in the days when Lord Shaftesbury had proposed the idea, the process of colonization might have been less complicated, and the displacement of the local population, as had been taking place in other colonial areas, could perhaps have been achieved with greater ease and fewer misgivings. However, in the mid-nineteenth century, devout Jews, primarily from Central and Eastern Europe, believed that immigrating to the Holy Land would result in its desecration and therefore had no desire to do so. The Jews living in the West were already secular enough not to fall into the pseudoreligious, nationalist trap beckoning them to a region that, from their perspective, offered no cultural or economic attractions. In addition, the birth pangs of the monstrous anti-Semitism that would grip Central and Eastern Europe had just begun, and the large Yiddish population awoke from their slumbers too late to extract themselves from the alienating surroundings that were about to regurgitate them.

Had it not been for the refusal of Western countries to accept massive immigration, it is doubtful whether this fictitious *ethnos* could have been constructed or whether a significant number of Jews and their descendants would have immigrated to Palestine. But the elimination of all other options forced a minority of the displaced to make their way to the Holy Land, which they initially regarded as an extremely unpromising destination. There, they had to displace a local population that had only recently, hesitantly, and quite belatedly assumed national attributes. The conflicts arising from colonization were inevitable, and those who thought they could be bypassed were only deluding themselves. The Second World War and the Jewish destruction it wreaked created circumstances that enabled the West to impose a settler state on the local population. The establishment of the State of Israel as a place of refuge for persecuted Jews took place during the last hours, or, to be more precise, at the final moments, of the dying colonial era.

Without its mobilizing mythos of ethnic colonization, the campaign for self-sovereignty would most likely not have been successful. Yet at a certain point, the logic that had helped establish the Israeli nation vanished, and the demon of mythic territoriality insolently overpowered its creators and their product. Its poisonous sting emerges at the beginning of the narrative, with the introduction of the consciousness of a homeland whose imagined borders far exceeded those of the true spaces of everyday life. This consciousness caused people to envision vast, almost limitless expanses, while the Palestinians' refusal to recognize the legitimacy of the foreign invasion of their land, and their violent resistance to it, have repeatedly provided the pretext for continuing expansion. Moreover, when in

2002, through the peace initiative proffered by the Arab League, the entire Middle East agreed to officially recognize the State of Israel and invited it to join the region, Israel responded with indifference. After all, it knew very well that such integration could come only at the price of parting with the Land of Israel and its ancient biblical sites, and that Israel would henceforth have to make do with a "small" State.

During every round of the national conflict over Palestine, which is the longest running conflict of its kind in the modern era, Zionism has tried to appropriate additional territory. And as we have seen, once such land became sacred from a nationalist perspective, it took immense effort to give it up. It was the 1967 war that finally ensnared Israel in a honeyed but bloody trap from which it has proved incapable of extricating itself on its own. Although it is true that all modern homelands are cultural constructions, the withdrawal from national territory is nonetheless a virtually impossible undertaking, particularly when attempted by choice. Even if the world could be convinced that Zionism has really been about finding a place of refuge for persecuted Jews, and not about the conquest of an imagined ancestral land, the ethnoterritorial mythos that motivated the Zionist enterprise and constituted one of its most powerful conceptual bases is neither able nor willing to retreat.

Ultimately, it will certainly wither away like the rest of history's nationalist mythologies. However, all those who are unwilling to espouse such a thoroughly fatalistic approach must ask themselves the following question: Will the demise of this mythos take with it Israeli society as a whole, along with all its neighbors, or will it leave signs of life in its wake? In other words, is the scorpion symbolic solely of the Zionist mythos, or is the entire nationalist cultural enterprise it created imbued with the scorpion's solitary, paranoid attributes, and therefore destined to continue swimming confidently toward its own, and others', ruin?

The bitter fate of the frog is not only a matter for the future. For quite some time now, the Palestinians have endured persistent suffering. This past and present suffering is what set the tone for this book and is also what inspired me to compose the afterword that follows.

In Memory of a Village

What are we doing in the villages that were abandoned . . . by friends
without a battle . . . ? Are we ready to protect these villages so that their
residents may return, or do we want to erase all evidence that a village
ever existed at the site?
—Golda Meyerson (Meir) before the central committee of the Mapai
(Land of Israel Workers Party), May 11, 1948

We also got on the trucks. The glow of emeralds
spoke to us through the night of our olive tree. The barking of
dogs at a fleeting moon over the church tower
But we weren't afraid. Because our childhood didn't
come with us. A song was enough for us: We'll return
in a little while, to our house . . . when the trucks empty
their extra load!
—Mahmoud Darwish, "Innocent Villagers," 1995

After our long and bumpy journey through the "ancestral Jewish homeland," I would now like to focus attention on a small piece of land within this larger geographic area. I believe it is important to dedicate these final pages to the story of this site—whose past remains with me like an open wound—because of the light it sheds on how remembrance and forgetting are constructed in Israel.

I teach history at Tel Aviv University and live not far from campus. Both my apartment and my place of work are located on the ruins of an Arab village that ceased to exist on March 30, 1948. On that spring day, the village's last frightened residents walked down the dirt road leading northward, bringing with them what belongings they could and slowly disappearing from the view of the enemies who had encircled the village. Women carried infants, and small children capable of walking on their own trailed behind them. The elderly were helped along by the young; the sick and handicapped were seated on donkeys. In their hasty, terrified flight, they left behind furniture, kitchen utensils, suitcases, and unraveled bundles, along with the forgotten and confused village idiot, who could not understand why he had been left behind.[1]

Within a few hours, the joyful besiegers had taken control of the village, on which their sights had been set for quite some time. Thus did the inhabitants of al-Sheikh Muwannis fade from the pages of the history of the Land of Israel and fall into the depths of forgetfulness.

The village's houses and fields no longer exist. All that remain are two or three rickety structures, some damaged and neglected graves, and a few particularly robust date trees that just happened not to interfere with the parking lot. My university was established right beside these last vestiges of the village. It evolved into the largest institution of higher education in Israel, extending across the land of the village that is no more. Indeed, parts of this book were written in an office within the university. It was from this strange, almost neighborly proximity between the built and the obliterated, and the intolerable friction between an illusive past and a mobile and constantly advancing present, that I derived a certain moral inspiration for some of the narrative strategies employed here.

As a historian, that is to say, as a certified agent of memory who makes a living by teaching about so many yesterdays, I was unable to finish this book without addressing the past of the physical space in which I conduct my everyday life. Although human hands have done almost everything possible to conceal and erase all that remained of the Arab village, it is still the same land and the same heavens, and the horizon above the sea that is visible to the west is the same horizon it always was, just seen through different eyes.

FORGETTING THE LAND

We do not know when the village of al-Sheikh Muwannis came into being. Homes of farmers always have less of a history than do centers of power, halls of capital, and commercial cities. On a map prepared by Pierre Jacotin, the well-trained head of the team of engineers, surveyors, and draftsmen who traveled with Napoleon Bonaparte's

---

1   One report of the *Haganah* stated: "an elderly and apparently stupid man was found hiding in one of the houses in the village . . . The state of the belongings that were left behind reflects the fact that they left the village suddenly." Quoted in Haim Fireberg, "Tel Aviv: Change, Continuity, and the Many Faces of Urban Culture and Society during War (1936–1948)," Ph.D. diss., Tel Aviv University, 2003, 62.

army during its conquest of the region in 1799, there are clear indications of a locality having existed at this location. Although the villages that appear on this groundbreaking French map are not identified by name, in the case of the village we are concerned with here, the drafter wrote the Arabic word *dahr*, most likely meaning "the slope of the hill." The village was located on a wide hill on the northern bank of the al-Auja River, which today is known as the Yarkon. In population and in land area, it was the largest village north of the city of Jaffa. Except for Jaffa itself, capital of the Palestinian coast, it likely also had one of the longest histories of continuous settlement in the region.

At the foot of the lands of al-Sheikh Muwannis, and not far from the river (which in ancient times ran slightly north of where it runs today), the remains of a magnificent site known as Tell Qasile were discovered in the late 1940s. In October 1948, just six months after the residents of the Arab village were forced out, excavations began on the calcareous sandstone hill some eight hundred meters south of the abandoned houses. Two shards of pottery with Hebrew writing, apparently dating from the seventh century BCE, happened to be found on the surface, leading excavators to believe initially that they were working on an ancient Jewish settlement from the "time of King Solomon."[2]

As in many later archaeological excavations undertaken in the Land of Israel, the findings were rich, but not Jewish. It turned out that during the twelfth century BCE, the Philistines—"those of the deep green," as they were referred to in Pharaonic documents—had established a port on the banks of the river. Around the wharf, a well-established settlement developed over an area of approximately sixteen *dunam*s. At the center of the hill stood a temple made of clay bricks, next to which were additional public and private structures. In the eleventh century BCE, the house of worship was destroyed and its

---

2   On December 24, 1948, the newspaper *Davar* reported that "an ancient Israelite city was discovered on the banks of the Yarkon." The paper also ran a poem composed by Nathan Alterman, the poet of the Zionist labor movement, in honor of the national discovery, part of which reads as follows: "The miracle here is not the mosaic floor on the hill from the ancient state of Israel . . . No! The miracle here is excavation of the floor and its structure under the authority of the Israeli state. Abba Eban [literally, Father Stone] explains to the nations the reasons for the Jewish battle that was justly fought. But it is also fortunate that from deep in the past, *Ima Eban* [Mother Stone] speaks this same thought." This initial enthusiasm was quickly forgotten when it became clear that *Ima Eban* was not Jewish.

walls rebuilt with stone. Excavators found large numbers of shards from objects ranging from food utensils to ritual articles. The streets of the settlement were straight and ran parallel to one another, suggesting a process of urban planning rather than spontaneous, haphazard construction. The site was conquered and set ablaze by the Pharaonic Egyptians at the end of the tenth century BCE, reducing activity at the site but not halting it altogether.

Remains from the fourth and fifth centuries BCE—that is to say, the period prior to the conquest by Alexander of Macedon—indicate relatively stable, continued habitation at the location. From the Hellenistic and Roman periods, we have evidence of diversified commercial activity and the existence of a bustling marketplace at the center of the locality. A structure remaining from the Byzantine period appears to have been a Samaritan synagogue, and the short-lived Sassanid conquest of the early seventh century CE left behind a rare silver coin. The beginning of Arab rule (late Umayyad and Fatimid dynasties) witnessed the construction of a large hostel, supported by pillars.

Because of the region's fertile land, we can assume that villagers continued to live in the area during the long period of Muslim dominance, although the focus of settlement shifted slightly northeast, most likely because of the flooding of the river during particularly rainy winters. On a nearby hill, slightly higher than Tell Qasile, another village began to take form. Over the years, its inhabitants converted to Islam and named the village after a local holy figure who was buried there.

The name al-Sheikh Muwannis already appears in the travel memoirs of Jacob Berggren, a well-educated priest from the Swedish embassy in Istanbul who visited Palestine in the early 1820s. In December 1821, he traveled from Jerusalem to Acre (known then as Akka) via Ramla, and passed by the village. According to his account, the village was located on a hill surrounded by muddy land that was flooded with water despite the moderate winter.[3]

We do not know what the village population was during this period, but we can reasonably assume that it was no less than 315, which was the population of the village according to the survey taken by the Palestine Exploration Fund (PEF) in 1879.[4] The significant

---

3 Jacob Berggren, *Resor i Europa och österländerne* 5.3, Stockholm: S. Rumstedt, 1828, 61.

4 I discuss this organization in chapter 3.

demographic revolution that affected some areas of the Middle East began during the last three decades of the nineteenth century and accelerated during the twentieth. According to the first British census in Palestine, which was completed in 1922, the village had 664 inhabitants, and by 1931 its population had risen to 1,154. In 1945, the village population stood at 1,930; three years later, on the eve of its depopulation, it was home to 2,160 men, women, and children.[5]

The increased rate of Palestinian natural reproduction, which can be credited primarily to conditions under the British Mandate, more or less paralleled the process that had taken place in Europe a century earlier. Increased food production extended the life expectancy of children, whereas the childbirth-curbing aspects of modernity—such as education, improvement in the status of women, and most important, the anticipated social mobility of the next generation—had not yet come into play. It is quite probable that during the final three decades of its existence, the wealthy village attracted peasant farmer migrants from the less fertile mountain regions. If such migrants did make their way to the village, they would have been incorporated into, and subsequently become an integral part of, the local population.

As al-Sheikh Muwannis continued to expand, some of its clay houses were replaced by houses made of stone bricks and even cement. Moshe Smilansky, an author and farmer who was well known throughout the Zionist community in Palestine and who wrote a considerable amount about the lives of Arabs in Palestine, described al-Sheikh Muwannis with admiration:

> All the farmers, except for a few exceptional ones, use Western plows. There are four harvesting machines in the village, as well as large equipment for threshing. They employ modern methods of organizing orange orchards and commercial fertilizers, in emulation of Jewish agricultural practices.[6]

5   Walid Khalidi (ed.) *All that Remains: The Palestinian Villages Occupied and Depopulated by Israel in 1948*, Washington, DC: Institute for Palestine Studies, 1992, 259–60. On the demographic increase all along the coastal plain, see Baruch Kimmerling and Joel S. Migdal, *Palestinians: The Making of a People*, Cambridge, MA: Harvard University Press, 1994, 44–51.

6   Moshe Smilansky, *Jewish Colonization and the Fellah*, Tel Aviv: Mischar v'Tasia, 1930, 27 (in Hebrew).

It was also one of the first villages to organize a citrus marketing coop-erative. Sa'id Baidas, a resident of the village, was chair of the Palestine Citrus Board (and an opponent of the mufti).[7] A regional school for boys was established in the village in 1932, and a comparable institu-tion for girls was set up eleven years later.

The village's economic prosperity may have also been responsible for its policy of moderation and tolerance toward the country's expanding Zionist settlements. Tel Aviv was growing at a phenomenal pace just to the south, and the village's relationship with its new neigh-bors was typically friendly. Children from the village sometimes rode their bicycles to the village of Summayl (al-Mas'udiyya), which was situated south of the river and where some Arab homes stood adja-cent to Jewish homes. The Jews also regularly purchased fruit and vegetables from the successful farmers. Although the residents of al-Sheikh Muwannis were displeased when at one point the Tel Aviv Municipal Council tried to tax some of its land, their complaints sounded more like the dissatisfaction of taxpayers than the protests of nationalists. The village elite, who owned a great deal of land, even agreed to sell the Jews more than three thousand *dunam*s in the northern section of the village; after the transaction, they retained 11,500 *dunam*s of fertile land, with many orchards, green banana groves, cereal crop fields, and grazing areas.

By the end of the First World War, a sizable share of the village's agricultural production was transported over the river to the port of Jaffa via a bridge known as Jisr al-Hadar. This bridge was blown up by the Ottomans during their retreat, and in its place the British built a barrel bridge, which was replaced in 1925 by the first cement bridge in Palestine, constructed by the pioneering Zionist Labor Battalion (Gdud Ha'avoda). The bridge was meant to link Tel Aviv and Herzliya, the new northern moshava that had been established the previous year, and to provide the village with a sturdier paved road for easier export of its produce.

We know nothing about the mood in the village during the Arab

---

7   Dan Yahav, *Cultural and Economic Life in Jaffa Before the Nakba (1948)*, Azur: Cherikover Publishing House, 2007, 63 (in Hebrew). In 1949, Sa'id Baidas was among twelve exiles in Beirut who signed a petition in the name of the Jaffa and Districts Inhabitants Council, asking the US government to support restitution of the refugees' rights to their property and land. See document in *Journal of Palestine Studies* 18:3 (1989), 96–109.

Revolt of the 1930s. However, based on the absence of any signs of agitation, we can cautiously conclude that the anticolonial protests that raged through Palestine during the period appear to have not had reverberations in al-Sheikh Muwannis and that a national consciousness had not yet emerged among its inhabitants.[8] During the Second World War, when many British soldiers resided in the area, Ibrahim Baidas, a member of the wealthiest family in the village, opened a large café next to the bridge in partnership with discharged soldiers from Tel Aviv. Because of its shaded pavilions by the water, the café was named the Hawaiian Garden. It hosted performances, and became enough of a landmark that local residents soon began referring to the bridge using the name of the café.[9] The serene life of a tropical island in the Pacific Ocean appeared to be within reach.

We do not know what Arabs and Jews discussed over tea and coffee in the café, and most likely we never will. However, we do know that the serenity of the establishment was first upset not by the national conflict but by a criminal offense: a robbery at the café on the night of August 10, 1947, perpetrated by young Abu Kishk bedouins who lived east of Herzliya. In the course of the break-in, three customers from Tel Aviv as well as the manager, a villager from al-Sheikh Muwannis, were killed. It was a strange prelude to the political shock waves that would disrupt the village just a few months later.

Immediately following the UN General Assembly vote of November 29, 1947, on the partition plan, tensions spiked throughout the region. According to the resolution, al-Sheikh Muwannis, like all other villages on the coastal plain, would lie within the borders of the Jewish state. The Palestinians around Tel Aviv were filled with consternation. What would it be like for Arabs to live in a state of new settlers, who continued to arrive in increasingly large numbers? How could they be confident that a regime of foreigners would treat the local inhabitants fairly? Most of the quiet villagers were almost certainly unaware of Zionism's claim of historic ownership to the "ancestral land" of the Jews, although it is safe to assume

---

8   Nevertheless, it is believed that one villager, Abd al-Qader Baidas, who was president of the Central Arab Farmers Union in Jaffa, joined the Palestinian Arab Party. My source for this information is "Al-Sheikh Muwannis: The Story of a Place," a seminar paper submitted to me by Asaad Zoabi in 2011.

9   The bridge's official name, according to the British, was El-Alamein. See Yehuda Ziv, *A Moment in Situ*, Jerusalem: Tzivonim, 2005, 143–4 (in Hebrew).

they had noticed the tendency of their uninvited neighbors to expand their landholdings.

Nonetheless, while violent clashes immediately broke out along the line between Tel Aviv and Jaffa (which, according to the partition plan, would remain an Arab enclave within the Jewish state), with dozens of casualties on both sides, the area north of Tel Aviv, the first all-Jewish city, stayed calm, though predictably saturated with tense anticipation.

At this point, the Haganah's first move was to exert heavy pressure on the residents of the three villages located south of the al-Auja (Yarkon) River and adjacent to the northern houses of Tel Aviv, in an effort to get them to abandon their homes. By the end of 1947, the residents of Summayl were forced to evacuate their homes and relocate to Jammasin. Then, during January 1948, the villagers of Jammasin abandoned their homes and, together with the refugees who had initially taken shelter in their village as well as the villagers of Jarisha, found temporary shelter in the large village of al-Sheikh Muwannis. As a result of the influx of displaced neighbors, the mood in the village went from bad to worse. Reports of fierce battles in Jaffa and nearby Salama added to the overall sense of fear. On January 28, 1948, Ibrahim Abu Khil, the village "diplomat," resolved along with the other local leaders of nearby localities to go to Petah Tikva to discuss the situation with Haganah officials. It was decided to hold the meeting in the home of Avraham Shapira, a mythical figure in the Zionist settlement community who enjoyed a high degree of trust among the local inhabitants of Palestine.

Despite open hostility toward the large Arab locality, Yosef Olitzky of the Haganah testified to the peaceable approach of the Palestinian representatives. According to his account of the meeting, the representatives of the villages expressed "their desire to maintain friendly relations, and said they would prevent all foreign Arabs and their own 'rioters' from entering their territory, and that if they were unable to overtake them, they would ask the Haganah for its assistance."[10] As a result of this productive discussion, Abu Khil stayed in close contact

---

10   Yosef Olitzky, *From "Incidents" to War: Chapters in the History of the Defense of Tel Aviv*, Tel Aviv: Haganah Command/IDF Cultural Service, 1950, 62 (in Hebrew). See also Yehuda Slutsky, *From Struggle to War: History of the Haganah*, vol. 3, Tel Aviv: Am Oved, 1972, 1375 (in Hebrew).

with the major Jewish force, neutralizing the friction and misunder-standings that arose from the growing tension. In February, the village came under fire and a few shots were fired in return, but these skir-mishes resulted in no casualties. The events were investigated and clarified, and both sides took measures to calm the hostile atmos-phere. And although young Arab villagers still dug defensive trenches, the entry of external fighting forces was prohibited and moderate villagers who favored peaceful relations continued to control all village actions.

But this state of calm was unacceptable to the leaders of the Haga-nah. Despite the village's peaceable disposition, they were concerned by the presence of such a large Arab locality in such close proximity to the Tel Aviv harbor—next to the electrical plant and the airport, both located along the shore. Moreover, during the same period, the Haganah was in the process of formulating Plan Dalet, which set the explicit goal of achieving territorial continuity under Zionist control. The view that a large Palestinian population was a threat to the exist-ence of a stable nation-state grew increasingly entrenched. We must remember that of the population designated for the Jewish state under the UN partition plan, more than 400,000, or 40 percent, were Arabs. And despite the best efforts of figures such as Israel Rokach, Tel Aviv's liberal mayor, and Gad Machnes, the moderate representative of the country's Jewish citrus growers, to prevent escalation, their pacifist initiatives were unsuccessful and, moreover, inconsistent with the policies of the Haganah.[11] We also have unconfirmed evidence that the Haganah made cash payouts to Arab collaborators to intention-ally disseminate rumors of Jewish plans to attack the village, in order to encourage the Arab residents to flee for their lives.[12]

It is therefore no wonder that the incitement and the false rumors mounted with every passing week. Reports spread that foreign fight-ers and "gangs" had penetrated the village and that a large supply of weapons had also been smuggled in. Some even maintained that armed German officers were present in al-Sheikh Muwannis.[13] The

---

11   Arnon Golan, *Wartime Spatial Changes*, Sede Boqer: Ben-Gurion University, 2001, 83 (in Hebrew).

12   Hillel Cohen, *Army of Shadows: Palestinian Collaboration with Zionism, 1917–1948*, Berkeley: University of California Press, 2008, 245.

13   Nechemia Ben-Tor, *History of the Fighters for Freedom of Israel (Lehi)*, vol. 4, Jerusalem: Yair, 2010, 414 (in Hebrew).

Haganah's efficient intelligence network and the organization's recon-
naissance flights over the village repeatedly confirmed the baselessness
of this information, but to no avail. Avraham Krinitzi, the mayor of
Ramat Gan, who coveted the lands of the neighboring village, was
among the chief inciters of false rumors. The Lehi organization ("Lehi"
is an acronym for "Fighters for the Freedom of Israel," a group led by
Avraham Stern), which participated relatively little in the fierce
clashes in south Tel Aviv, joined the campaign of intimidation in the
north, aimed at driving away the local Arab population. Ya'akov Banai,
a commander of another militant group, the Irgun secessionists,
recorded the following recollections:

> This village sprawls between Tel Aviv, Ramat Gan, and Petah Tikva.
> Although this situation forces it to act wisely and quietly, it main-
> tains constant contact with the Arab population centers. Shmuel
> Halevy [an official of the Tel Aviv municipality] suggests conquering
> the village, and we have started to take preparatory measures. A
> demonstrative patrol was conducted in which sixty men partici-
> pated. We passed by the village and tried to make sure they knew we
> were from "Jama'at Shtern" [Arabic: the Stern Gang]. They were
> terror-struck. The second measure was to issue an invitation to the
> *mukhtar* to come to a meeting the next day at the Musrara Bridge on
> the outskirts of Tel Aviv. Two *mukhtars* arrived for the meeting: that
> of al-Sheikh Muwannis and one from the village of Jalil [today,
> Gelilot]. They arrived on horseback in formal attire. Shmuel Halevy
> informed them that they had twenty-four hours to collect all the
> weapons in the village and bring them to a designated location. They
> claimed that all they had were personal weapons, pistols [to be used
> at weddings]. But these two shows, the patrol and the meeting, were
> enough to fill them with fear. They started to abandon the village,
> and we continued pressuring the villagers.[14]

The next act of "pressure" was a typical terrorist attack. Lehi fighter
Elisha Ibzov (Avraham Cohen) was captured on his way to Nablus
with a truck filled with explosives that was supposed to be detonated
at the city's Arab headquarters. In retaliation, Lehi fighters abducted

---

14   Ya'akov Banai, *Anonymous Soldiers: The Book of Lehi Operations*, Tel Aviv:
Hug Yedidim, 1958, 652 (in Hebrew).

four adult villagers from al-Sheikh Muwannis, who happened to be accompanied by a youth and who had set out toward Jalil in search of food and fuel. Although the five hostages had no connection to Ibzov's capture in Nablus, their Lehi abductors threatened to kill them if their comrade-in-arms was not released. Rumors spread through the village that the captors had already killed the hostages, and the panic reached new heights. As a result of persuasion, deterrence, and mediation by the Haganah, the five villagers were released (in the meantime, it turned out that Ibzov had been executed immediately after being captured), but the terrorist act had its desired effect. "The village was increasingly abandoned," Banai continues with a sense of satisfaction. "We left them a route of exit. Most wandered with their belongings toward Tulkarm and Qalqilya."[15]

The fiery heroes of Lehi were not alone in leaving the residents of al-Sheikh Muwannis a "route of exit" northward. They were working alongside moderate members of the Haganah. Despite the previous unwritten agreement, the hesitations, and the moral issues involved, the Haganah's Tel Aviv command decided to join the secessionist group in imposing a siege on all routes into the village. Although the British Mandate was still in force at the time and His Majesty's forces were still in the area, their presence did not prevent the thirty-third battalion of the Alexandroni Brigade from encircling the village during the daylight hours of March 20 and occupying a number of village homes. From that point on, all Arab passage and movement required the authorization of their enemy, and all provisions entering the village were subject to thorough inspection. It became impossible for villagers to reach their fields or to care for the crop that was almost ready for harvest. The next step was to prohibit the return of anyone who left the village. The economic stranglehold, combined with the lack of fuel necessary to operate the generators, quickly resulted in a shortage not only of food but of water. During the village's last days, the last few inhabitants evacuated their homes, led by Ibrahim Abu Khil, who, until the last moment, had naïvely believed the promises of his Jewish "friends."

---

15   Ibid. See also Nathan Yalin-Mor's report in *Lohamey Herut Israel: People, Ideas, Deeds*, Jerusalem: Shekmuna, 1975, 478–9 (in Hebrew). This former Lehi commander had the following melancholy thought to offer: "I have often asked myself whether the *mukhtars* of al-Sheikh Muwannis and Jalil were among the notables of the villages who approached Gad Machnes at the end of '43 to offer refuge to the Lehi fugitives. Those were different times." Ibid.

Once the last inhabitants had left the village—except, of course, for the elderly village idiot whose fate remains unknown—Lehi fighters quickly seized control of its main buildings. There they set up their main base, which they named Ramat Yair, in memory of their deceased commander Avraham Stern, whose code name was "Yair."[16] It was from this base that the order for Lehi fighters to take part in the conquest of Deir Yassin near Jerusalem was issued just a few days later. As we know, the brief spurt of fighting at Deir Yassin ended on April 9 with the killing of more than one hundred inhabitants of the mountain village, and the public humiliation of all those who remained. Ramat Yair remained operational until May 29, when Stern's successors were inducted into the IDF. At this point, the site became one of Israel's new military bases, but it was not long before the authorities began to populate it with Jewish immigrants out of concern that refugees might try to return to the village.

By this time, however, the frightened residents of al-Sheikh Muwannis who had been forced into exile were already miles away. Some had reached Tulkarm and Qalqilya, which came under Jordanian control after the war. Others were dispersed among villages in the Triangle region, such as Tira and Jaljulia, which were ultimately included in the territory incorporated into the State of Israel. Still others found themselves in the refugee camps of the Gaza Strip. In Israel, with no source of income, they initially lived in tents and were subject to travel restrictions. Some left the West Bank and Israel and began wandering the Middle East. A small number managed to reach the United States and Canada. The land they left behind in al-Sheikh Muwannis was expropriated by the Israeli authorities. Those who remained in Israel were legally classified as "absentees" despite their presence in the country, and were stripped of all property rights for their land and their homes. It goes without saying that none of the villagers received compensation.

Years later, the former inhabitants of al-Sheikh Muwannis would make secret pilgrimages to get a glimpse of their homes from afar. Refugees who became Israeli citizens were able to do so prior to 1967, while those who found themselves living in the West Bank arrived in tears at the old calcareous sandstone hill only after the Six-Day War.

---

16 Micky Banai, *Walking on Memories: al-Sheikh Muwannis*, Tel Aviv, Ashkelon: Banai, 1995, 30–3 (in Hebrew).

A LAND OF FORGETTING

The experience of the residents of al-Sheikh Muwannis was preferable to the bitter fate of the residents of Deir Yassin, Ein al-Zeitun, Balad al-Shaykh, and other villages in which many of the inhabitants paid with their lives for daring to support the armed resistance against the establishment of a Jewish state in their country. However, it was undoubtedly worse than the experience of certain other villagers, such as the inhabitants of Ein Houd.

Like the inhabitants of al-Sheikh Muwannis, the people who lived in this serene village located on a hillside overlooking the northern coastal plain chose not to come into conflict with Zionist military forces and yet were nonetheless displaced from their homes. Surprisingly, some were allowed to continue living on a hill not far from their village, enabling them to gaze at it for the rest of their days. Their former homes became a Jewish Israeli artists village, and for many years the Israeli authorities considered the new, relocated "Ein Houd" to be an unrecognized locality. Finally, however, luck worked in their favor. Fifty-two years after the establishment of their new village on the hill, they received official government recognition and, in 2006, were even hooked up to the Israeli electrical grid.[17] The refugees of al-Sheikh Muwannis, in contrast, were unable to continue living together as a community, and most ended up scattered around the world.

The story of al-Sheikh Muwannis is not unusual. As noted in chapter four, in addition to the depopulation of Arab neighborhoods in the cities, more than four hundred villages were obliterated—deleted—from the Land of Israel during and following the 1948 war.[18] All told, in the course of the Nakba, some seven hundred thousand people were displaced, their lands and homes appropriated without compensation. Many of them and their descendants still live in

17   On these two neighboring villages and the relationship between landscape and memory, see Susan Slyomovics, *The Object of Memory: Arab and Jew Narrate the Palestinian Village*, Philadelphia: University of Pennsylvania Press, 1998.

18   See Noga Kadman's outstanding book *Erased from Space and Consciousness*, Jerusalem: November Books, 2008 (in Hebrew). This study provides a broad understanding of the produced forgetting within Israel of the human landscape that once existed in Palestine.

refugee camps throughout the Middle East. Why, then, take an interest in one isolated village?

As I explained at the beginning of this afterword, I have an uneasy feeling about the place itself, which, I contend, should be shared by all historians who work at Tel Aviv University. My primary occupation is to try cautiously to fashion memories out of forgotten documentation from the past. I teach history as a profession, and my students expect me to display a reasonable degree of unbiased academic integrity. At the outset of each new course, I therefore make sure to teach them that collective remembering is to some degree a product of cultural engineering, which is almost always contingent on the mood and the needs of the present. I also place special emphasis on the fact that just as the past is responsible for creating the present, the national present freely molds its own past, which, we must always remember, contains vast empty space of forgetting.

I live within a nation and a territory that are both clear constructions of remembering four thousand years into the past. This processed and reconstructed Jewish memory became the food of sustenance of the Zionist movement and served as the primary basis for legitimizing its enterprise of colonization. This, among other things, helped shape the Israeli political mentality, which holds that the "brevity" of the Palestinians' condition cannot be compared to the prolongation that of the Jews. After all, how can we compare an exile of six or seven decades to an exile of two millennia? How can we compare the yearnings of simple farmers to the longings of Jewish eternity? What are the claims of homeless refugees worth when compared to a divine promise, even if God does not exist?

This abbreviated history of al-Sheikh Muwannis can be understood as analogous to the young child's exclamation in Hans Christian Andersen's tale of the newly clothed emperor: "The king is naked!" To justify this categorical, offensive assertion, we now turn our attention to the politics of national memory that find such symbolic expression on the former lands of the village itself. This area, which is now the site of a number of upscale Israeli neighborhoods,[19] contains an intriguing and rare concentration of four agencies of Zionist Israeli

---

19   It is worth noting that three Israeli prime ministers—Golda Meir, Yitzhak Rabin, and Shimon Peres—all chose to reside on the former lands of al-Sheikh Muwannis.

commemoration: the Eretz Israel Museum, the Palmach Museum, the Israeli Museum at the Yitzhak Rabin Center, and, of course, Beit Hatfutsot, the Museum of the Jewish People. These four bastions of memory have been charged with preserving and documenting a Jewish, Zionist, and Israeli past.

The oldest of the four institutions is the Eretz Israel Museum, which was founded in 1958 on the southern edge of the village near the Tell Qasile excavations, which, as we know, began ten years earlier. In addition to its archaeological findings that, according to historical periodization, belong to the "biblical period," the museum seeks to present the entire "history of the Land and its culture." Among its permanent exhibitions is "The Land of the Baron," which offers a detailed exploration of Edmond James de Rothschild's settlement enterprise and the "establishment of Jewish settlement in the Land of Israel." Quite symbolically, the museum's ethnography and folklore pavilion, which is dedicated to the memory of "Jewish ways of life in different communities around the world," is located in one of the houses of old al-Sheikh Muwannis, without making a reference to the history of the structure or the "ways of life" of its previous residents.

The institution was initially known as the Land of Israel Museum (*Muzeon Eretz Israel*), but, with the appointment of Major General (Res.) Rehavam Ze'evi as its director, its name was changed to the Land of Israel Museum. During his tenure, the museum was revitalized, and Ze'evi's great love for his expanding homeland was manifested in the focus and content of its exhibitions. In 1988 the former general established the Moledet Party, which called for the "transfer" of Arab Israelis out of Israel; nevertheless, this political activity did not prevent him from continuing to direct the museum until 1991, when he was appointed to serve as a minister in the Israeli government. At the time of writing, the museum's chairperson is Dov Tamari, a former brigadier general who also holds a Ph.D. in history.

The Palmach Museum is located a bit higher up on the sandstone hill and is as isolated as a fortress. On the building's façade appears the motto "The righteousness of the path," taken from a well-known poem by Nathan Alterman, the same poet who in 1948 reacted with such great enthusiasm to the discovery of "Jewish" Tell Qasile and in 1967 was among the founders of the Whole Land of Israel Movement. At the time of writing, the chairperson of the association responsible for running the museum is the former major general Yeshayahu

Gavish, and the institution operates under the auspices of the Israeli Defense Ministry. The museum was established in the year 2000 to commemorate the historical military enterprise of the Palmach, the elite strike force of the Haganah. The Palmach played a pivotal role in the victory of 1948, though not on the al-Sheikh Muwannis front. For the first few decades of Israeli statehood, a large proportion of senior IDF officers came from the ranks of this force. Of these officers, the most well known in the international realm was Yitzhak Rabin, who was murdered in 1995 while serving as prime minister of Israel.

The Yitzhak Rabin Center, located behind the Palmach Museum, was established by law in 1997 to commemorate the prime minister who had been murdered two years earlier. At the center of the complex stands the Israeli Museum, which opened in 2010 and was established, among other reasons, to paint "a picture of the Zionist enterprise as a success story . . ." The conception for the museum came from Anita Shapira, head of the Weizmann Institute for the Study of Zionism at Tel Aviv University, who also headed the team responsible for its exhibition content. The chairperson of the public council that initiated the project, as well as its most prominent figure, is former General Security Service (Shin Bet) chief Jacob Perry, who a few years later, in 2009, was also appointed as chair of the board of directors of Beit Hatfutsot, which is located on the Tel Aviv University campus, adjacent to the Yitzhak Rabin Center.

Founded in 1978, Beit Hatfutsot is located at the heart of the Tel Aviv University campus. Its International Board of Governors is currently chaired by Leonid Nevzlin, a successful Russian businessman who fled to Israel in 2003 after being convicted in absentia by the Russian authorities of contracting murders and of evading billions of dollars in taxes. Nevzlin's friend Ariel Sharon called upon him to save this stronghold of Jewish memory from financial collapse, and indeed, with the help of savings he had brought from Russia, Nevzlin succeeded in the task.[20]

The official aim of the museum is to "present and display the ongoing 4,000-year-old story of the Jewish people—past, present and

---

20   On the Russian billionaire's image as the "savior of Beit Hatfutsot" and his ties to the Israeli political and economic elite, see Maya Zeinshtein, "'We Love You,' Prof. Rabinovich Told the Happy Oligarch Leonid Nevzlin," *Haaretz*, September 29, 2009 (in Hebrew).

future," "to nurture a sense of belonging among Jewish visitors and to strengthen Jewish identity," and "to foster understanding of the Jewish people and support for Israel as the Jewish state among all visitors." Among other components, the museum has a Jewish Genealogical Center with a database that already contains more than three million names. The center enables visitors to "explore their ancestry, record and preserve their own family trees for future generations, thus adding their own 'branch' to the family tree of the Jewish People" not only by using names but also through the use of DNA testing. The genetic pool already contains 300,000 samples, and the number continues to grow due to the fact that "genetic genealogy is of particular importance for the Jewish people."

In addition to prominent businessmen and former security officials, the museum's International Board of Governors and board of directors include respected historians representing the Hebrew University of Jerusalem and Tel Aviv University. At the time of writing, these positions were held by professors Israel Bartal, Jeremy Cohen, Itamar Rabinovich, and Raanan Rein. As reflected in the other museums discussed briefly above, such a social profile is typical of almost all important cultural institutions in Israel.

The lands of al-Sheikh Muwannis have been invaded and inundated by a flood of Jewish memory—rising out of the low river like a massive wave, sweeping up to the top of the hill, and bursting powerfully across its crest through the center of the obliterated village. Its institutions hold reams of information, countless displays and exhibits, a myriad of addresses and photographs. Much capital was invested in commemorating the fate, the suffering, and the success of the Jews. Hundreds of people visit these institutions each day to learn from them, including Israeli schoolchildren, soldiers of the IDF, ordinary Israeli visitors, and numerous international tourists. They all tend to leave with a deep sense of satisfaction, convinced that their consciousness of the Jewish past is now firmer and more solid.

It goes without saying that none of these glorious temples of memory makes mention of the history of the site on which they were built. Because the old Arab village does not belong to a Jewish, Zionist, or Israeli past, we find no trace of it in this large and bustling cluster of museums.

The Tel Aviv University campus was built at the top of the sandstone hill, helping to facilitate the slow but steady erasure of al-Sheikh

Muwannis. Its official date of establishment is 1964, but the cornerstone of its first academic building, which protruded defiantly above the relatively low village structures, was already laid in 1955. As noted above, the village structures were populated by displaced, poverty-stricken Jews in 1948. Within a few years, a battle of attrition began between Tel Aviv University and these new, low-income local residents. Only in 2004, after the payment of 108 million shekels, were most of the residents removed from the area, enabling the university to grow ever stronger and expand southward, systematically flattening the remaining houses.[21] Clearly, no one involved in these changes ever considered the possibility of compensating the original, non-Jewish owners of the land.

Tel Aviv University employs more than sixty history lecturers in three different departments; a comparable number of historians worked there in the past and retired. Nowhere else in Israeli academia is it possible to find such a large and productive community of memory. These scholars have authored dozens upon dozens of volumes on a diverse array of subjects in international, Middle Eastern, Jewish, and Israeli history. Their academic achievements are praised both in Israel and abroad, and some of these scholars are permanent guests at the world's most prestigious universities. Still, not one of them thought it necessary to write a book, or even a single academic article, on the history of the land lying beneath the asphalt and cement on which their capital of prestige continued to accumulate. None of them advised M.A. or Ph.D. research on the tragedy of the voiceless villagers who were displaced from the site. As is typical of national histories, the dark side of the past was shoved into the subconscious to wait, in the best-case scenario, for future generations to bring it to the surface. The barons of memory must always be academic but have never been required to be ethical.[22]

In 2003 a fascinating Israeli group of activists known as Zokhrot, whose goal is to make the Nakba part of public consciousness, sent a letter to Professor Itamar Rabinovich, who was then serving as president of Tel Aviv University. The letter requested that the university

---

21   *The Marker News*, June 30, 2004 (in Hebrew).

22   The only relevant work appears to be a final project, completed by Nurit Moscovitz for the university's School of Architecture, which contains a note briefly acknowledging the existence of the village.

acknowledge, "in a modest fashion, the deleted past" of al-Sheikh Muwannis.[23] The petition was signed by twenty university lecturers as well as dozens of students and descendants of former village residents. Rabinovich, who served as a lieutenant colonel in the IDF intelligence corps and as the Israeli ambassador to the United States, is also a historian of the Middle East and a recipient of the Jewish Book Award in the United States for one of his academic studies. Despite his role as an agent of memory and a member of the Board of Directors of "Beit Hatfutsot: The Museum of the Jewish People," he did not even respond to the request of the lecturers and students to commemorate the recent past. To the extent that it was possible to clarify his position, he appears to have simply chosen to ignore it. The questions of insistent journalists met with the following response by the university's spokespeople: "A project on the University's history is currently being written and will also address al-Sheikh Muwannis."[24] However, by 2012, at the time of writing, the long-awaited project has still not been published, and Tel Aviv University and the land on which it sits still lack a written history.

Yet despite all this, one remnant of the village's suppressed past does remain. On the southern side of the university sits a magnificently renovated Arab structure known as the Green House. Although this structure is officially designated as a faculty club, owing to its high prices it is typically not frequented by the lecturers for whom it was ostensibly intended. Instead it serves as a profit-generating banquet hall and a restaurant to which distinguished guests from abroad are invited during academic conferences and for fund-raising events. Its Hebrew-language Web site recently described the establishment as follows (translated from the Hebrew):

> The house is a one-of-a-kind architectural treasure that remains from the village al-Sheikh Muwannis. The village al-Sheikh Muwannis was located on the edge of an ancient Philistine settlement that existed as early as the twelfth century B.C. (Tell Qasile). The village's

---

23   Quoted from the Hebrew text of the letter. Hebrew, English, and Arabic versions of the letter and the names of its signers can be found in the booklet *Remembering al-Shaykh Muwannis*, at http://www.zochrot.org/sites/default/files/zoc_muwannis_final_2.pdf.

24   Ran Harnevo, "Tel Aviv: A Demand to Commemorate al-Sheikh Muwannis," *Yedioth Aharonot*, November 10, 2003.

growth and expansion during the first half of the nineteenth century resulted in the construction of large houses made from chiseled stone alongside its simple stone houses. At the end of the First World War, the British reached the outskirts of the Turkish-controlled village, and in a surprise attack on the night of December 2, 1917, the village came under British control. The onset of the British Mandate resulted in the development of the entire region: Tel Aviv and Jaffa, as well as al-Sheikh Muwannis. The Green House could be seen prominently from afar because of its color and the stunning arcade that adorned its façade. At that time, its two upper floors served as residences, and its lower floor was used for commerce and the production of handicrafts.

Beginning in 1924, the situation of the village changed. Some of its lands were sold, and negotiations for the purchase of additional land began. In March 1948, the village was designated as a Lehi base of operations, known as Ramat Yair. It was the location of the major assembly of all Lehi soldiers, where the order was issued regarding the integration of Lehi forces into the IDF. In June 1948, after the establishment of the state, al-Sheikh Muwannis was used to house air force and Machal (overseas volunteers) personnel. Beginning in 1949, the houses of the village were used to house Jewish immigrants and refugees who had suffered injury from the war, as well as fighters back from the battles of the War of Independence who had not been provided with another place to live. 1964 marked the inauguration of the university campus at Ramat Aviv. As the university continued to develop, the Green House was designated to serve as its faculty club.[25]

The identity of the Tel Aviv University historians who volunteered to write this excerpt is unknown. However, I present it here almost in its entirety because of how effectively it reflects Israeli consciousness regarding the past: The land was purchased and not taken by force, and the emptied Arab homes and localities miraculously provided necessary refuge for the Jewish victims. The village, parts of which started to be sold in the 1920s, became a base of Lehi operations in the late 1940s, and ultimately became the distinguished university.

---

25   http://www.tau.ac.il/university-club/description.html

Today there is no trace of what happened to the original residents in March 1948—neither of the siege, the economic strangulation, or the abduction. This concealment of the past of the Other is one precondition of the righteousness of the Zionist colonization's historical path.

The great irony of the story of the Green House is that it was in fact the home of Ibrahim Abu Khil, the Haganah ally who was the last to leave the village because of his trust in his Jewish friends. The construction of the beautiful, carefully designed house was a major investment, apparently based on its owners' firm belief that they would be living there for many years to come. Abu Khil's conciliatory diplomacy was consistent with this approach. He made a bitter mistake, however. He did not know that he, his ancestors, and his children had been born in the "Land of Israel," and that their residence in it was destined to be only temporary.

"How easy it had been to be seduced, to be knowingly led astray and join the great general mass of liars—that mass compounded of crass ignorance, utilitarian indifference, and shameless self-interest."[26] These words by S. Yizhar (Yizhar Smilansky), which directly address the tragic situation of the refugees of 1948, have remained with me over the years. But I, too, have no reason to be proud. Although I, too, signed the letter to the president of Tel Aviv University in 2009, I failed—until now, that is—to make known the history of the village on whose former lands I continue to work. I was too busy with other subjects that were more distant in time and space. As I worked on shaping the content of this book, it became clear to me that, this time, I would not be able to skip over such a nearby place whose wound has not yet healed.

Over the years, I have learned much from my many cultural and research journeys. But the most important thing I have learned is that, after all is said and done, remembering and acknowledging victims that we ourselves create is much more effective in bringing about human reconciliation and the living of an ethical life than incessantly recalling that we are the descendants of people who were once victimized by others. A brave and generous memory, even one tainted by hypocrisy, is still a necessary condition for all enlightened

---

26   S. Yizhar, *Khirbet Khizeh*, London: Granta, 2011, 7.

civilizations. How much more must we learn before we understand that victims never forgive their victimizers as long as they remain unwilling to acknowledge the injustices they have committed and to offer compensation for them?

At the end of 2003 I observed the destruction of the large, unique house of Mahmoud Baidas, which for many years stood at the bottom of the calcareous sandstone hill, just across from the Land of Israel Museum. I was standing not far from his granddaughter, Magdalene Sebakhi Baidas, who had come there for the occasion from the city of Lod. When the bulldozer had cleared away the last of the collapsed walls to make way for a prestigious Tel Aviv neighborhood, she reeled with sorrow and finally burst into tears. It was hard for me to imagine her emotions at that moment, as I had never experienced such a situation. Perhaps my father, who by then was no longer alive, could have understood her better. In 1945 he went back and stood before the destroyed home of his mother in Lodz, Poland. Years later, after another visit to the city of his birth, he told me that plaques had been erected in the area of his former neighborhood to commemorate the past existence of a Jewish community. These plaques did not dull his longing for his past, which had been taken away from him so abruptly.

I have been working at Tel Aviv University for twenty-seven years, and the institution means a great deal to me. I love to teach there, and it is one of the reasons I was finally able to write this book. To eliminate all doubts and misunderstandings, I would like to make absolutely clear that I do not believe the university should be removed and replaced with a new village, replete with fields and orchards. Nor do I believe that the descendants of the Palestinian refugees will ever be able to return en masse to the hometowns and villages of their parents and grandparents. However, just as the State of Israel bears responsibility for acknowledging the tragedy suffered by others as a result of its own establishment, and paying a price for that in the longed-for peace process, it is only fitting that my university erect a plaque commemorating the uprooted inhabitants of al-Sheikh Muwannis, the peaceful village that vanished as thoroughly as if it had never existed.

It would also be fitting for the four major museums of Ramat Aviv's campus of memory, which commemorate the "long history of the Land of Israel" and "the past and the present of the eternal Jewish people," to be joined by a fifth institution, one that documents the fate of the refugees of the territorial space of the old subdistrict of Jaffa.

And what structure could be better suited for this function than the Green House? After all, the ethical profits to be earned by the university through such an undertaking would greatly outweigh the financial losses incurred by the closure of the banquet hall. It would also make my university a flagship icebreaker of the historical forgetting that continues to preserve the conflict in a frozen block of misrepresentations.

But perhaps I am completely mistaken. Perhaps the Zionist philanthropists from around the world, whose generous support facilitated the construction of the university buildings as well as the museums in their midst, would not be pleased by a Palestinian commemoration in the very heart of their Land of Israel. After all, wouldn't publicizing the Nakba and the struggle against those who deny it impair their sense of ownership over the land of their "forefathers"? And for this reason, might they not reduce their grants, halt their donations, grow disillusioned with their Jewish state?

Every turning point in the politics of memory is the product of contending with the fields of hegemonic power that determine the culture and identity of a society. Memory and identity always depend on the character of the national consciousness that envelops them. For the sake of their future in the Middle East, will Judeo-Israelis be capable of redefining their sovereignty and, by doing so, changing their attitude toward the Land, its history, and, most important, those who were displaced from it?

This is a question that historians cannot answer. All they can do is hope that their books may somehow help to bring about the beginning of change.

Acknowledgments

I would like to extend my heartfelt gratitude to the many friends and acquaintances who helped me complete this book: Yehonatan Alsheh, Nitza Erel, Yoseph Barnea, Michel Bilis, Yael Dagan, Richard Desserame, Eran Elhaik, Alexander Eterman, Boas Evron, Israel Gershoni, Noa Greenberg, Yuval Laor, Gerardo Leibner, Ran Menahemi, Mahmoud Mosa, Linda Nezri, Nia Perivolaropoulou, Christophe Prochasson, Anna Sergeyenkova, Bianka Speidl, Stavit Sinai, and Asaad Zoabi.

I am extremely grateful to my wife, Varda, and my daughters, Edith and Liel, to whom I owe more thanks than I could ever express in words.

I would also like to thank Jean Boutier, Yves Doazan, and Arundhati Virmani, all from the Marseille campus of the School for Advanced Studies in the Social Sciences (EHESS), for their hospitality and their warmhearted friendliness.

I am grateful to Geremy Forman, who translated this book into English, and to all those at Verso Books (especially Avis Lang) who treated the book with such professional care, trying to the best of their ability to rectify flaws, iron out wrinkles, and make it into an accessible, readable text. I would also like to thank my students for repeatedly challenging my own historical imagination, as well as those who were forced to listen patiently for me to state my piece even when they were really waiting impatiently for me to shut my mouth.

To all those who criticized or panned my previous book—and by doing so provoked, inspired, and steered me into writing this book—I owe more than they could (or would like to) imagine. The major claim of all my detractors was that everything I presented was already known and had already been written by them, and, at the same time, that none of it was correct. I must admit that there is some truth to this assertion: many things that were known at a certain point in time but were subsequently pushed into the margins or swept under the rug did play a central role in the critical narrative I re-created here. In this way, it necessarily became politically incorrect and historically flawed. I remain hopeful that this book will succeed, if only partly, to repeat the same process.

All errors, mistakes, inaccuracies, unnecessary embellishment, and unconventional views are the result of my hand alone, and I of course bear sole responsibility for them.

Index